Borrowed Forms
The Music and Ethics of Transnational Fiction

Borrowed Forms

The Music and Ethics
of Transnational Fiction

Kathryn Lachman

LIVERPOOL UNIVERSITY PRESS

First published 2014 by
Liverpool University Press
4 Cambridge Street
Liverpool
L69 7ZU

British Library Cataloguing-in-Publication data
A British Library CIP record is available

ISBN 978-1-78138-030-7

Typeset by Carnegie Book Production, Lancaster
Printed and bound by Booksfactory.co.uk

Contents

Acknowledgements

I completed this book at the University of Massachusetts Amherst, where I have benefited greatly from the support and generosity of my chairs: Julie Hayes, Bill Moebius, Patrick Mensah, David Lenson, and Jim Hicks. Maryse Condé has been an inspiring mentor and a model of how artfully to negotiate the roles of writer, critic, teacher, public intellectual, and matriarch. I am grateful to Dominic Thomas, Cathy Portuges, Maria Tymozco, Ronnie Scharfman, Leah Hewitt, Bruce Baird, Michael Papio, Laura Doyle, and Stephen Clingman for contributing insights and expertise. I thank Rhona Trauvitch for her efficient research assistance during my summers abroad, and Patricia Matthews for providing careful copy-editing in the book's final stages. Many other colleagues and students throughout the Five Colleges have engaged with these ideas and provided inspiring and collegial community.

I remain indebted to Thomas Trezise for his guidance throughout my graduate studies at Princeton University, where this book began. I am grateful also to Michael Wood, Marie-Hélène Huet, Suzanne Nash, André Benhaim, Simon Gikandi, David Bellos, François Rigolot, Caryl Emerson, Gyan Prakash, and Göran Blix for furthering my development as a scholar. Samuel Webber and Sylvie Pebrier in Paris, and Ngugi wa Thiong'o, Lynne Huffer, Shoshana Felman, Cathy Caruth, and Susan Blood at Yale University sparked my interest in many of the questions I pursue here. I feel fortunate to have had the opportunity to participate in Assia Djebar's seminar at New York University and to exchange ideas on music and democracy. Of the many teachers and mentors who influenced my understanding of music over the years, Mischa Koskoff and Erick Friedmann at Yale marked me profoundly. I feel their absence acutely.

I gratefully acknowledge the generous research support provided by a George Lurcy Fellowship, the Princeton Institute for International and Regional Studies, the UMass Amherst Interdisciplinary Studies Institute, and the UMass Amherst Faculty Research Intensive Semester Program. A Henry Hart Rice Fellowship from Yale University funded my residency in Beirut, Lebanon from 1998–1999, where my interests in Francophone writing and multilingualism coalesced.

An earlier version of Chapter Two was published previously in *Research in African Literatures*; it is reproduced here with kind permission.

At Liverpool University Press, Alison Welsby has nurtured the book with exceptional professionalism and care. Sue Barnes, Patrick Brereton and their staff helped to shepherd the manuscript through to timely completion. David Luljak provided expert assistance in preparing the index. I extend particular thanks to the two anonymous readers whose substantive responses allowed me to sharpen the argument.

Although we are spread out across different continents and all too rarely together, I am immensely grateful to my parents, Anthony and Margaret, for their love and encouragement, and to my brothers, David, Jamie, and Adam, who never fail to inspire, provoke, and challenge me. I greatly appreciate the support that my in-laws, Susan and Barry Ferris, have provided at various stages. Finally, I owe a special debt to Bettina Lerner and Kerry Bystrom whose friendship and ideas have enriched my scholarship in countless ways.

I dedicate this book to Noah and Eli, who have grown up alongside it. And to Jesse, whose love and commitment have lit the way.

Introduction

I cannot reduce my thoughts about life to the music
of a single voice and a single point of view—I am,
after all, a novelist.

—*Orhan Pamuk*

Borrowed Forms considers the impact of musical forms on late twentieth-century literature. The book looks closely at four musical concepts that have significantly influenced the novel and critical theory: polyphony, or the art of combining multiple, interdependent voices; counterpoint, the carefully regulated setting of one voice against another; variation, the virtuosic exploration of the diverse possibilities contained within a single theme; and opera, the dramatic setting of a story to a musical score. Although these musical forms took shape in the European Renaissance and Baroque, novelists have appropriated them as literary strategies because they open up alternative ways of conceiving relations among different subjectivities, histories, and positions, and provide a dynamic means to challenge and renew literary forms.

In our cultural moment, novels circulate more widely than any other literary genre, and possess an exceptional plasticity that readily accommodates multiple perspectives, languages, styles, and registers. Not surprisingly, the novel has emerged as the privileged literary vehicle for expressing plurality and difference. How the novel reflects this increasingly transnational consciousness, and more precisely, how novelists and critics deploy musical forms to respond to new ethical and aesthetic demands, are among the principal questions this book addresses.

The short novella, "Clone," by Argentine author Julio Cortázar, offers a compelling example of the kind of formal experimentation that music has inspired among contemporary writers. Published in 1980, "Clone" follows a group of eight madrigal singers on tour throughout South America. Problems arise as the ensemble's hot-tempered lead singer, Sandro, comes to suspect his wife, soprano Franca, of having an affair with another singer. His mounting jealousy increasingly compromises the collaborative spirit of their rehearsals, and threatens to derail their performances. The situation comes to a head on the evening of the group's final concert in Buenos Aires, where they are to perform the notoriously difficult music of Carlo Gesualdo, an eccentric early Baroque composer known as much for his audacious use of dissonance as for having murdered his wife and her lover in the conjugal bed.[1] As the curtain rises for the performance, Franca fails to appear. Sandro has re-enacted Gesualdo's crime of passion, murdering his wife offstage and delivering a stunning blow to singers and audience alike.

Cortázar's story presents a highly unusual—and unanticipated—musical construction that is emblematic of the novels we will examine throughout this work. As he reveals in an afterword entitled "Note on the Theme of a King and the Vengeance of a Prince," Cortázar borrows the structure of Johann Sebastian Bach's Musical Offering. The eight protagonists represent the eight instruments in an orchestrated version of Bach's suite. Mimicking the Musical Offering's thirteen contrasting movements, the story contains thirteen sections that closely follow Bach's pattern of voicing. The final movement of the Musical Offering includes all eight instruments, save one. By extension, the closing scene of Cortázar's story assembles all eight singers, with the exception of the murder victim, Franca. The structure of an eighteenth-century Baroque suite thus governs the organization and voicing of a contemporary Argentine novella: it determines the number and types of characters, as well as the mood and trajectory of the narrative, right up to its violent dénouement. At the same time, Gesualdo's fabled history exerts a thematic pressure on the narrative: the composer is a frequent subject of conversation among the musicians, and his tumultuous history comes literally to repeat itself through Sandro and Franca. In this manner, two musical source texts from the European Baroque determine the demise of Cortázar's unfortunate soprano in Buenos Aires. Gesualdo's legendary past, which is repeatedly evoked in the story, plays out on the thematic level, while the Musical Offering—a work which is not once mentioned in the narrative itself, apart from in the afterword—operates at the level of structure and form.[2]

It turns out that Cortázar is far from alone in appropriating Baroque musical forms and redeploying them as formal strategies in transnational narratives. However, the title he gives to the story, "Clone," immediately problematizes what it means to create a literary response to a work of music. When scientists produce a clone, they analyze the genetic code that makes up an entity, and use it to fashion a full or partial copy thereof. Roberto, one of the characters in the novella, uses the word "clone" to describe the impression of seamless unity the musicians aspire to achieve in performance as they give unified expression to the music in a score: "El otro día leyendo ciencia-ficción encontré la palabra justa: éramos un *clone* [...] el canto y la vida y hasta los pensamientos eran una sola cosa en ocho cuerpos" (Cortázar, 1980, 110). ['The other day, reading some science fiction, I found the exact word: we were a *clone* [...] singing, living, and even thinking were all one single thing in eight bodies" (Cortázar, tr. Rabassa, 1983, 45)]. Ironically, however, by the beginning of the novella, this unity is already a thing of the past, as jealousy and desire have destroyed it. Instead of the clonelike unity promised in the title, the story recounts the gradual dissolution of the ensemble and the fatal elimination of one of its members. It is also worth noting that Roberto borrows the notion of "cloning" from science-fiction novels, as it indicates just how closely imbricated music and fiction are in this text. Music determines the course of the novella, but literature has already shaped the protagonists' perceptions.

To pursue the genetic metaphor further, Bach's Musical Offering functions as the determining code that generates Cortázar's story. Its role only becomes visible through the author's afterword, despite the pervasive thematic presence of music throughout the story. In this sense, the code is hidden in the text, much like the mathematical patterns and lipograms adopted experimentally by Oulipo writers of the mid-twentieth century in Europe and the United States, particularly Georges Perec, Harry Matthews, and Italo Calvino. These writers used formal constraints to produce literary texts, often embedding them into narratives unbeknownst to readers.[3] Cortázar's constant thematic references to Gesualdo's madrigals obscure the formal relation between the story and the Musical Offering. The technical explanations of his afterword thus come as a great surprise, and to some degree displace the catharsis of the story from the thematic level (the murder) to its fascinating formal construction (its imitation of the musical structure of the Musical Offering).

At the same time, Cortázar's story alerts us to the dangers of what Hayden White (1992, 288) calls the "structuralist fallacy: namely, the belief that when we have identified a structure in an artistic work, we have also found its meaning." Recognizing the role of the Musical Offering does not necessarily bring readers any closer to seizing the significance of the story. In fact, while the title may seem to offer a commentary on the work's borrowing of musical form, it actually misleads readers into pursuing formal connections that are not supported by the text. The author takes pains in his afterword to list the sequence of contrapuntal movements to which each section of his story corresponds, only to proclaim subsequently his lack of musical expertise. He even quips that he simply read the movements (and their instrumentation) off the record jacket of Millicent Silver's orchestral recording of the Musical Offering during an afternoon at the beach, thereby revealing that the source on which he modeled the story is not the authoritative original, but an orchestrated adaptation. Cortázar thus undermines the temptation to read the story itself as a "clone," by asserting its necessary difference from the musical model, which itself already differs from an original text that recedes into the distance. Even for an author fully versed in musical composition, it would be an impossible project to render the multiple contrapuntal genres that make up the Musical Offering—crab canons, canons in contrary motion, and so on—in any literary text, let alone such an economical piece as a short story.

Cortázar thus brings virtuosity and experimental verve to "borrowed" material, just as Bach did before him. Bach produced the Musical Offering at the request of Frederick the Great who set him the task of extemporizing a fugue on a particularly unwieldy and chromatic theme. Bach improvised an impressive three-part fugue in the king's presence, and later sent him a collection of thirteen elaborations of the theme, far surpassing his expectations. Cortázar in turn responds with his own extravagant elaboration of Bach's work. Mario Vargas Llosa (2011, 145–46) observes that "no other writer has bestowed on the game the literary dignity that Cortázar gave it, or made the game such a flexible and profitable instrument of artistic creation and exploration." Along with the game, Vargas Llosa sees freedom as vital to any discussion of Cortázar's fiction: "Freedom to violate the established norms of writing and narrative structure, [...] to revolutionize [...] narrative time, the psychology of the characters, the spatial organization of the story and the relationships within it. To unwrite the novel, to destroy literature." "Clone" illustrates Cortázar's affinity for puzzles and radical approach to form, as does his earlier novel *Rayuela* (*Hopscotch*), whose chapters the author encouraged readers to read out of order, either according to their whim or following a sequence suggested in the text.

Through his formal and thematic appropriation of these different musical sources, Cortázar develops a transnational and interdisciplinary aesthetic, while demonstrating the impossibility—and the undesirability—of achieving true coincidence of forms. As we have seen, the story is a hybrid creation rather than a perfect clone. Cortázar borrows the structural apparatus from Bach, while thematically embracing the darkness and murderous passion of Gesualdo's biography. "Clone" thus stages an encounter—in Buenos Aires, no less—between multiple musical and literary sources. The author uses sixteenth-century Italian scandals, the contrapuntal voicing of a masterwork of the German Baroque, and the experimental spirit of the Oulipo movement of the mid-twentieth century to spin a contemporary murder story while asserting the essential difference between literature and music. In this sense, the story works against the very notions of uniformity and repetition invoked in its title, "Clone," to affirm instead an aesthetics—and ethics—of difference as fundamental to creative expression.

In the context of this study, it is especially important to take note of what "Clone" reveals about the relationship between a musical "voice" and a voice in literature. Cortázar realizes each "voice" in Bach's musical score through a corresponding literary character. By twinning a character to each instrument, he rewrites the contrapuntal lines of Bach's work as dialogues or larger conversations. Virtually all the action takes place through verbal confrontations between characters, whose spirit is predetermined by the music.

"Clone" demonstrates the kind of innovative and virtuosic experimentation with musical form that this book locates in the novels of writers such as Maryse Condé, Assia Djebar, Nancy Huston, and J. M. Coetzee. The turn to musical form in transnational fiction must be understood as a move of both aesthetic and ethical dimensions: it reflects an effort to challenge the conventions of genre and form, an interest in bringing new perspectives to the fore, a desire for new ways to engage conflicting viewpoints and histories, and a commitment to preserving difference. Furthermore, it indicates a refusal to identify with any single national tradition and an understanding of artistic and cultural heritage as hybrid, multilayered, and complex.

The appropriation of musical forms by contemporary novelists goes hand in hand with the intense interest that literary and cultural critics have accorded to music throughout the twentieth century. Baroque forms, in particular, play a striking and explicit role in postmodern and postcolonial critical theory. As early as the 1930s, Catalan critic Eugenio d'Ors defined the Baroque as a revolutionary and destabilizing current that traverses every historical period. The atemporality and unbounded inventiveness of the Baroque similarly captivated Alejo Carpentier, Gilles Deleuze, Antonio Benítez-Rojo, Wilson Harris, and Édouard Glissant. Like d'Ors, Carpentier identified the Baroque as an aesthetic that surfaces in all times and that accommodates the proliferation of forms and accumulation of styles. For Deleuze (1993, 5), the "Baroque refers not to an essence but rather to an operative function, to a trait. It endlessly produces folds. It does not invent things: there are all kinds of folds coming from the East, Greek, Roman, Romanesque, Gothic, Classical folds... Yet the Baroque trait twists and turns its folds, pushing them to infinity, fold over fold, one upon the other. The Baroque fold unfurls all the way to infinity." Benítez-Rojo (1992) later lays claim to the Baroque as a creolizing aesthetic that spirals out from the Caribbean to touch the furthest reaches of the world. He locates traces of Caribbean dance—the swaying rhythm of a creole woman's walk—in the florid, expressive gestures and repetition in European Baroque art and architecture. Glissant likewise embraces the Baroque "as a rebellious [...] decolonizing strategy to deform—creolize—the metropolitan standard" (Zamora and Kaup, 2009, 622). Significantly, all of these critics undermine European claims to Baroque forms and ideas, and seek to locate them instead within a dynamic, transcultural framework. While scholars have increasingly attended to the phenomenon of a New World or alternative Baroque that emerges from the Caribbean and Latin America (Kaup, 2005; Lambert, 2004), this book deterritorializes the Baroque even more radically to show how novelists deploy its forms transnationally across borders, forging new connections among diverse locations and historical contexts.

Voice

It is impossible to address polyphony, counterpoint, variation, and opera, without first engaging the question of voice. The term "voice" signifies differently in music and literature, and is the subject of debate within both fields. In "Clone," we saw how Cortázar transposes each of the various musical voices that constitute Bach's (instrumental) counterpoint into a corresponding literary character. And yet, as the novels examined in this book reveal, the act of translating the concept of voice from music to literature is far from simple. Between the musical and literary understanding of voice lies a crucial divide: a musical voice implies sound, while a literary voice is invariably silent. A musical score encodes a performance, whereas a literary text occasions a reading. A performance often involves multiple actors who occupy a common space and time; reading, by contrast, is an intimate act. Music can *simultaneously* deploy multiple voices in relations of harmony, unison, or dissonance, while works of literature necessarily alternate voices in succession.[4]

The notion of voice is extremely multifaceted, as even standard dictionary definitions attest. For instance, the first entry on "voice" in the *Oxford English Dictionary* places emphasis on sound. The voice is the "sound formed in or emitted from the human larynx in speaking, singing, or other utterance." Significantly, the second entry on voice emphasizes the political: "the right or privilege of speaking or voting in a legislative assembly, or of taking part in, or exercising control or influence over, some particular matter; part or share in the control, government, or deciding of something." Another entry links the voice to questions of singularity and alterity, and defines it as the mark of an individual: "sounds regarded as characteristic of the person and as distinguishing him from another or others." "To voice," in the verbal form, is "to act as the mouthpiece or spokesman," "to give voice, utterance, or expression to," and "to endow with voice, or the faculty of speech or song." These definitions point to the tensions between voice as agency and singularity, on one hand, and voice in the sense of "to speak for" and "to take the place of," on the other.

In music, there are also multiple dimensions to the understanding of voice. In one sense, "each of the melodic lines in polyphonic music, whether sung or not" constitute a voice, and thus voice is synonymous with a musical part. In another, the voice is the physical, resonant production of a human body, "the specific, irreplaceable quality of human vocal cords, membranes stretched across the larynx in song. [...] not reproducible in symbols and thus fixable on the page" (Abbate and Parker, 2012, 7–11). Deleuze and Guattari (1987, 96) argue that "as long as the voice is song, its main role is to hold sound." The operatic voice is an extreme instance of voice, as the singer generates an unparalleled range of volume and expression.

These definitions indicate the fundamental ambivalence that haunts the notion of voice. On one level, voice connotes political agency and presence. Having a voice entails a capacity to communicate needs, desires and thoughts. This necessitates an audience, for as Gayatri Spivak (1988) demonstrated in her seminal essay on subaltern subjectivity, a subject who goes unheard or unacknowledged cannot be said to possess voice.[5] At the same time, the voice rests on the precarious premise of a unified speaking or singing subject, a notion upended by the linguistic and psychoanalytic revolutions of the early twentieth century that revealed the fractured and unstable nature of subjectivity. In *De la grammatologie,* one of the founding texts of deconstruction, Derrida revisits eighteenth-century works on the evolution of music and language to question the phonocentric bias of Western philosophy and the privileged status accorded to voice as an indicator of presence. Derrida unravels the binary distinction between writing and voice to show how writing and difference always already inhabit speech, and even thought itself.

Nonetheless, there has been an unmistakable resurgence of the term "voice" in literary criticism since the 1990s. The reinvestment of literary scholars in questions pertaining to the voice has often been understood in relation to the discovery of anti-Semitic publications authored by preeminent Yale critic Paul de Man. The revelation that de Man had contributed more than one hundred literary articles to Belgian collaborationist newspapers between 1940 and 1942, and never retracted the positions he espoused in these pieces, led many to question the ethical and ideological underpinnings of his critical approach. Deconstruction insists on the indeterminacy of the text, and affirms the capacity of language to produce meaning independent of authorial intention, which its opponents saw as highly problematic because it risks evacuating human responsibility and negating "the possibility of action and political opposition" (Bernstein, 1998). Ann Banfield (1991, 22) observes that "to linguistics, there was an 'anti-linguistic response' [called alternatively discourse analysis, pragmatics, speech act theory, communications theory]— that turns instead to the 'human voice divine' within linguistic performance, substituting communication for language. It provides the justification for the return of a unified authorial voice, in the guise of the speaker, to literature." The renewed critical interest in the voice signals an effort to re-inscribe political responsibility and agency into texts in response to deconstruction and the postmodern fragmentation of the subject as a function of language.[6] In addition, it stems from the translation of Bakhtin's critical work into English and French in the late 1980s, and the introduction into the critical vocabulary of terms like polyphony that explicitly focus on "voice."[7]

The issue of voice—what it is, who has access to it, how it is understood across different genres and disciplines—is of particular importance with respect to transnational fiction. As recent scholarship attests, the transnational experience is divided along lines of class. The growth of transnational corporations and the development of new communication technologies have led to the unprecedented global movement of people and ideas, but they have also increased inequality, widening the divide between "those who circulate capital" and "those whom capital circulates" (Žižek, 1999). While the cosmopolitan elite elect their affiliations and determine their movements between different cultural contexts, this is not the case for working-class immigrants and refugees whose displacements are dictated by economic, environmental, and political pressures. Indeed, as Vertovec and Cohen argue, while capital, merchandise, and information move freely across the globe, restrictions on the movement of people—travellers, labor migrants, and asylum seekers—are tightening (Ezra and Rowden, 2006). Whose voices do not come across in transnational fiction? As David James (2011, 191) asks, "have modern and contemporary novelists offered stories about belonging that unsettle the outright celebration of perpetual relocation, complicating the model of global citizenship upheld by those of an economically comfortable cosmopolitan class?" The novels addressed in this book show access to voice to be both unequal and mediated. Alongside the concept of voice, these texts explore the possibilities and problems of "voicing": how agency and voice are assigned within the text, who speaks for whom, and which voices remain underrepresented or excluded.

The Music of the Transnational Novel

Condé, Djebar, Huston, and Coetzee are among the most prolific and visible figures on the stage of contemporary transnational literature. The musical dimension in their work is emblematic of an ongoing engagement with multiple literary traditions, in local and global issues, and in a virtuosic experimentation with narrative form. Moreover, in spite of their success, each of these writers lays claim to a kind of marginality, because of the creative freedom such marginality confers. Educated abroad, subject to multiple displacements, and currently residing in voluntary exile, they claim "transnational" affiliations. Djebar, born in the coastal town of Cherchell, Algeria in 1936, moves between Paris and New York; Condé, born on the French Antillean island of Guadeloupe in 1937, worked for many years between New York and Paris; Huston, born in Calgary, Canada in 1953, writes from Paris in both French and English; and Coetzee, born in Cape Town, South Africa in 1940, currently writes from Australia and has long maintained a formidable presence in publishing, book reviews, and academia both in Britain and the United States. All four writers have engaged in multifaceted careers as writers, scholars, teachers, and public intellectuals, and maintain a subversive and independent distance from fixed ideological positions. Their novels convey skepticism toward collective identities, an uneasy relationship with tradition, and a sense of being out of place and out of time.

Their deployment of musical forms to express complex, transnational affiliations recalls Edward Said's (1993, 248) discussion of the Trinidadian scholar C. L. R. James:

> Well after *négritude*, Black nationalism, and the nativism of the 1960s and 1970s, James stubbornly supported the Western heritage at the same time that he belonged to the insurrectionary anti-imperialist moment which he shared with Fanon, Cabral and Rodney. In an interview he said: "How am I to return to non-European roots? If it means that Caribbean writers today should be aware that there are emphases in their writing that we owe to non-European, non-Shakespearean root, and the past in music that is not Beethoven, that I agree. But I don't like them posed there in the way they have been posed *either-or*. I don't think so. I think *both* of them. And fundamentally we are a people whose literacy and aesthetic past is rooted in Western European civilization."

James turns to music—and to Beethoven, specifically—to lay claim to a broad, aesthetic tradition, as does each of the writers considered here.

These writers were born between the late 1930s and 1950s, at a time when music was still very much part of a liberal, humanist education. They came of age before "the mass entertainment media eroded the culture of home performance and musical amateurism" (Kramer, 1995, 4). Djebar studied classical piano and has been identified as an unusually musical writer since the publication of *L'amour, la fantasia* [1985, *Fantasia, an Algerian Cavalcade*], an epic novel that deploys personal autobiography, oral testimonies, and historical accounts of Algeria's colonization and struggle for independence, all the while making reference to the structural transgressions and expressive excess of Beethoven's fantasies and to the traditional North African cavalry formations called fantasias. In more recent years, operatic adaptations of Djebar's novel *Loin de Médine* [*Far from Medina*] have been premiered on stages in Italy and the Netherlands.

Said, as is well known, was a highly accomplished pianist and the music critic of *Nation* magazine. In addition to his extensive writing on music, which includes *Musical Elaborations* and a volume of essays entitled *Music at the Limits,* Said co-authored *Paradoxes and Parallels* with Daniel Barenboim, the world-class pianist and conductor. The two also partnered in establishing in 1999 the West-Eastern Divan Symphony Orchestra to bring together Middle Eastern young musicians across political divides. Said wrote insightfully about his own position as an Arab intellectual who questioned the West's imposition of its authority—political, cultural, economic—over the Middle East, and who nonetheless remained deeply committed to the performance and consideration of Western classical music.

Condé, though not a musician, asserts the importance of music to her writing. She claims she always writes to music, favoring artists as diverse as Vivaldi and Kassav.[8] Many of her novels feature musicians, and again exhibit the same diversity in styles: the protagonist of *Victoire, les saveurs et le mots* (2006) is obsessed with classical music; *La vie scélérate* (1987) features a celebrated Gwoka musician engaged in the preservation of Guadeloupean traditions,[9] while Marie Noëlle in *Desirada* (1997) marries an innovative Jazz musician whose compositions fail because they are too ahead of the times.

Huston has a particularly close relationship to music, as she studied piano and harpsichord. Her novels engage with music on all kinds of levels: thematically, they include many musicians; formally, they enact principles and narrative structures borrowed from music; philosophically, they explore the differences between music and language, and probe the social conventions that govern how music is produced and received. Huston has ventured into musical recording as well. In the early 1990s, she assembled an eclectic group of Baroque and jazz musicians to produce a musical reading of her novel *Les variations Goldberg*, which she released on disc as *Pérégrinations Goldberg* [*Goldberg Wanderings*], and which bears striking resemblance to Glenn Gould's experiments in contrapuntal radio.

Coetzee came to music much later; by his own account, he was fifteen years old when he first heard Bach's music wafting over from a neighbor's garden. He later completed a doctoral thesis on Samuel Beckett's writing and thus developed a rare intimacy with the work of one of the most interesting musical writers of the early twentieth century. Coetzee's fiction, like that of Djebar, has inspired adaptations for the operatic stage: the Theatre of Erfurt, Germany in 2005 commissioned an operatic version of his novel, *Waiting for the Barbarians* (1980), with a musical score composed by the prominent American composer Philip Glass. *Disgrace* inspired a film version in 2008, for which Antony Partos and Graeme Koehne wrote original music to represent the opera that Coetzee's protagonist is writing.[10]

As each of these writers elects transnational affinities over national identities, musical forms provide a means of addressing the complexities of their experience. This makes them vulnerable to Benita Parry's (1996, 39) critique that "despite the fictions' disruptions of colonialist modes, the social authority on which their rhetoric relies and which they exert is grounded in the cognitive systems of the West." While their engagement with Western classical music[11] undeniably brings into view the influence of their Western education, these authors self-consciously inflect this tradition and allow it to interact, overlap, and relate with others. It would be too simple to regard these forms as remnants of an elitist, imperial world order and an indication of a pervasive neocolonial aesthetics. In the act of borrowing and reappropriating forms, these novelists bring them into vastly new contexts, making visible new relations, and thus performing the kind of radical, relational poetics that Glissant advocates. Multiple musical traditions intersect in the novels of Djebar and Condé, including traditional Andalucían song, Berber chants, and North African military fantasias in the case of Djebar, and Zouk and reggae in that of Condé. Huston constantly probes the distinctions between "high" and "low" culture, juxtaposing classical music and genres such as popular folksongs, blues, and jazz, and evaluating spontaneous forms of music against those that require extensive instruction and practice. Coetzee incessantly calls into question the validity and relevance of all inherited forms, whether lyric poetry, the African griot tradition, opera, or the novel itself. The authors examined in this book thus self-consciously confront the possibilities and problems that arise in the "translation and transformation of borrowed or inherited categories"—musical, linguistic, philosophical, aesthetic, social, and political—which Gikandi (1992, 44) identifies as the primary task of postcolonial writing.

The novels under consideration here span the last decade of the twentieth century, and occupy pivotal roles in the literary production of each author. *Traversée de la mangrove* (1989) is Condé's first work to be set in Guadeloupe following the author's symbolic "return" to the island. *Les nuits de Strasbourg* (1997) is the first novel by Djebar to be entirely set in Europe, and to grapple with the entangled legacies of World War II and the Algerian War. *Les variations Goldberg* (1981) is Huston's first novel, often seen as an act of homage to her teacher and mentor Roland Barthes. Finally, *Disgrace* (1999) is Coetzee's first novel to address post-apartheid South Africa. *Disgrace* provides a particularly illuminating counterpoint to the fiction of Djebar, Condé, and Huston not only through its engagement with music (opera), but more broadly because of Coetzee's interest in and frequent references to the

French literary tradition, particularly to Rousseau and Beckett.[12] Despite this affinity, this is the first time Coetzee's work has been placed in dialogue with francophone fiction.

Transnational Studies

This study engages with a wide range of scholarship on transnational literature and on the interdisciplinary relations between music and literature. Benedict Anderson (1983) persuasively linked the rise of the novel to nation formation and to the constitution of national identities, showing how novels played a vital role in enriching European national languages by disseminating shared ideas about national history and shoring up collective identity. Novels legitimized certain voices and experiences, while relegating others to silence. Transnationalism shifts focus from the nation as the determining frame of experience, to consider the dynamic movement "within, beyond, and between nations" (Ashcroft, 2010, 22), as individuals and communities navigate multiple pulls of belonging and identification. Accordingly, scholars of transnational literature have sought to determine how the genre of the novel has changed to account for the different tiers of transnational experience, from migrant workers to refugees of political violence or environmental disaster, international students, employees of global corporations, and artists. Does the transnational novel require a new set of critical terms, or can existing theories of the novel adequately account for such developments in transnational fiction as the diversity and multiplicity of voices, wide-ranging cultural references, and shifts between vastly different geographies and temporalities? What part does music play in meeting the aesthetic challenges and priorities of transnational fiction?

Stephen Clingman (2009) and Peter Hitchcock (2010) both offer insightful responses to transnational writing. Clingman adopts a "navigational approach" to reading that attends to the temporal and geographical shifts in transnational fiction, and explores the status of boundaries. Hitchcock studies the issue of scale and duration, noting the tendency of transnational writers to exceed the spatial and temporal limits of the traditional novel and to produce series of trilogies and quartets. Accordingly, he uses Bakhtin's notion of the chronotope to consider the extended duration and serialized form of Djebar's Algerian Quartet, an expansive project that interweaves Algerian history and autobiography over the course of four novels. The chronotope enables

Hitchcock to consider the extended duration and serialized form of Djebar's project as a response to decolonization and transnationalism. Musical forms similarly open up spatial and temporal dimensions in the novel.

In fact, music is an important device in transnational fiction because it provides formal strategies to address the aching disparities and rich contradictions of the transnational experience, as well as the spatial and temporal disjointedness it entails. To some extent, Paul Gilroy has already shown music to be integral to understanding transnationalism, as music is one of the key modes of expression that constitute the dynamic cultural and historical space he outlines in *The Black Atlantic*. Gilroy demonstrates how black musical expression played a role in reproducing "a distinctive counterculture of modernity" (36). For Gilroy, the "vitality and complexity of this musical culture offers a means to get beyond the related oppositions between essentialists and pseudo-pluralists on the one hand and between totalizing conceptions of tradition, modernity and post-modernity on the other" (36). Jazz occupies a complex status as an "important repository of black cultural values" and transnational historical experience and a highly intellectual, restlessly creative, and self-conscious mode of expression (97). Accordingly, writers from the Caribbean and North America appropriate and engage with jazz. Nick Nesbitt (2003), for instance, illustrates how Antillean writers reference jazz in their writing, showing how Daniel Maximin, in particular, dialogues with the history of jazz and introduces a jazz-like poetics into his novels.

African American authors have also experimented with musical forms. A striking example is Toni Morrison's 1992 novel *Jazz*, a breathtaking evocation of Harlem in the 1920s. The novel recounts the story of a young couple who migrate from the rural South to New York City, and endure betrayal, murder, and madness. Morrison brings multiple elements of jazz into the novel—vernacular language, repetition, call and response patterns, scatting, or instances of wordless vocalization where the voice functions as a musical instrument—according to a willful strategy of appropriation and hybridization. As Morrison (1985, 342) explains, "I try to incorporate into that traditional genre, the novel, unorthodox novelistic characteristics—so that it is in my view Black, because it uses the characteristics of Black art." By infusing the novel's language and structure with a jazz-like aesthetic and explicitly calling the text "Jazz," the author remakes the novel into an expressive vehicle for African American experience. As the novel unfolds in New York during the jazz age, this turn to jazz is also deeply consonant with the time, place, and ethos of the text.

The resurgence of Baroque musical forms in contemporary transnational writing poses a particular kind of challenge, as the application of these forms in twentieth-century contexts suggests a temporal and geographical disjunction. Yet it indicates the currency that key aesthetic values of Baroque art hold for contemporary writing: irregularity, multiplicity, dynamism, extravagance, undecidability, and simultaneity. D'Ors (1935, 23), anticipating Deleuze, highlights the impossibility of defining the Baroque in opposition to other periods by showing how elements of the Baroque pervade all periods and are manifest in the most diverse regions, from the Occident to the Orient: "The style of civilization is called classicism. Should we not then give the name Baroque to the style of barbarity that persists in permanence beneath culture? We call a large irregular pearl baroque. But still more baroque, still more irregular is the ocean water that the oyster transforms into a pearl."[13] He thus links the Baroque to processes of transformation, of becoming.

In a deliberate effort to read transnationally, this book crosses disciplinary divides by considering South African and Canadian writers alongside their Antillean and Algerian counterparts. These novelists do not fit neatly into either a postcolonial or a francophone framework. As Coetzee observed in March 1997 at a French-sponsored conference for francophone and anglophone African writers in Djibouti, the question "who speaks?" cannot be disconnected from "who listens?" Coetzee's readership—like that of Djebar and Condé—cuts across national boundaries. Such a transnational readership necessarily complicates an author's affiliations and commitments. Who is considered a South African writer today? Or, as Coetzee frames the question:

> What about someone who was born in South Africa, who perhaps resides there, who writes in English, is published in England and the United States, and who is widely read throughout these countries and translated across Europe, in such a way that for each reader he has in South Africa, he has hundreds or thousands elsewhere; someone who maybe considers himself a witness to his country of origin for the world, while at home he is accused of disseminating a foreigner's vision of his country, or at least a vision comforting to foreigners?[14]

And what of an Algerian or Guadeloupean author, who writes in French, lives in New York, publishes in Paris, and is translated throughout Europe and the United States? In Algeria, Guadeloupe, and South Africa, respectively, critics constantly call into question the authenticity—and by extension the

authority—of writers like Djebar, Condé, and Coetzee, as though international success were the marker of fraud and betrayal. Critics reproach Djebar
because she lived abroad throughout the Algerian civil war of the 1990s and
writes in French, Condé for her imperfect mastery of Creole, and Coetzee
because he eschews the overtly political, realist tradition embraced by authors
such as Nadine Gordimer. Huston also upsets categories of national and
linguistic belonging. She is an anglophone Canadian who resides in Paris
and who writes interchangeably in both French and English, translating her
own work between these languages and confounding readers in her refusal to
sanction either the French or English version as the original.

As Françoise Lionnet argues, the standard understanding of the term
"postcolonial" fails to account for the differences between nations that
emerged from the colonial experience at vastly different moments in history,
and those still under metropolitan rule: the United States, for instance,
became a postcolonial nation following the American Revolution in the
eighteenth century, centuries before the wave of decolonization movements
in Africa and Asia in the mid-twentieth century.[15] The islands of the French
Antilles, Guadeloupe and Martinique, have been departments of France
since 1946; because they remain politically and economically dependent on
the metropolis, they cannot properly be termed "postcolonial." Algeria, by
contrast, achieved independence from France in 1962, but the postcolonial
regime's exclusive monopoly on power and program of enforced Arabicization
in turn marginalized constituent cultures, including Berbers, Jews, and French
speakers. South Africa poses yet another set of problems: recognized in 1910
as a republic independent from Great Britain, the apartheid regime institu-
tionalized a system of internal colonization from 1948 to 1994, relegating the
majority of the population, Blacks and Coloureds, to a subordinate, circumscribed existence. At what point, and for whom, did South Africa become a
postcolonial nation? Certainly, the end of apartheid in 1994 marks a watershed
moment in South African history, but it signals not the end of a colonial era,
rather the passage from an exploitative, discriminatory, and racist system
to an inclusive, multicultural democracy.[16] If the term "postcolonial" can
still be useful, it is because it occasions this kind of comparative discussion
of the colonial experience and its legacy on contemporary politics, and, as
K. Anthony Appiah (1991, 353) observes, it facilitates the construction of
"*transnational* rather than a *national* solidarity."[17]

Huston, Condé, and Djebar are generally categorized under the label
of francophone studies, a category that many now regard as "a form of

neo-colonialism through which France continues to assert cultural (and perhaps even political) hegemony over formerly colonized peoples" (Hargreaves and McKinney, 1997, 4).[18] Condé maintains that "the word francophone encompasses people who have nothing in common, apart from the fact that they speak French. None of these linguistic groups has anything to do with the others. Speaking French in Ivory Coast and speaking French in Guadeloupe does not foster a connection. The label 'francophone' is extremely fragile" (Broichhagen et al, 2006, 19). Christopher Miller (2006, 235) emphasizes that the literature called "francophone" emerges "from a thin veneer at the top of postcolonial societies and its authors strive to represent in an international idiom the experience of every day lives that are lived in hundreds of other languages." Djebar's essays speak vividly to this tension, as she seeks out modes of representing Algerian women without betraying or supplanting their voices. Djebar displays an acute awareness of her privilege as one of the few Algerian women of her generation to be educated in French, and to possess the freedom to navigate the public sphere. She argues that the label "francophone" has placed her in a "no-man's land," "on the margins," in oscillation between languages, between the North and the South, between body and voice, between the solitary self and a collective history (Djebar, 1999, 29–30). In the late 1990s Djebar proposed the term *"francographie"* in place of *francophonie*, thereby shifting the emphasis from voice (*phonè*) to writing (*graphe*). This notion of *francographie* captures the interior struggle with multiple languages—colloquial Arabic, Berber, the body—that necessarily precedes and informs her writing in French.

In 2007, resistance to the term "francophone" coalesced into a movement of authors who demanded a more radical reassessment of *francophonie*, and who published an incendiary piece, "Le Manifeste des quarante-quatre," in the French newspaper *Le Monde* on March 16, 2007. These writers clamored for the abandon of *francophonie* in favor of a *"littérature monde,"* a world literature in French that would liberate the French language from its "exclusive pact with the nation" (Le Bris and Rouaud, 2007). Like Djebar, they argue that "francophone" is an invalid term for writing in French: "l'émergence d'une littérature-monde en langue française consciemment affirmée, ouverte sur le monde, transnationale, signe l'acte de décès de la francophonie. Personne ne parle le francophone, ni n'écrit en francophone." ["The emergence of a self-declared world literature in the French language, open to the world, transnational, seals the death certificate of Francophonie. No one speaks francophone, nor writes in francophone."] As Paris remains unrivalled as the center of French publishing, the movement has yet to achieve real autonomy and critics have an important role to play in eroding these disciplinary boundaries.

In her contribution to the volume *Pour une littérature monde* (2007), Condé calls on music to challenge the integrity of the French language. The author claims she worked hard to appropriate and reinvent the French she inherited from her parents and schooling, a French of submission, silence, and conformity. Significantly, she sees music as a more flexible, expressive register:

> Je n'avais pas choisi cette langue. Elle m'avait été donnée. Non pas par la colonisation. C'est une absurdité de le prétendre. La colonisation ne sait que réduire les peuples au silence. C'est contrainte et forcée qu'elle bâtit quelques écoles dans l'intention de former les subalternes dont elle a besoin. Le français avait été marronné par des parents aimants qui me l'avaient offert, voulant me parer au mieux pour l'existence. Comme j'aurais aimé être poète ou chansonnier pour plier la rebelle à mes jeux! [...] Ou griot pour allier la parole à la musique et au rythme. Jean-Jacques Rousseau avait raison: l'écrit n'a pas de vie. Il faut lui restituer la chaleur qu'il a perdue. Comment? Je m'essayai à mille stratagèmes. (Condé, 2007, 213)

> [I didn't choose this language. It was given to me. Not by colonization. It would be absurd to make that claim. Colonization only knows how to reduce people to silence. It was through sheer necessity that colonization built a few schools in view of shaping the subalterns it needed. The French language was stolen away (marooned) by loving parents who gave it to me, wanting to equip me as best as possible for life. How I would have loved to be a poet or singer in order to bend the rebel language to my games! [...] Or a griot who could join speech to music and rhythm. Jean-Jacques Rousseau was correct: writing has no life. You have to restore the warmth it has lost. How? I tried a thousand strategies.]

Condé's desire to ally her writing to music and rhythm speaks to the desire of authors to reappropriate the sonorous fullness of speech. While literature has been preoccupied with the tension between writing and orality since classical Antiquity—Socrates famously did not write, and Plato advocated the exclusion of poets from the republic—these issues become especially charged in the colonial and postcolonial contexts, where the language of writing was often imposed by a colonial power, and remains disconnected from the multiple registers of everyday life.[19] Orality presupposes direct contact with others. Writing, by contrast, is divisive, "breaks presence," and mediates across distance. As Condé attests, the challenge is to give writing life and warmth.[20]

Coetzee particularly attends to the status of colonial languages in Africa. He portrays English as morally and expressively "exhausted" in contrast to African languages that retain warmth and immediacy. In *Disgrace*, theater and storytelling stand out as literary genres that still manage to reach audiences, whereas the novel, opera, and poetry are in crisis in a world increasingly driven by consumerism and corporate interests. Coetzee nonetheless insists that the task facing writers is to create novels despite this irrelevance, to write while fully conscious of living beyond one's time, to write in the very face of failure and alienation.

Taking a different approach, Djebar reclaims and valorizes writing primarily by asserting its historical place in North African culture. She recounts that her mother inherited a collection of notebooks containing musical settings of medieval Andalucían Arabic poetry. French soldiers mistook the notebooks for subversive tracts and destroyed them during the Algerian War, leaving her mother inconsolable, despite the fact that she knew every poem by heart. The notebooks represented a treasured family heirloom that had been passed down by generations of women. Djebar explains how these musical texts embodied "the culture of [her] mother. One speaks so often of orality but there is a written culture, a whole patrimony of writing in the Maghreb."[21] Djebar uses this story on one hand to assert the rich musical culture of Algeria, and on the other, to render visible a longstanding tradition of writing. She claims writing as the legitimate heritage of North African women, who belong to "a culture of learning and poetic inscription." By asserting writing as the traditional inheritance of North African women, Djebar rejects the prevailing understanding of postcolonial writing as secondary, foreign, and borrowed. Her revisionary stance challenges preconceived notions about the relationship between written and oral culture, and aligns with Derrida's critique (1976, 28–29) of the longstanding association of orality with fullness, presence, and authenticity.

Word and Music Studies

While the field of word and music studies has blossomed in the past two decades with important scholarly interventions, music remains marginalized in literary criticism. By contrast, music is by no means marginal to the novel tradition. In an impressive study of music in British fiction, Gerry Smyth (2008, 7) argues that "[m]usic looms surprisingly large in the history of British fiction. Novelists from every generation, working within every genre, have responded to the power of music by incorporating it into their narratives, by trying to harness its techniques and effects, and by attempting to recreate the emotions that come to be associated with particular musical styles, forms or texts. In fact, music represents a recurring feature of the canon." This observation holds true outside the British tradition as well. A salient example is Marcel Proust's attempt in *A la recherche du temps perdu* to emulate Wagner's *Gesamtkunstwerk*, the totalizing, epic fusion of drama, poetry and music. In *Doktor Faustus,* Thomas Mann similarly takes on the music of his contemporary, Arnold Schoenberg, and proceeds to analyze and critique his controversial approach to composition, twelve-tone serialism.

This book attends to a different phenomenon: it examines the engagement of twentieth-century writers and critics with Baroque forms that are radically incongruous with the time and space they address. It also calls attention to two problematic tendencies among literary critics as far as music is concerned: on one hand, the tendency to treat music as a universal language that transcends the political, and on the other, to ascribe democratizing and emancipatory properties to music. Music, on the most basic level, is "organized noise," and it is beset with political, social, and ideological implications. Musicologists and cultural critics have increasingly studied the relationship between music, ideology, and power. Jacques Attali, for example, argues that music is prophecy, because of its capacity to express social forces before they become visible elsewhere. Musical "styles and economic organization are ahead of the rest of society because it explores, much faster than material reality can, the entire range of possibilities in a given code" (Smyth, 2008, 3). The exceptional plasticity of music, its entanglement in economic and cultural discourses, its direct popular appeal, and its capacity to incorporate and layer diverse voices have fascinated many twentieth-century literary and cultural critics—including Bakhtin, Barthes, Deleuze, Milan Kundera, Gilroy, and Said[22]—who have looked to musical forms for new conceptual models to understand narrative voice, multilayered narrative structures, diasporic cultural production, and the relationship between overlapping and conflicting histories.

It is thus essential to evaluate the ideological tenor of the literary engagement with music more critically. On what grounds do critics refer to contemporary novels as polyphonic, participatory, and multivoiced? What can musical counterpoint teach us about conflict resolution and cosmopolitan coexistence? How far can we extend counterpoint and polyphony as metaphors in literary criticism before the terms break down? How does musical performance shed light on such literary issues as the tensions between textual authority and interpretative freedom, between the pressures to maintain social conventions and the desire for change? How might the literary representation of opera enable us to rethink not only the relationship between music and language, but also the encounter with alterity more broadly? Why do the Western European concepts of polyphony, counterpoint, variation, and opera continue to play a role in the contemporary novel? What do musical ideas that coalesced during the Baroque period offer contemporary transnational writing? Do these forms support efforts to challenge boundaries, transform notions of community, undermine dominant ideologies, and affirm the right to difference, or are they, as Cameron Fae Bushnell (2013) claims, indicative of the pervasive impact of colonialism and the continued hold of Western aesthetic forms? To what extent do musical forms provide a means of dislodging dominant ideologies, as Mai al-Nakib (2005) suggests?[23] How are musical forms creolized in the process?

Criticism on music and literature tends to fall into three general categories: studies that examine *representations* of music in literary texts; those that treat music as a *metaphor* in order to address existential, linguistic, or philosophical questions; and those that explore the potential of musical *forms* in literature. In recent years, the field of musico-literary criticism has seen the publication of several important works by Lawrence Kramer (1989), Werner Wolf (1999), Eric Prieto (2002), Stephen Benson (2003), Alison Rice (2006), Smyth (2008), Julie Huntington (2009), and Bushnell (2013), several of which exemplify the aforementioned categories. Wolf considers the relationship between music and fiction as a privileged instance of "intermediality," a kind of intertextuality that emerges from the rapport not simply between multiple texts, but between different media. By revisiting English novels by Laurence Sterne, Aldous Huxley, Samuel Beckett, Virginia Woolf, and Anthony Burgess, he offers a set of criteria for determining whether a particular work of fiction truly engages with music, and for evaluating how music functions within the text. Wolf's study is remarkable in its attempt to redefine the discipline of musico-literary criticism. However, although Wolf calls for further analysis of the *function* of musical forms in literature, he gives very little consideration to the political or ethical dimensions of intermediality. Wolf focuses on writing in English, but neglects postcolonial fiction by non-Western authors. Smyth and Bushnell also address the influence of musical form on the anglophone literary tradition. Bushnell focuses exclusively on postcolonial anglophone writing, and argues that the use of classical forms indicates the persistence of Empire and the deep hold of Western cultural values on writers from around the world.[24] Smyth offers a helpful and wide-ranging overview of developments in the field of word and music studies from 1940 to the present. He demonstrates how music is integral to the canon and to recent British fiction, proposing incisive readings of canonical and contemporary texts. Benson, by contrast, is concerned principally with the representation of music in contemporary literary texts, and with the limits of language to capture and express musical experience. He presents an extensive and thoughtful consideration of the strategies through which novels construct an encounter with music.

Writing in the context of French and francophone criticism, Rice tunes a musical ear to the work of three North African francophone writers: Hélène Cixous, Assia Djebar, and Abdelkebir Khatibi. She explores music as a supple metaphor in order to illuminate key aspects of their writing: their situation between languages, hybrid subjectivity, and self-conscious poetics. Huntington studies the role of rhythm and sound in francophone writing from Africa and the Caribbean, drawing particular attention to the drumbeat. Of these works, Prieto's *Listening In* merits particular attention as an impressive attempt to account for the importance of music in modernist narratives. Prieto traces the history of the relationship between music and letters from Classical Greece to the early twentieth century. He argues that music came to play a major role in the writing of Samuel Beckett, Michel Leiris, Roger Pinget, and Claude Levi-Strauss precisely because it provided a literary model for emerging ideas on consciousness itself, a fluid way of representing subjectivity. Prieto (2004, 99) sees the modernist turn to music in relation to the burgeoning interest in subjectivity, psychoanalysis, and the workings of memory: music for modernist writers provided "a model for thought in its temporal dimension, opposed to the synchronic, spatializing dimension of the linguistic sign."

Each of these studies has inspired this book in various ways, and laid the ground for a consideration of the influence of musical form in contemporary transnational writing. The prevalence of musical forms in fiction is the expression of a distinct historical and intellectual moment: the close of the twentieth century, the shift from postcolonial frameworks to theories of globalization and transnationalism, and the search for hybridized, multivoiced artistic forms that convey the complexities of transnational experience and subjectivity.

Music as Political Agency: the Transnational Legacy of Rousseau

The writers addressed here, like many authors shaped by the colonial experience, claim an affiliation to the eighteenth-century philosopher and musician Jean-Jacques Rousseau: Condé, Huston, and Coetzee all cite him liberally, and Coetzee even fashions the character of David Lurie in satirical homage to Rousseau. The fact that Lurie presumes to write an opera despite his evident lack of musical experience recalls Rousseau's own entry into operatic composition. Returning from a disappointing evening at the opera where he found the music "faible, sans chaleur, sans invention" [weak, lacking warmth and originality], Rousseau determines he could do better: "A force d'y penser, et même malgré moi, je voulus [...] tenter de faire à moi seul un opera, paroles et musique" [The thought of it made me determined, despite myself, to try to write an opera alone, words and music] (*Confessions* II.7).

Rousseau argues that writing impoverishes speech and robs it of its inherent musicality, making it impossible to mobilize people in the public square. Stripped of accent and intonation, writing completely obscures the link between words and a particular speaker and situation. Although Derrida deconstructs this binary opposition of speech and writing, Rousseau's thought continues to resonate with writers who experienced the imposition of a colonial language and whose relationship to oral culture was irrevocably disrupted and mediated. Moreover, Rousseau identifies a North–South divide well before such notions had currency, and gives thought to the issues of migration and colonization. In the *Essai sur l'origine des langues,* he conjectures that language must have originated simultaneously in the North and South, but in response to different situations. Northern languages developed out of necessity, as harsh environmental conditions and scarcity of food compelled people to work together to build technical skills for survival; as a result, these languages emphasized precision. By contrast, given the more hospitable climates and constant abundance of food in the South, Southern languages emerged out of passion, not of necessity, and privileged expression over technical exactitude. In a remarkable attempt to account for history, migration, global inequality, and the ascendancy of written culture over music and speech, Rousseau imagines that a catastrophic event must have "tipped" the Earth on its axis to produce different climates and regional temperaments. Faced with increased scarcity and hardship, the people of the North migrated to the South, where they supplanted the musical, accented, vocalic languages of the meridian with their abstract, mute languages and writing. For the people of the Southern hemisphere, the language inherited from the North was a foreign imposition. Writing was doubly foreign, as it came from the Phoenicians and was tainted by commerce. Harmony, like writing, arrived from the North and displaced melody.

Rousseau takes an impassioned stance against harmony, insisting that the melodic line holds moral importance, whereas harmonic counterpoint and polyphony alienate the public and lead to anomie. In the *Dictionnaire de musique* (1768), Rousseau dismisses harmony as noise, "sans écho, sensuel mais pas spiritual" ["without echo, sensual but not spiritual"]. By contrast, he attributes immediate moral effects to melody: "c'est d'elle que dérive tout le pouvoir de la musique sur l'âme" ["The power music has on the soul derives from melody"].[25] Rousseau laments the predominance of harmony in French music under the influence of Jean-Philippe Rameau, as he links it to undemo-cratic developments in the political and social spheres: the decline of political agency, the absence of debate, and alienation. He goes so far as to declare that where harmony "engulfs melody and philosophy consumes language, social and political freedom are lost to servitude" (Thomas, 1995, 141).

For Rousseau, melody offers a possible remedy to social and political problems, while harmony aggravates inequity and autocracy. Ironically, in keeping with Rousseau's assertion that every problem contains its own remedy ("le remède dans le mal"), contemporary authors *write* to recover voice, and the musical forms and concepts they deploy are Baroque, multivoiced, and *harmonic*. As the following readings demonstrate, novelists borrow multilayered musical forms in order to account for the entanglements and contradictions of contemporary transnational experience.

                                     *   *   *

The chapters that follow each consider a particular musical concept in relation to a distinct ethical and narratological concern: polyphony and representation, counterpoint and history, variations and performance, opera and alterity. Why are these musical forms—which one might expect to find associated with elite, conservative, and Eurocentric values—instead seen to offer such radical democratic and liberating potential for literature? What happens in the translation of musical concepts to the literary domain? In pursuing such questions, this book seeks to re-evaluate some of the utopian and celebratory claims of recent literary theory.[26] Notions like hybridity and polyphony have become clichés—associated with positive, liberal values like multiculturalism, cosmopolitanism, and pluralism—rather than useful tools for textual analysis. By examining the way music has informed these theoretical ideas, this book develops a more nuanced critical vocabulary for addressing contemporary narrative form.

Postcolonial novels are often described as "polyphonic," with little consideration of what precisely this entails. Chapter 1 accordingly seeks to define polyphony, by reading Condé's canonical novel, *Traversée de la mangrove* [1989, *Crossing the Mangrove*], against leading theorists of literary polyphony, Bakhtin and Kundera. Bakhtin developed the concept of literary polyphony in order to highlight the unique capacity of the novel to hold together multiple, sociohistorical perspectives without allowing any particular voice to dominate, an aesthetic he located in Dostoevsky's novels.[27] Kundera later used the term to describe the narrative technique of combining multiple simultaneous, interconnected plotlines that engage a common theme, as in Dostoevsky's *Demons* and Broch's *Sleepwalkers*. Bakhtin understands polyphony as the interplay of multiple perspectives and ideologies; for Kundera it is a question of multiple plotlines. Bakhtin's conception is largely phonocentric and moral, whereas Kundera's is both spatial and thematic.

One of the most prolific and widely read novelists of the Antilles and a formidable and uncompromising critic, Condé challenges a common misperception about literary polyphony in postcolonial criticism, namely the idea that the novel can approximate oral culture and give voice to disenfranchised subjects. The novel stages a ritual wake in the rural village of Rivière au Sel. Prompted by the sudden, inexplicable death of a tall, mysterious stranger, the local people come together in order to honor the dead man and to try to make sense of his unusual story. One by one, each of the inhabitants occupies the position of narrator, offering memories and speculations regarding the deceased. The text holds together their stories, refusing to privilege any particular account, and creating the illusion of a community event that unites the villagers. When one looks more closely at the novel, however, it becomes clear that there is no actual exchange between the villagers, who are deeply divided along lines of race, class, and gender. The silent monologues laid out in the text are only available to the reader, who by the same token, is shut out of much of what actually transpires at the wake. The novel thus gives the impression of intimacy and community, while maintaining an aesthetic of opacity. Reading this novel against the criticism surrounding it demonstrates how the uncritical use of the term "polyphony" actually obscures our understanding of ethics and representation, and mutes the social critique present in Condé's texts.

Chapter 2, "Edward Said and Assia Djebar: Counterpoint and the Practice of Comparative Literature," moves from polyphony to consider the closely related term, counterpoint. Musicologists may well hold counterpoint and polyphony to be nearly identical, but the fact remains that they have had very different applications in literary theory and cultural studies. This chapter examines Said's theory of counterpoint as developed in *Culture and Imperialism* (1993) in relation to Assia Djebar's novel *Les nuits de Strasbourg* (1997). Counterpoint is a practice of reading transnationally and transhistorically that challenges the literary canon by opening it to include texts relegated to the margins, thus undermining the very idea of the center and radically shifting the relations of power to foster reciproqual and equal exchange. In the years since Said's untimely death in 2003, the musical dimension of his work has drawn critical attention. *Les nuits de Strasbourg* provides fertile terrain to extend this work. Djebar's novel uses counterpoint in order to revisit the fraught relationship between France and Algeria. Instead of pairing the former colony with the metropolitan center, Djebar instead relates Algeria to Alsace, and highlights their similar histories of political and linguistic instability, occupation, and hybridity. The novel stages the crosscultural romance between Thelja, a young Algerian scholar and François, a native of Strasbourg who served in the French army during the Algerian War. The lovers' probing conversations bring divisive historical issues down to a more manageable, human scale. Djebar revisits Franco-Algerian history within the context of an increasingly multicultural Europe, in which communities are faced with multiple conflicting histories. The novel's contrapuntal approach consists of four principal dimensions: firstly, it juxtaposes conflicting histories to reveal their unexpected points of contact; second, it dialogues with a diverse array of writers who have been excluded from dominant canons; third, in a more poetic sense, it explores the contrapuntal possibilities of language, the ability of words to signify in multiple ways; and finally, it exploits the transnational influence of the Antigone myth. Djebar's use of the Antigone story to address the conflict between memory and national history relates significantly to strategies adopted by Jacques Derrida in *De l'hospitalité* (1997) and Leila Sebbar in *La Seine était rouge* (1999), texts similarly written during the time of the Algerian civil war of the 1990s.

The third chapter, "Glenn Gould and the Birth of the Author: Variation and Performance in Nancy Huston's *Les variations Goldberg*," examines the relationship between performance and authority in music and literature. In *Les variations Goldberg* (1981), an amateur harpsichordist invites thirty friends into her bedroom for an intimate performance of Bach's Goldberg Variations on a midsummer evening in Paris. Huston structures the novel according to Bach's theme and variations. The text consists of thirty-two loosely connected sections, the first and last of which are narrated by the performer, while each of the intervening chapters explore the thoughts of a different audience member in keeping with the mood of the corresponding musical variation. This chapter argues that Huston's choice of the Goldberg Variations participates in ongoing debates about performance instigated by her compatriot, Canadian pianist Glenn Gould, who at the time of writing had just issued his second recording of the Goldberg Variations, the work with which he launched his career some twenty-five years earlier. Gould shook up the classical music world by withdrawing from the concert stage at the peak of his career to advocate recording as more democratic than live performance. Arguing that performance subjected musical interpretation to the vagaries of chance and to the unreliability of the human body, Gould held that recording allowed the artist more control over their interpretation *and* that it that it emancipated the musical experience by according the listener greater autonomy in shaping their experience of music. This reading of Huston shows how Gould's revolutionary ideas on performance are inseparable from—and anticipate—important shifts in literary theory regarding the relation among author, text, and reader expressed in such seminal essays as Roland Barthes's "The Death of the Author" and realized in the *nouveau roman*. Situated at the interstices between music and literature, Huston's novel examines changing attitudes to performance and authority in both fields, and points to an unacknowledged but fertile exchange across disciplinary borders.

Chapter 4, "Opera and the Limits of Representation in J. M. Coetzee's *Disgrace*," considers the role of opera in J. M. Coetzee's *Disgrace* (1999). In the tradition of modernist novels such as Proust's *A la recherche du temps perdu* and Sartre's *La nausée*, *Disgrace* is a meditation on artistic creation that uses music in order to stage the problems of writing. With unflinching irony, Coetzee interrogates the value of the English language novel in contemporary post-apartheid South Africa, particularly in light of linguistic diversity, the vibrancy of African popular forms, and the aspiration for rapid political and economic transformation. The novel's protagonist, David Lurie, is an aging English professor at Cape Town University who, weary of writing academic studies of Wordsworth and Romantic poets, decides to try his hand at an opera about Lord Byron's late romance with an Italian countess. His careless pursuit and rape of a student leads to his dismissal from the university, forcing him to take refuge at the home of his daughter Lucy in the rural Eastern Cape. A brutal attack unsettles Lurie's sense of place in the post-apartheid South Africa, and challenges his assumptions about justice, entitlement, sexual violence, and representation. In the aftermath of the incident, he continues to work on the opera, but the project undergoes profound changes. Critics generally read the opera as an embedded narrative in the novel and take its progress as evidence of Lurie's developing ethical sensibilities. I argue, on the contrary, that the opera is not a simple *mise en abyme*; the opera radically disrupts the text, opening a space of opacity and unreadability in the narrative, much like the story of rape that constitutes the center of violence in the novel. This chapter situates Coetzee's engagement with opera in *Disgrace* in relation to his critique of classical forms in *Age of Iron*, and ongoing exploration of the limits of narrative production and authority in *Waiting for the Barbarians,* and the later novels *Elizabeth Costello* and *Diary of a Bad Year.* Coetzee critiques both opera and the novel in order to make the case for their enduring and immeasurable value.

Ultimately, the deep engagement with classical forms that is evinced in the literary production of Condé, Djebar, Huston, and Coetzee reflects a particular moment in the history of ideas and in the ongoing transformation of the novel. While younger authors, including Chris Abani, Chimamanda Adichie, and Fatou Diome, deploy diverse musical strategies in their novels, the Baroque continues to exert a powerful hold on contemporary artists, as Kyle Abraham's stunning dance production, *Pavement* (2012), illustrates. Abraham's dance piece layers Baroque *castrato* arias with sound bites from John Singleton's *Boyz n the Hood* (1991) to interrogate gang violence and the constuction of masculinity in urban Black neighborhoods of Pittsburgh. This startling juxtaposition provokes new reflection on the broader cultural history of these issues across vastly different contexts.

When this book was already well underway, the editor of a leading literary journal published a call for "renewed scholarly interest in polyphony, dialogism and intertextuality: categories that have been superseded by materialist and historicist categories of reading" (Yaeger, 2007, 434). And yet, like so many others, her subsequent analysis leaves out music. It is my aim to bring music back into the discussion, and to develop a more cogent understanding of the interplay between musical form, narrative, and ethics in the transnational novel.

CHAPTER ONE

From Mikhail Bakhtin to Maryse Condé

The Problems of Literary Polyphony

> Each person who enters the labyrinth of the
> polyphonic novel somehow loses his way in it and
> fails to hear the whole behind the individual voices.
>
> — *Mikhail Bakhtin*

> On ne traverse pas la mangrove. On s'empale sur
> les racines des palétuviers. On s'enterre et s'étouffe
> dans la boue saumâtre.
>
> — *Maryse Condé*

Literary critics today invoke polyphony in order to characterize virtually any text that employs multiple narrative voices, languages, or storylines. Mikhail Bakhtin introduced polyphony into literary criticism in the late 1920s in relation to Dostoevsky's novels, and Milan Kundera later popularized the term in *The Art of the Novel*. However, despite its extensive applications in contemporary criticism, and particularly in discussions of African and Caribbean fiction, it is still unclear what precisely polyphony means to different critics and what kinds of novels it best describes. This chapter takes up the task of situating polyphony, clarifying its mechanics, and attending to the political work it is called on to perform in the novel.

Bakhtin lays out his theory of polyphony in the seminal essay *Problems of Dostoevsky's Poetics* (1929/1973). In his reading, polyphony evokes the particular capacity of the novel to accommodate contradictory positions and multiple discourses without imposing any central authoritative view. Whereas a "monophonic" text affirms the point of view of its author, polyphonic writing embraces dissonance and moral ambiguity. Several of Bakhtin's readers emphasize that polyphony is best understood as a loose metaphor, as an attempt to engage the "aural" and "oral" qualities of language and to account for the simultaneous interplay of voices within a text (Benson, 2003; Emerson, 2004). Jennifer Judkins (2011, 140) suggests that "musical forms themselves are generally soft concepts that are stretched and manipulated."

The malleability and multidimensionality of polyphony have made it a particularly appealing term for critics, as it facilitates a consideration of sound, space, and time in relation to the novel, aspects that surface more readily in discussions of poetry than of prose. Yet polyphony implies an act of interdisciplinary translation, as we move from the "simultaneous and harmonious" melodic lines that sound in a work of music to the "multiplicity of independent and often antithetic narrative voices" that interact sequentially and silently in a text.[1] Whereas the polyphonic voices in a piece of music can unfold simultaneously, a literary text relies inevitably on the horizontal juxtaposition or alternation of voices or plotlines whose simultaneity—and vocality—must always be constructed or imagined by way of some narrative conceit.

Of particular concern is the tendency of scholars to invoke polyphony in relation to Caribbean and African texts, often without clarification or reference to music (or to Bakhtin, for that matter). For instance, Gérard Meudal (2000) claims that Maryse Condé writes with "the sovereign ease of a novelist who has reached the perfect mastery of a polyphonic art of narration." David and Nicole Ball describe Djiboutian writer Abdourahman Waberi's novel *Passage of Tears* (2009/2012) as "a polyphonic novel," pointing to its "tense counterpoint between two totally different voices."[2] Odile Cazenave and Patricia Célérier (2011, 133) also identify Waberi's treatment of the narrative voice as polyphonic, and go further to assert that this type of narration articulates an ethics of "individual responsibility to the collective." H. Adlai Murdoch (2001, 8) notes the presence of polyphony in the works of Caribbean authors Daniel Maximin, Patrick Chamoiseau, Édouard Glissant, and Maryse Condé, which he reads as part of a willful aesthetic of ambiguity, displacement, and narrative fragmentation that engages "the elusive core of an undefinable creoleness." Delphine Perret (1995, 664), similarly, sees polyphony as a "typically Creole and doubtless postmodern phenomenon." These instances convey a very broad, generalized understanding of polyphony. For Ball, the presence of even two voices is enough to constitute polyphony. Cazenave and Célérier are interested in how polyphony highlights the relation of the part to the whole, the individual to the collective. Murdoch understands polyphony as a vehicle for a distinctly Caribbean aesthetic, while Perret sees it as both Caribbean and postmodern. Critics assume they are talking about the same thing when they use the term "polyphony," but they rarely break down the textual mechanics of polyphony, and ascribe diverse properties to the term. The fact that polyphony resonates in disparate ways in contemporary criticism, and that it is so often applied to texts by authors of color from Africa or the African diaspora, illustrates the need for a much more critical definition of the term.

This chapter engages Maryse Condé's *Traversée de la mangrove* [1989, *Crossing the Mangrove*] to show how a more situated account of polyphony shifts our understanding of authorial voice, plot development, sound, and space in the novel. Although thoroughly criss-crossed by scholars since its publication, Condé's novel continues to present critical challenges. Hailed as her most "Antillean" work (Philcox, 2001), marking both a creative and physical return to her native island of Guadeloupe,[3] the novel stages the fictional wake of Francis Sancher, a tall, charismatic stranger of mysterious Cuban origins who spends the last months of his life in the rural Guadeloupean village of Rivière au Sel. The novel opens as an elderly woman, Léocadie Timothée, stumbles upon Sancher's corpse. The news of his death spreads through the village, but no one can make head or tail of it. There are no wounds on the body; the man was seemingly in perfect health. Suspecting Sancher has fallen victim to crime, the local authorities take the corpse to the capital and attempt to determine cause of death through an autopsy, to no avail.[4] The body is then returned to the village, where the inhabitants assemble to perform the ritual wake. Throughout the night, each villager seeks to explain Sancher and his untimely death; their successive narrations draw a complex, contradictory portrait of the deceased, and show how the stranger's brief sojourn in the remote, insular village has profoundly unsettled their lives.[5] Ostensibly structured like a crime novel, the text offers no definitive answers for Sancher's death, only a multiplicity of possible interpretations, each one undermined by the narrator's acerbic irony.

Critics have generally read Condé's novel as a critique of the Martinican-led *créolité* movement because of its subversive depiction of contemporary Caribbean community (Britton 2004; Dash 2003). Whereas the leading proponents of Créolité, Patrick Chamoiseau, Raphaël Confiant, and Jean Bernabé, celebrate the harmonious coexistence of the diverse communities who inhabit the Caribbean and argue for the literary use of Creole, *Traversée de la mangrove* draws attention to the deep fractures among these groups, as well as their parochialism and xenophobia. The novel's unique, circular structure has also drawn a good deal of attention, but has frequently been misread. Critics emphasize the "orality" of the text, pointing to its diversity of narrators, creative appropriation of the ritual time and space of the wake, and seeming emphasis on storytelling. They miss the crucial fact that the novel stages instead a sequence of silent interior monologues to which only the reader is privy.[6] The people in this divided community neither speak to nor hear one another; they are competitive, jealous, xenophobic, and self-centered. The novel holds together their stories, through the artful narrative structure of the vigil, while nonetheless preserving the animosity between them. In other words, community and voice are illusory; they only come into being through the reading of the novel. As the following discussion sets out to illustrate, Condé's text critiques not only the celebratory rhetoric of Caribbean community, but more importantly for our discussion here, the clichéd and often exoticizing discourse on polyphony and voice.

As is the case with many transnational writers, it is impossible to position Condé either at the periphery or the center because both she and her novels move so fluidly between worlds. Born in Guadeloupe in 1937, she went to Paris in 1953 to complete her education at the Lycée Fénelon and the Sorbonne, like many Antillean intellectuals of her generation. Following her marriage to Guinean actor Mamadou Condé in 1960, she left Paris to work as a teacher in the Ivory Coast, only later reuniting with her husband in newly independent Guinea. She remained in West Africa for twelve years, teaching in Guinea, Ghana, and Senegal while raising her four children, a period she revisits in her recent memoir, *La vie sans fards* (2012). In 1972, she moved to London with her present husband, translator Richard Philcox. She earned a doctoral degree in Caribbean literature at the Sorbonne in 1975, and published her first novel *Hérémakhonon* the following year. Her increasing acclaim as a novelist, especially after the publication of the epic novel *Ségou* in 1984, brought invitations to teach at universities in the United States, including the University of California at Berkeley, the University of Virginia, Princeton University, and finally, Columbia University, where she developed a vibrant program in francophone studies and remains an Emeritus Professor. For nearly twenty years, Condé divided her time between New York and Guadeloupe, while also maintaining a visible presence in Paris. Her work has garnered numerous international literary prizes, including the Grand Prix Littéraire de la Femme (1987), Prix de l'Académie Française (1988), Prix

Marguerite Yourcenar (1999), Prix Tropiques (2007), and the Grand Prix du Roman Métis (2010). In 2004, she received the title Chevalier de la Légion d'Honneur from the French government, and was called upon to preside over the Commission for the History and Remembrance of Slavery.

Condé's fiction is dizzyingly transnational in scope, mapping out the complex web of interconnections between Guadeloupe, the Caribbean archipelago, West Africa, South Africa, the Americas, Europe, and Asia. Although *Traversée de la mangrove* unfolds in a tiny Guadeloupean village, it highlights the transnational diversity of the Antilles through characters of Indian, Syrian–Lebanese, Chinese, and Haitian heritage. As mentioned above, however, the novel does not offer a banal celebration of transnationalism, because it illustrates that not everyone has equal access to mobility. In fact, while the island elite may vacation in Paris and educate their children abroad, most of the subjects within the novel are enmeshed in circumstances from which they cannot escape, despite their transnational family histories. They are also prone to prejudice and intolerance. The novel exposes the tensions between global and local forces, most notably by juxtaposing Sancher's global travels with the inexorable historical responsibility that ties him to Rivière au Sel.[7] Despite the villagers' attempts to classify Sancher, his exotic origins, extensive travels, writerly vocation, and worldly knowledge exceed their categories. Like numerous other characters in Condé's fiction who engage in writing, art, or music, Sancher illustrates the problematic status of the writer in the Caribbean. As Lydie Moudileno (1995, 626) observes, the "artist serves to unveil the dynamic of their communities, while simultaneously revealing his inability to represent that community."

Condé's own resistance to classification has become one of her hallmarks as an artist and critic. She has been extremely vocal in protesting the application of European and North American theory to Caribbean literature. She argues that the use of theory often amounts to yet another form of intellectual colonization and stems from a misplaced arrogance on the part of Western critics, a will to render the text transparent. Following Martinican poet Glissant, Condé upholds opacity as a vital quality of Caribbean literature. Opacity constitutes the freedom not to be understood, and constitutes a strategy of resistance against a system of thought that reduces the other to an "*object* of knowledge."[8] Condé defends the opacity of her own texts through her resistance to glossing local expressions for an international audience, as well as through her refusal to authenticate any interpretation of her work. She asserts, "Ever since *Crossing the Mangrove*, I have been writing much less didactically, bringing in more and more derision, humor, and mockery, so that the message, if there ever was a message, has become so muddled that it is difficult to perceive" (Broichhagen et al., 2006, 21). Cilas Kemedjio (2013, 185–87) sees the pervasive derision in Condé's work as a marking of "postcolonial feminism," a willful effort to prevent "the novel from being established as an edifying model. The intention to destabilize certainties is translated in a speculative writing that, by dint of suggesting a plurality of interpretations, instates indeterminacy in the reading process." As Kemedjio astutely observes, however, critics have fallen under the spell of the writer's notorious dissidence and refusal of classification, which ironically has resulted in a uniform critical response. For Kemedjio, this constitutes an ethical failing on the part of Condé's critics. Condé "attempt[s] to formulate a voice that incarnates subaltern ones even while resisting any reduction into established categories. The dissidence that almost all critics detect in Condé's oeuvre becomes, so to speak, the writer's trademark. The unanimity in criticism regarding the transgressive dimension ends up being suspect." To put this in slightly different terms, such a critical response ironically flattens out the polyphonic dimensions of Condé's project. It reproduces an ambivalence that some see as already present in Bakhtin's own position, the lingering desire for answers and authenticity that many of us share: "Even as we rejoice in polyphony, we prick up our ears for the Word' (Erdinast-Vulcan, 1997, 267)—in this case, for Condé's authoritative word.

In *Traversée de la mangrove* as in her other novels, Condé draws on an arsenal of stylistic strategies to undermine simple truths: these include a proliferation of narrators, a nonlinear narrative structure, a frequent recourse to the impersonal voice to express gossip and public opinion, and a savvy manipulation of irony and double-talk in order to cast doubt on virtually any statement. She is renowned for seeking "words and plot situations that provoke, tease, extort, dialogize," to borrow Bakhtin's terms (Bakhtin, 1973, 39). The author incorporates popular expressions and neologisms, along with constant references to music, film, polemical debates, and other literary texts. More importantly, it is often difficult to distinguish between what is merely being thought and what is spoken. The successive interventions of the different narrators give off the impression of spoken dialogue, leading readers to perceive the novel as an instance of theatricality (Perret, 1995), and to emphasize the role of storytelling in the text (Fulton, 2001). In fact, however, the characters' narrations are fragmented, interior monologues that are not actually spoken out loud within the realm of the text.

If critics have largely failed to pick up on the subversively non-vocal dimension of the narratives in *Traversé de la mangrove*, a striking ambivalence between silence and vocality nonetheless haunts many critical readings of the novel. Critics interchangeably refer to acts of reading and hearing, demonstrating their uncertainty as to the ontological status of the narratives (Morrison, 1995; Fulton, 2001). Murdoch (2001) notes the slippery indeterminacy of voice in many of Condé's texts, pointing to the impossibility of pinning down discourse to a particular speaker. Only Crosta (1992) pursues this investigation further and insightfully separates out the distinctive narrative planes of the text, to delineate two levels of representation: the diegetic level of action, consisting of all the externalized happenings and conversations at the wake, which for the most part are inaccessible to the reader; and what she calls the meta-diegetic level comprising the internal thoughts of the characters and which, conversely, are exposed to the reader's gaze.

To put the case more clearly, Condé's novel does not demonstrably privilege the voice, although it deploys multiple narrators and has been interpreted by most critics as a text that comes remarkably close to approximating oral culture. Instead, the novel reveals the problematic status of the voice and points to the limits of literary polyphony, even while deploying many of its characteristic features. Revisiting the novel's structure allows us to develop a more rigorous notion of what polyphony entails, particularly in the transnational context, and to reflect critically on why the term has been applied so liberally to African and Caribbean authors. As we have seen, the critical consensus maintains that Condé's work is "polyphonic," but it is unclear what precisely this means. Polyphony functions something like the other labels attached to her work, like "francophone," "feminist," and "postcolonial" (Moudileno, 2006). This is symptomatic of a more general problem: the lack of clarity and precision in the current use of musical terms in literary criticism. On one hand, this ambiguity reflects the equivocal status of music in literary studies, where music is all too often associated with "the physical, the immediate, the bodily, the emotional as opposed to the rational and cognitive character of language" (Tolbert, 2001, 451). On the other, it reinforces Thomas Pavel's (1998, 580) claim that "such typically Bakhtinian notions as 'polyphony,' 'dialogism,' and 'carnival,' are unreliably defined, imperfectly defended, and, as a result, can easily be challenged" and appropriated. Emerson (2004, 113) arrives at a similar conclusion to assert that Bakhtin's influence is due in part to the porous nature of the concepts he proposed. His terms "are highly suggestive, but many potentials [are] left undeveloped." On a more significant level, the cavalier use of the term indicates the exoticizing and essentializing tendencies in criticism on African fiction.

The popular, egalitarian dimensions of Bakhtin's thought have made it appealing to postcolonial and postmodern scholars. Homi Bhabha, Henry Louis Gates, Jr., Stuart Hall, and Robert Young have taken up and extended the Bakhtinian concepts of hybridity and heteroglossia (Young, 1995, 21–22); Peter Hitchcock and Sanders deploy the chronotope; while numerous critics, including Glissant, Benítez-Rojo, Gilles Deleuze, and Félix Guattari, have appropriated the term "polyphony." Despite its wide resonance in theory and criticism, however, there have been few serious attempts to think about literary polyphony in relation to music. As Stephen Benson (2003, 293) contends, "Nowhere in the literature has any attention been paid to the work of polyphony as metaphor, to the nonliterary discursive sphere it implicates, as opposed to the concept that it passively enables." Dale Peterson (1993, 761–68), writing on African-American literature, argues that the adoption of Bakhtin's theoretical notions by North American scholars has been far too facile, celebratory, and commercial. Peterson claims that the incorporation of Bakhtin by such theorists as Gates and Houston Baker, Jr., has amounted to "serving" up a "Russian-American Creole." In the hasty consumption of Bakhtin, immense differences in contexts—historical, cultural, and geographic—have been erased. Furthermore, critics have neglected to examine the tensions between "the author's willed monologue and a character's zone of speech." Peterson demonstrates how Zora Neale Hurston's *Their Eyes Were Watching God,* like many other so-called "speakerly texts," is actually a writerly tour de force exhibiting stunning "literary ventriloquisms of orality."[9] Who does such a text actually empower? This question suggests another related issue: Do polyphonic novels equip readers to attend more closely to the diversity of voices within their own communities, and make them more conscious of their relations with others?

Polyphony in literature carries seductive and misleading associations with orality and democracy because it refers to a sonorous, complex, and collective phenomenon. But whether the polyphonic text holds special "democratic" or "emancipatory" potential is highly debatable, because of the masterful authorial control polyphonic writing implies. Ken Hirschkop (2001, 3) notes that for many scholars, Bakhtin became "a philosophical spokesperson for humanity at large," without adequate attention to the precise textual, political, and social implications of his thought. "We have to ask: What is this 'dialogism' that so many celebrate as liberating and democratic: what are its actual cultural forms, its social and political preconditions, its participants, methods and goals?" (Hirschkop, 1989, 2). How can we distinguish between the organized pluralism of democracy and the chaos of cacophony? In the context of postcolonial and transnational fiction, what specific techniques contribute to creating polyphony in the novel, and to what ends?

On the most basic level, polyphony means "many voices" or "many sounds"; the term is derived from the Greek *polyphonia*. In Western musical composition, polyphony refers to the simultaneous combination of several vocal or instrumental parts. The *Oxford English Dictionary* defines polyphony as a "multiplicity of independent and often antithetic narrative voices, none of which is given predominance; [also] the use of this narrative technique."[10] Polyphony brings our attention back to the voice, highlighting the potential of music—and by extension, narrative—to be multivoiced, and to inscribe a plurality of equal and unmerged voices. Yet, as we saw in the Introduction, the voice itself is an ambiguous term, and continues to preoccupy philosophers and linguists. In *Of Grammatology*, Jacques Derrida shows voice to be a deeply problematic metaphor, with only a tenuous connection to sound, exteriority, and language. Derrida (1976, 20–22) submits Heidegger's discussion of voice to a rigorous critique in order to dislodge the prevailing association of voice with sound and immediacy. He particularly points to the contradictions between Heidegger's claim that the voice is "*heard* (understood) [...] as the unique experience of the signified producing itself spontaneously from the self [...]," and his notion of the "voice of being" as "silent, mute, insonorous, worldless, a-phonic." Derrida thus points to a fundamental rupture between "meaning and the voice, between 'the voice of being' and the '*phonè*,' between 'the call of being,' and articulated sound." For our purposes here, it can also be helpful to consider voice against the related concept of "voicing," which Bakhtin refers to as "orchestration." In music and literature, "voicing" refers to how an author or composer distributes musical or fictional material to different instruments, singers, or subject positions. Voicing implies differential relationships of power and subservience, as the author or composer has the capacity to "animate" or "give voice" to others. Polyphony—except when spontaneous, collectively improvised, and *unwritten*—is produced through an act of voicing, so it inevitably becomes a site of tension between these contradictory elements of agency and submission.

Bakhtin (1973, 6–7) defines the polyphonic novel as "a plurality of independent and unmerged voices and consciousnesses [...] with equal rights and each with its own world." Each character's word "sounds, as it were, alongside the author's word and in a special way combines both with it and with the fully and equally valid voices of other characters." Thus defined, polyphony places emphasis on sound and voice, equality and plurality, independence and interdependence. Several key elements come into Bakhtin's understanding of literary polyphony: the equality and independence of each narrative voice; the importance of conflict and opposition even at the level of each individual utterance; the absence of teleology or overarching ideology; the positioning of the authorial voice on the same level as the characters, who each carry a truth equal to that of the author; the interweaving of different kinds of extra-literary material into the narrative; and the prevalence of mass-scenes where as diverse an array of characters as possible is assembled.

These attributes come into play in Condé's novel. The vigil, for instance, has elements of an unruly dinner party that unites "motley" guests from different social classes and generations, and successively explores their various points of view without producing any fixed, definitive conclusions. Different narrators intervene in turn, much like the passing of a motif among voices in a fugue. In addition, Condé incorporates disparate texts, from fragments of Ecclesiastes to newspaper articles, catalogues, citations from operas, and off-color jokes, bringing them into irreverent proximity. She works to expose the contradictions and dissonances within the very cultural forms that others (and particularly the critics associated with the *créolité* movement) celebrate as uniting Antilleans across their differences. Condé thus writes against the self-congratulatory rhetoric that has characterized both postcolonial studies and Caribbean criticism.

Before turning to a detailed analysis of how this plays out in the novel, we need first to map out the contours of the theoretical debate a bit further, by examining how Kundera appropriates and redefines polyphony.

The Polyphony of Storylines

Kundera popularized the concept of literary polyphony in his treatise on the novel, *L'art du roman* [1986, *The Art of the Novel*]. Kundera argues that the most important quality of the novel is its capacity for ambiguity and uncertainty. Surprisingly, although he engages many of the same fictional works that Bakhtin uses to develop his ideas, Kundera never credits Bakhtin as a precursor. The parallels between their writings on literary polyphony have not escaped scholarly attention.[11] Benson (2003, 300) observes that both Bakhtin and Kundera experienced the oppressive Soviet state and are passionate advocates of the "ethical significance of the modern European novel." Both critics foreground the novel's capacity to raise questions, regard polyphony as a stage in the ongoing evolution of the European novel, and define it against other forms. Bakhtin places the polyphonic novel in opposition to the "monological" fiction of Tolstoy that champions a single ideology. Kundera (1988, 17–18) contrasts the novel to the media, which he sees as the agent of "unification of the planet's history," distributing throughout the world "the same simplifications and stereotypes."[12] For both Bakhtin and Kundera, the polyphonic novel holds ethical value because it preserves uncertainty and difference.

There are, however, key differences in how Bakhtin and Kundera situate polyphony in the novel. For Bakhtin, polyphony refers to multiple, divergent voices within a sentence or even a word, while Kundera thinks of polyphony on a much larger compositional scale, in terms of the grand plotlines of the novel.[13] Bakhtin positions the author in the role of an orchestrator. For Kundera, the polyphonic author is a "poet and philosopher," spinning out different plotlines without ever losing the essential connection between them. This points to an important distinction in their vocabulary. Bakhtin's sense of polyphony is highly phonocentric, as he frequently refers to narrative "voices" that "sound" in the novel. Kundera evokes narrative "lines," and compares the horizontal unfolding of plot to melody. Kundera draws on his formal training as a musician to make precise comparisons between music and literature, whereas music plays a metaphorical and vague role in Bakhtin's thought (Emerson, 2004).

Kundera sees the polyphonic novel as consisting of multiple, equal plotlines that are unified in such a way that none of these storylines can be removed without destroying the meaning and intelligibility of the whole.[14] Kundera (1988, 82–83) regards Dostoevsky's *Demons* as an exemplary polyphonic text, because it consists of three distinct narrative lines that evolve simultaneously and that consider the same abstract theme from a different angle, "like a thing reflected in three mirrors. [This] gives the novel as a whole an internal coherence." Hermann Broch's Sleepwalkers presents another instance of polyphonic writing, even though it satisfies only one of the three conditions Kundera posits as essential to the genre, multiple plotlines. The novel's five narratives are of unequal importance in the text. The first storyline dominates to the point that the others function as "a simple accompaniment," and one could easily eliminate one narrative from the novel without compromising the rest of the work. Furthermore, the different storylines are only tenuously interconnected; characters from one thread do not reappear in the others. In Kundera's assessment, Broch's novel fails to achieve the fully fledged polyphony of a Bach fugue, which he holds up as the ideal illustration of polyphonic form since not one note of Bach's music is superfluous. Ultimately, however, Kundera's desire for indivisibility is problematic because it sustains the very values of unity and wholeness that the novel is meant to question. He ascribes an untenable perfection to Bach's work, idealizing music rather than submitting it to the same rigorous analysis he brings to the novel.[15]

This is not the only inconsistency in Kundera's discussion of literary polyphony. The author is unclear as to whether literary polyphony amounts to a poetic intention, a style, a technique, or a form. In one instance, Kundera (1996, 95) claims that "La polyphonie romanesque est beaucoup plus poésie que technique." ["Novelistic polyphony is much more [like] poetry than technique."][16] Later, however, he emphasizes the importance of technique when he seeks to explain why the polyphonic novel only fully came into being in the nineteenth century. Kundera locates the beginnings of novelistic polyphony in the embedded narratives of sixteenth- and eighteenth-century novels such as *Don Quixote*, *Jacques le fataliste*, and *Tristram Shandy*, but holds that these early instances fall short of true polyphony because the stories they contain do not unfold simultaneously, but instead sequentially. Kundera credits nineteenth-century novelists as having been the first to develop the compositional *techniques* necessary to sustaining multiple, simultaneous lines.[17] In many ways, the term "polygraphy"[18] suits Kundera's purposes better than polyphony, as he never mentions voice or sound, but rather lays out a technical approach to writing that treats the text like a score with multiple, simultaneously evolving lines.

Despite these inconsistencies, Kundera's treatment of polyphony helps to sharpen the questions we need to bring to Condé's novel and other texts. Where precisely does multivoicedness play out in the novel: on the level of the utterance or through long plotlines? Are all of the constituent voices or lines absolutely essential to the novel? What role does authorial intervention play in a novel, and is it ever possible to tease out authorial voice from the other voices within a text? Does the text place emphasis on sound, or on spatiality?

Authorship and Voice

This brings us to the thorny question of authorial voice, one of the places where the comparison between music and literature is most fraught. Bakhtin portrays the author as an orchestrator who strategically assigns voices and ideas to a cast of characters. This analogy is difficult to reconcile with his other claim that the author is "just one of the many voices in the text." In other words, can the authorial voice really be *equal* to the other voices within a text, while at the same time exercising creative *authority* over those other voices? Bakhtin's claims concerning the position of the author are difficult for a contemporary critic to evaluate, because his terms are so outdated. Generally speaking, literary critics no longer regard the author as a unified voice or persona, but instead either as a function of language (Barthes), or produced by the text (Foucault). As criticism on Condé reveals, however, critics often fall into the trap of reifying authorial voice when engaging with African or Caribbean writers. By contast, music entails a much more marked separation between the composer and the musical work. Few musicologists seek to locate a composer's voice within a musical composition, with the striking exception of Edward Cone whose controversial position on the subject distinguishes him from the bulk of his colleagues.[19] Composers may have a recognizable musical style, but even in the case of *Lieder,* or songs, listeners rarely confuse the singing voice with that of the composer. The status of the author's voice in a literary text is far more misleading, since a narrative voice feels so alluringly immediate, especially where first-person narration is used. Readers animate the voices of a text in their own heads; by contrast, music is generally experienced as coming from the outside, except when one silently reads a score.

The lingering fascination with authorial voice is particularly evident in the immense interest on the part of critics in the persona of Maryse Condé. Scholars have not given up on trying to situate her voice with respect to her novels.[20] At the same time, much has been made of the author's famous irreverence and refusal to confirm readings of her work. Nearly all of her novels test the boundaries of voice. Condé plays this up in her comments on *Histoire de la femme cannibale* [2003, *Story of the Cannibal Woman*]: "It rejects, in fact, the trio formed by the author, narrator, and main character. I wanted to create a work in which you don't really know where all these voices you hear are coming from. Is it Maryse Condé talking? Is it Rosélie? Is it the narrator who's expressing an opinion?" (Broichhagen et al., 2006,

25–26). In fact, Condé's description of *Histoire de la femme cannibale* comes remarkably close to Bakhtin's (1981, 77) definition of the modern novel in 1940: "One often does not know where the direct authorial word ends and where a parodic or stylized playing with the characters' language begins."

Bakhtin (1973, 49) asserts that the polyphonic novel "is not a multitude of characters and fates in a single objective world illuminated by a single authorial consciousness; rather, a plurality of consciousnesses with equal rights and each with its own world combine but are not merged in the unity of the event." The characters within the polyphonic world exceed the author's control; each of their voices carries a truth that rivals that of the author. For Bakhtin, this represents a revolutionary shift as to where authority is situated in a text: "What the author used to do is now done by the hero who illuminates himself from all possible points of view." In a sense, Bakhtin anticipates here the poststructuralist turn in the middle of the twentieth century: "For Dostoevsky as Bakhtin understands him, and for Bakhtin himself, 'secondhand' definitions of others are fundamentally *unethical*. One must approach another as a 'personality,' that is, as someone 'who has not yet uttered his ultimate word'" (Morson and Emerson, 1990, 265). This concern for the other's irreducible alterity is central to Condé's work, and illustrated in the opacity that Francis Sancher retains throughout the novel.

The issues of authorial voice and responsibility are particulary contentious in the Caribbean. When Condé "returned" to Guadeloupe in the late eighties, she found herself confronted with a local audience who preferred "lived culture" to writing and who regarded her as a foreign import with little relevance. As she describes it, they saw her as "published in France, written in French" with a reputation developed in the French- and English-speaking press and in American universities (Clark, 1989, 111). The shock of this initial encounter motivated her to redefine her relation to that public.[21] In "Habiter ce pays" [1989, "To Inhabit This Land"], Condé argues that the principal role of the Caribbean writer is to listen:

> Dans un pays comme le nôtre, l'écrivain c'est une femme, un homme parmi les autres, à l'écoute du pays d'une manière un peu particulière, essayant d'exprimer la voix du pays avec ses mots, avec son imaginaire, avec sa sensibilité. Mais le temps de l'écrivain, être privilégié, n'existe plus. Habiter ce pays nous ramène donc à cette humilité. (Condé, 1989b, 14)

[In a country like ours, a writer is a woman, a man, among others, who listens to the land in a rather particular way, trying to express the voice of the land with her words, her imagination, her sensitivity. But the time of the writer as a privileged being no longer exists. To live in this country brings us back to this humility.]

Through this statement, Condé adds her voice to the longstanding debate over the responsibility of the Caribbean writer. Martinican poet Aimé Césaire saw it as the duty of the Caribbean writer to speak for those who cannot. In the *Cahier d'un retour au pays natal* (1939), Césaire declares: "Ma bouche sera la bouche des malheurs qui n'ont point de bouche, ma voix, la liberté de celles qui s'affaissent au cachot du désespoir." ["My mouth will be the mouth of misfortunes that have no mouth, my voice, the liberty of those who are sinking in the dungeon of despair."] Abiola Irele (2008, 124) observes that these lines are a "gesture of identification and of self-dedication. [...] Césaire lent the extraordinary energy of his poetry to voicing the existential predicament of the black race." Three decades later, Glissant redefined the role of the Caribbean writer to reflect a new commitment to alterity. In *L'intention poétique*, Glissant (1969, 197) claims to write for "ceux qui n'ont pas eu de voix et dont nous ne saurions être la voix" ["those who had no voice and for whom we would not know how to be the voice"]. Glissant thus contests Césaire's notion that the writer can speak *for* others. Condé takes this one step further. She asserts that the writer must listen to the land, but that her ultimate function is not to serve as a voice for others, but to seek her own voice.

This claim allows the writer to mark her distance from Guadeloupeans, even as she asserts her connectedness to the island and its history. In an interview in 1989, Condé admitted to VèVè Clark that her relationship to other Guadeloupeans was not easy. Her efforts to reconnect with the local people were not always reciprocated. Condé recalled, "I went out and met with not so much the people but with the island itself. I learned how the island speaks to your mind; how it smells. It has a life of its own despite the meanness of individuals or their limitations" (Clark, 1989, 133). More than a decade later, in conversation with Emily Apter (2001, 96), Condé described her ongoing experimentation with language, form, and voice as a personal artistic venture: "More than the layering of languages, I'm interested in the polyphony of voice. I've worked with mixing first- and third-person voices, but I'm still not satisfied with the results. I'm still looking for the right form of the novel, the right voice; I'd like to create a 'Maryse Condé language.' I haven't found it yet; I'm still searching."

Condé's willful search for her own writing voice in French has multiple implications. As outlined above, it represents her impatience with the prescriptive doctrines through which Martinican writers have successively sought to define Caribbean writing, namely *négritude*, *antillanité*, and *créolité*. It articulates a defense of authorial freedom, and vindicates the value of fiction as art, outside of its capacity to serve as a political weapon. At the same time, however, the statement flirts dangerously with myths of authenticity and originality. Condé is by no means blind to this: she seems to play this up, by fashioning a "Maryse Condé language" that is richly intertextual, often cannibalistic, bitingly ironic, fragmentary, and contradictory, pitting different voices and positions against one another.

The question of what constitutes a Guadeloupean voice is a constant obsession throughout *Traversée de la mangrove*. The novel presents twenty "voices" who alternate as narrators and who are far from unified, but "multiple, located, contradictory" (Smyth, 2002, 22). An implicit narrator interjects ironic commentary throughout these accounts, casting doubt on each one's authenticity and authority. Condé's fictional narrators themselves refuse responsibility for their words, and instead claim merely to relay what others say. The text stages an incessant pattern of statement and negation. Phrases such as "Les gens prétendent que" ["People claim that"] are followed closely by their refutation, "Mais les gens racontent n'importe quoi" ["But people say anything"] (34). The use of impersonal expressions such as "on," "certains," and "les gens" constantly obscures the source of information. A variety of metaphors evacuate human agency from statements: gossip is a flowering plant,[22] rumors are attributed to the wind, and news items to a storm. Moreover, the text frequently leaves us no way to distinguish between rumor and "truth": "Les histoires les plus folles se mirent à circuler. En réalité, Francis Sancher aurait tué un homme dans son pays [...] Ce serait un trafiquant de la drogue dure, un de ceux que la police [...] recherchait en vain. Un trafiquant d'armes ravitaillant les guérillas de l'Amérique latine" (Condé, 1989a, 38–39). ["The craziest stories started to circulate. In reality, they supposed Francis Sancher had killed a man in his country [...] that he was a drug dealer, one of those the police [...] sought in vain. An arms dealer supplying South American guerillas."] As these examples illustrate, nothing separates the wildest rumors from the supposedly "real" accounts that oppose them. No one voice speaks from a position of unquestionable authority; there are contrary claims for each utterance and everything is the site of social contestation.

Multivoicedness thus emerges at the level of each statement in Condé's text, reflecting what amounts to a "microtextual," dialogic approach to polyphony. In Julia Kristeva's reading (1970, 16–18), Bakhtin sees Dostoevsky as a scribe who confronts points of view, consciences, voices, and texts. Ideologies are not organized according to a hierarchy in the novel, nor are they thought out or judged; instead, they function only as material. In this sense, the polyphonic text has only one ideology, that of form; the polyphonic novel puts multiple ideologies on display, only to empty them out in their confrontation. Kristeva suggests that Dostoevsky's influence in the French tradition is most strongly felt in the *nouveau roman*, which marks "the dissolution of the character novel towards novels that stage the intersection of multiple voices." In fact, more than any of Condé's other novels, *Traversée de la mangrove* demonstrates an affinity to the *nouveau roman* because it is structured precisely as a confrontation between different narrators and their conflicting interpretations.[23]

The discontinuous structure of *Traversée de la mangrove* has elicited a variety of metaphors, such as the mosaic (Perret), the patchwork quilt (Ramsay), and the creole garden (Rosello). Christopher Miller (1996, 180) describes it as an "egalitarian parceling out of the style." All of these metaphors reflect the eclectic distribution of material throughout the novel, but they are also essentially all static and fail to account for the dynamic interaction between narrative voices. The narrations of the various characters do not simply follow one another in neat succession, as the novel's table of contents seems to indicate; the characters' interventions are silent and internal, and as such can easily unfold simultaneously. The metaphor of polyphony, unlike any of the analogies above, allows us to address the mutual interpenetration and interdependence of the voices in the text and to consider the possibility of their simultaneity. There are, however, several other issues that remain to be considered before we can establish more precisely how polyphony functions in the novel.

The Spatial Configurations of Polyphony

One of the most radical attributes of polyphony is the potential for temporal simultaneity. A polyphonic score consists of a horizontal and vertical dimension: individual lines can be read horizontally, or the lines can be read together vertically, point by point. This multidirectionality is especially important in the context of postcolonial literature. Postcolonial critics Ashcroft, Griffiths, and Tiffin (1989, 34) argue that "history, ancestry, and the past" have constituted a powerful reference point for European epistemology; postcolonial thought challenges this by emphasizing how "time broadens into space. [...] Hybridity in the present is constantly struggling to free itself from a past which stressed ancestry and which valued the 'pure' over its threatening opposite, the 'composite.' [Postcolonial thought] replaces a temporal linearity with a spatial plurality." Derrida notes a similar shift in linguistics, contrasting Ferdinand de Saussure's linear and horizontal view of speech and writing, to the innovative musical paradigms Roman Jakobson proposed a few years later that accommodate horizontality *and* verticality. Saussure (1959, 70) argues that "auditory signifiers have at their command only the dimension of time. Their elements are presented in succession; they form a chain. This feature becomes readily apparent when they are represented in writing and the spatial line of graphic marks is substituted for succession in time." By contrast, Jakobson (1966, 15) proposes that writing can break free of linear constraints by substituting "for the homogeneousness of the line the structure of the musical staff, the chord in music."

Bakhtin emphasizes the spatial dimensions of polyphony by describing how voices in the novel do not merely follow one another in sequence, but "spread out in one place, standing alongside one another" (Benson, 2003: 299). Bakhtin thus likens the polyphonic novel to a "labyrinth" in which readers inevitably lose their way. Condé's tangled mangrove gives a distinctly Antillean twist to Bakhtin's image of the polyphonic labyrinth. The title of the novel juxtaposes two contradictory notions: the linear idea of crossing and the messy circularity of the mangrove swamp, whose knotted roots and branches actively resist navigation.[24] The novel itself offers an ironic commentary on its title: Sancher announces he is writing a novel called *Traversée de la mangrove* which he claims he will never finish because it was prematurely named. Vilma retorts that the novel will fail for other reasons, namely that its title stands on an impossible premise: "On ne traverse pas la mangrove. On s'empale sur les racines des palétuviers. On s'enterre et s'étouffe dans la boue saumâtre" (Condé, 1989a, 192). ["You can't cross the mangrove. You'd get stuck on the mangrove roots. You'd suffocate in the brackish mud."]

The title drew criticism from Chamoiseau, whom Condé invited to serve as the novel's first public reader.[25] Chamoiseau (1991, 390) argues that the title "Tracée dans la mangrove" would have been more productive, as it would have allowed Condé to evoke the paths forged by runaway slaves (nèg mawon) in the island forests, which he sees as a more significant aspect of the Caribbean experience. To be sure, the trace is an important term in the Caribbean imaginary. In Glissant's poetics of antillanité, for instance, the trace connotes poetic freedom, the capacity to forge transnational alliances and reject the constraints of possession and belonging.[26] Furthermore, in psychoanalysis and trauma theory, the trace indicates the inscription of experience on the psychic apparatus. The trace thus speaks not only to the traumatic histories of displacement, enslavement and exploitation, but also to the historical resistance practiced by slaves and the poetic freedom claimed by Caribbean writers. Chamoiseau's critique, however, exhibits the prescriptive agenda for Caribbean literature that Condé so adamantly resists, and puts forth certain words and images as more "Caribbean" than others. It also illustrates the pettiness of some of these debates, as Condé's title already evokes a distinctive dimension of Antillean history. Crossing recalls the transnational crossings that mark Caribbean experience: the Atlantic crossing that brought slaves from Africa to the Caribbean plantations; the later migrations of Indians and Lebanese who came to work the plantations after the abolition of slavery; the privileged, repeated crossings of the island elite who vacation in the metropolis and send their children to obtain advanced degrees abroad; the inbound waves of Haitians and Dominicans who come to Guadeloupe in hope of work; and the outbound waves of West Indians who leave the archipelago for the United States in pursuit of the American Dream.

While the title places emphasis on the act of crossing, the novel itself takes on a circular structure that reflects Condé's search for an aesthetic that would transcend particular Caribbean literary movements. As she indicated to Apter (2001, 96), "I disagree with créolité. What matters much more to me are problems of finding the right structure for the story, of translating cultural practices. I used a circular language to render the ritual of the night vigil."[27] She identifies Traversée de la mangrove as her most circular narrative: "In place of a linear story with a beginning and end, the narrative is defined by the sunset and the sunrise. Within these contours, there is circularity. I don't think this recurs in any of my books" (Broichhagen et al., 2006, 26). The novel's three sections—le serein, la nuit, le devant-jour—denote the cyclical passage of night into day. The wake resembles a concentrated theatrical experience whereby spectator and actor share the same temporal and spatial confines for the duration of the representation. The story unfolds between evening and daybreak, and the action is confined entirely to a house (Fulton, 2001, 301–9).

The alternation of narrators constitutes a critical aspect of the novel's circularity. The narrative progresses like a revolving wheel, whereby each movement or revolution brings a different point on the circle to the top. As in polyphonic music, no voice dominates except momentarily. A chorus of prayer circulates beneath the individual narratives, functioning throughout the novel like the continually repeated "ground" or bass line in polyphonic music. Taken from the book of Ecclesiastes, the prayer itself emphasizes eternal cycles of renewal and healing: "To everything there is a season, a time for every purpose under heaven, / There is a time to be born, a time to die, / There is a time to sow, a time to reap" (Ecclesiastes, 3.1–11). Against this constant refrain, Condé animates the thoughts of twenty individuals. Sancher is "the symbolic point to which everyone converges in their differences" (Rosello, 1995, 572). His foreign origins excite both admiration and derision. Romantic speculations circulate about his fortune, his involvement in anticolonial struggles, the historic curse that has plagued his family, and his vocation as a writer. Women project their desires on him, are tempted to nurture and console him, and see in him the possibility of self-liberation.[28] In this sense, Condé's narrative exemplifies yet another of the definitions Bakhtin proposes for literary polyphony: "different voices singing variously on a single theme" (Bakhtin, 1973, 4). To further complicate matters, however, the novel's main subject, Sancher, constitutes yet another "voice." Far from a static focal point, he is repeatedly described as a talking windmill, a *"moulin à paroles,"* propelling words in all directions (Condé, 1989a, 30). Moreover, as we will see in a moment, the text subverts the very idea of vocality. The narrations are only "heard" by the reader; they are otherwise silent, set against the noise of prayer, jokes, eating, and howling dogs.

What Constitutes a Caribbean Aesthetic? Who Decides?

Condé's invitation to Chamoiseau to serve as the novel's first public reader attests to a literary dialogue between the two writers that was already underway, and which erupts in places throughout the text like a palimpsest. *Traversée de la mangrove* is partly a rejoinder to the novel Chamoiseau published the preceding year, *Solibo magnifique*.[29] Both novels open with the inexplicable death of a symbolic figure. In *Solibo magnifique,* the highly revered storyteller Solibo drops dead in mid-sentence and the writer, represented in the text as a scribe ["scripteur"] or "marqueur de paroles," attempts to prolong his legacy. *Traversée de la mangrove* turns instead on the discovery of a writer's corpse; the writer, moreover, is a stranger to the community. Chamoiseau builds on the mythic tradition of the storyteller in Caribbean culture, and positions the writer in the same lineage. Condé pushes aside both the storyteller and the writer in order to facilitate the emergence of other subject positions. Her irreverent act demolishes the traditional hierarchies in Caribbean society and creates space for a more radical polyphony in the novel, making it possible for anyone to become a storyteller.

Chamoiseau praises Condé for staging the novel as a vigil, a trope he sees as quintessential of Caribbean history and literature. In Chamoiseau's view, the wake is *the* space from which a Caribbean collective identity emerges, the space of the storytellers, of intrigues, of rebellion:

> The wake is for us a melting pot of Creole culture, of its speech, of its orality, and it gave the extraordinary pretext that would allow plantation slaves to gather without spreading the fear that they were plotting to revolt or burn down a plantation. I even have the feeling that the Creole language, in its whispers, that the Creole culture, in its ruses and detours, and the Creole philosophy, in its underground, clandestine and fatalist character, all were shaped in the wake's contours; there, too, was shaped our most painful subjectivity. The wake also is the space of the storyteller, our first literary figure, the one who in the silence, gave us his voice, and who, facing death in the night, laughed, sang, challenged, as if to teach us how to resist our collective death and night... (Chamoiseau, 1991, 390–91)

Condé, however, harnesses the wake's history to very different ends: she uses its historic significance as a space of defiance in order to stage her own resistance to the prescriptive agenda of the *créolité* movement spearheaded by Chamoiseau and his Martinican colleagues. Instead of presenting the wake as a "melting pot of Creole culture," she uses it to reveal a profoundly fractured community of alienated individuals, linked by their tenuous relationships to a dead man, who is, moreover, a stranger. The novel presents "a community of differences that must be negotiated and tested, in the midst of, in some cases, intransigent conflicts and power differences. [...] It is a contemporary view of creolization [...] that allows for the changing dynamics of continual immigration and diasporic movement, as well as the cultural leaching caused by departmentalization" (Smyth, 2002, 22).

Condé radically undercuts the figure of the storyteller. Cyril is a minor character and what is more, he stumbles and stutters inexpertly in his speech.[30] His modest genealogy is no match for Sancher's exotic ancestry and impressive experience with foreign lands, freedom struggles, and unmentionable crimes (Condé, 1989a, 156). Condé's parodic portrayal of the storyteller has led several critics to read the novel as a thorough emasculation of "the male figure of *créolité*, the *contour*" (Smyth, 2002, 22–23). It demonstrates her unwillingness to spin nostalgic eulogies for a past she views as complex and imperfect.

If the storyteller no longer functions as the mouthpiece of collective consciousness in Condé's novel, the "writer" fares little better. The implicit narrator represents writers, would-be writers, and historians with a hearty dose of skepticism and critique. The fictional writers in the novel, Francis Sancher, Émile Etienne, and Lucien Évariste, are all paralyzed by self-doubt, identity politics, and the linguistic and aesthetic prescriptions of the media. Lucien, for instance, anticipates the media's critical response to his as yet unwritten book, "As-tu comme le talentueux Martiniquais Patrick Chamoiseau, déconstruit le français-français?" (Condé, 1989a, 228). ['Have you deconstructed proper French, like the talented Martinican Patrick Chamoiseau?'] Fulton (2001, 303) calls attention to the novel's "cynical disempowering of the role of the author," pointing to how "the people of Rivière au Sel express a profound mistrust of this mysterious occupation which involves 'sitting and doing nothing'." Such contempt for writing—and particularly for the genre of "politically correct," "cultural studies" writing that celebrates Caribbean folklore and oral traditions—recalls the caustic portrait in Condé's *La vie scélérate* (1987) of a writer who struggles to produce a volume, *La Guadeloupe inconnue*, that hardly anyone will read (Clark, 1989, 106). These derisive representations of writing poke fun at prevailing doctrines in Caribbean literature, while further problematizing what it means to be a Guadeloupean "voice." Such remarks de-fetishize literature, using humor and irony to bring writers down to an accessible level.

Condé also parodies select passages from *Solibo magnifique*, to critique Chamoiseau's simplistic veneration of origins. In *Solibo magnifique*, the storyteller advises the writer to pay attention to roots: "Z'Oiseau, tu dis:

La tradition, la tradition..., tu mets pleurer par terre sur le pied-bois qui perd ses feuilles, comme si la feuille était la racine! ... Laisse la tradition, pitite, et surveille la racine...!" (Chamoiseau, 1988, 63). ["Z'Oiseau, you say: Tradition, tradition..., you get down and weep for the tree that loses its leaves, as if the leaf were the root! ... Leave off tradition, my son, and keep an eye on the root...!"] In *Traversée de la mangrove*, Condé rewrites this passage to transform the root from a source of origin into something much more rhizomatic: "Les problèmes de la vie, c'est comme les arbres. On voit le tronc, on voit les branches et les feuilles. Mais on ne voit pas les racines, cachées dans le fin fond de la terre. Or ce qu'il faudrait connaître, c'est leur forme, leur nature, jusqu'où elles s'enfoncent pour chercher l'eau, le terreau gras. Alors peut-être, on comprendrait" (Condé, 1989a, 170). ["Life's problems, they're like trees. You see the trunk, you see the branches and the leaves. But you do not see the roots, hidden in the depth of the earth. And yet, what you have to experience is their form, their nature, to where they dig down to seek water, rich compost. Then perhaps you'll understand."] Condé thus suggests that one needs to take into account the broader environment that nourishes these roots: by extension, one needs to engage the dynamic interplay of transnational influences on Caribbean subjectivity.

Roots and trees constitute privileged metaphors in the Caribbean literary imagination, and their evolution in the work of successive authors reflects key shifts in the understanding of identity and history. Césaire promised to "plant a tree of sulfur and lava among a vanquished people," demonstrating his view of the intellectual as a pillar of power and strength.[31] He portrayed the tree as "an explosive, plunging shaft," a link to authenticity and origins. In Glissant's writing, by contrast, trees project outwards, and are a locus of "confusing, contradictory forces,"[32] reflecting an emphasis on relation and diversity. Chamoiseau tellingly stages *Solibo magnifique* at the foot of a tamarind tree, whereas Condé privileges the tangled mangrove swamp. While Chamoiseau establishes an artistic genealogy whereby the writer inherits the legacy and cultural authenticity of the *conteur*, Condé rejects this simplistic paradigm. As Smyth (2002, 18–19) notes, "Condé's use of the mangrove swamp image confounds a celebratory creoleness that seeks to trace well-defined roots to an earlier, more authentic, cultural identity."[33] The mangrove connotes new, artistic potential, as opposed to the forest that has been exploited and ravaged by the French. Condé (1989a, 67) portrays the Guadeloupean forest as a "cathédrale saccagée," a "sacked cathedral" that has been brutally deflowered by colonization.[34]

Condé ultimately caricatures Chamoiseau's view of writing as always secondary and inferior to orality. Solibo maintains that writing is detached from reality: "Ecrire, c'est comme sortir le lambi de la mer pour dire voici le lambi" (Chamoiseau, 1988, 53). ["Writing is like taking the mollusk from the sea in order to say, here is the mollusk."] In this view, writing reflects the loss of immediacy and presence. Within the environment of the sea, and by extension in oral culture, the meaning of the shell is immediately evident. Writing rips words from their social and lived context, and then tries to compensate for the rupture. In *Traversée de la mangrove,* Condé playfully inverts Chamoiseau's statement to produce an enigmatic Creole refrain of her own: "Chobet di paloud/ Sé an lan mè/ An ké kontréw" "La chaubette dit à la palourde, c'est dans la mer que je te rencontrerai" (Condé, 1989a, 190). ["The whelk said to the clam, I'll meet you in the sea."] The rebellious young Mira sings the refrain when she routinely arrives late for school, preferring leisurely detours through the forest to the monotony and efficiency of the direct route. Her whimsical Creole song contrasts with the quiet obedience of her classmates who apply themselves to their assigned math problems. Mira's resistance to the ordered logic and discipline of the school mirrors Condé's own refusal to follow the dictates of the Créolistes, and to celebrate oral culture as a source of plenitude and meaning. As Anthea Morrison (1995, 620) notes, the novel "avoids dichotomizing 'parole' and 'écriture'."[35] In fact, as we will now see, Condé explodes the limits between vocality and silence, in such a way that it becomes difficult to separate out these different dimensions of the text.

Silence and Opacity

The confusion between speech and silence in the text brings us to the crux of what is most problematic in existing criticism of the novel. Even the most discerning critics have misread the alternating narratives in *Traversée de la mangrove* as oral testimonies, and seen the wake as a liberating *prise de parole* (speech act) on the part of the community. Fulton (2001, 307) writes, "Story-telling itself thus becomes the link between characters." However, this vocal dimension is unsupported—and even actively undermined—by the text itself.

While the structure of the novel seems to suggest a circle of mourners who come forward one by one to commemorate the deceased, their narrative interventions are not spoken, but constitute instead internal monologues set against a clamor of prayer and drunken laughter. When one attends carefully to Condé's representation of the vigil, one "hears" persistent rainfall, the howling of dogs, the chorus of prayer led by Dinah and other women around the body of Francis Sancher, the raucous sounds of men drinking on the veranda, people partaking in the traditional *soupe grasse*, the occasional belch, off-color jokes, and the weak improvisations of Cyrille, the storyteller—not a succession of vocal performances.[36] In fact, the twenty narratives in the novel are *not* vocal performances in any sense, but instances of silent retrospection. By stringing out these reflections in succession, Condé demarcates a distinct narrative plane, a level of silent, interiority that underlies the external happenings of the wake. In theatrical terms, this constitutes a level of dramatic irony, as only the reader partakes in these otherwise private reflections.

The transitions between "speakers" clearly expose the status of the interventions as unspoken and silent. When the postman Moïse concludes his reflections on the deceased, for instance, the implicit narrator tells us that he joins his voice to the choir which presumably has been singing the entire time: "Dinah Lameaulnes entonnait un nouveau psaume. [Moïse] inclina très bas la tête et mêla sa voix à celle du chœur" (Condé, 1989a, 48). ["Dinah Lameaulnes launched into a new psalm. [Moïse] tilted his head way back and joined his voice to the chorus."] Moïse's thoughts on Sancher, like those of the other characters, are *silent*, indicating his alienation from a community that is otherwise occupied. Similarly, when the hermit Xantippe arrives at the wake, we are told that the other villagers are engaged in either raucous celebration or silent introspection. His entrance causes the others momentarily to cease their activities: "Immédiatement, les bruits s'éteignirent dans un lac glacé de silence et certains envisagèrent de le pousser aux épaules. [...] Bientôt donc, certains reprirent leurs blagues et leurs rires. D'autres *en silence* se mirent à *penser* à Francis Sancher, suçotant leurs souvenirs comme des dents creuses" (26). ["Immediately, the sounds ceased in a frozen lake of silence and some contemplated shoving him on the shoulders [...] Then soon they went back to their jokes and laughter. Others *silently* began to *think* about Francis Sancher, sucking on their memories like hollow teeth."][37] The narrator uses repeated "s" sounds in this passage to represent audibly the villagers' chewing over their memories. As this passage makes clear, the villagers are either busy in their own thoughts or joking around, and certainly not listening to each other's monologues on Sancher. There is a palpable hostility between them; they are all shoulders and teeth, hardly a warm endorsement of community.

Condé's text thus unravels the "vocality" associated with polyphony. This, of course, does not necessarily make the novel less "polyphonic"; it illustrates instead that literary polyphony does not have a privileged connection with the voice, or with sound. To return momentarily to Bakhtin, Emerson suggests that there is nothing particularly "verbal" about Bakhtin's understanding of dialogism: "The whole dynamic between I and Other could be a dialogue in space conducted through gestures, images, and shifting perspectives. [...] The three-dimensional context in which bodies interact—the entire 'scene' or 'scenario'—is crucial" (Emerson, 2005, 4). This concurs with Henri Meschonnic's (1982, 72) expansive definition of language as made up of "communication, signs, but also actions, creations, the relationships between bodies, the hidden unveiling of the unconscious." Throughout *Traversée de la mangrove,* there is a physical, nonverbal dimension to communication that reflects Condé's interest in the stage and cinema.[38] These nonverbal forms of communication, however, often prove as opaque as speech. Fulton (2001, 309) shows how a collective sigh raises multiple possible interpretations: "Il y eut un chœur de soupirs d'approbation sans qu'on sût très bien si c'était le commentaire sur la vie ou le commentaire sur Francis Sancher qui faisait l'unanimité" (Condé, 1989a, 251). ["There was a chorus of sighs of approval although one couldn't tell if it was a commentary on life or a commentary on Francis Sancher that won unanimous agreement."] Even though the sigh is produced in unison, it does not indicate unity or homogeneity. Instead, it too yields numerous conflicting interpretations.

In a particularly perceptive reading of the novel, Crosta discerns two distinct concurrent planes of narration in the text: a diegetic level encompassing the implicit narrator/author's discourse about the wake, and a meta-diegetic level consisting of the "characters' thoughts, impressions and recollections" about the deceased.[39] She thus stands out as one of the few critics to have understood the private, introspective nature of the narratives themselves. Rosemary Erlam also refers to the different dimensions in the text. She notes that a vibrant "décor sonore" (background noise) often replaces the narrative thread itself, creating the impression of multiple levels of reality. But she goes on to assert that "Loin d'être une cérémonie polyphonique, c'est au moyen d'une sorte de cacophonie que nous sont communiqués les sentiments et les souvenirs de ceux qui connaissaient Sancher" (Erlam, 1997, 36). ["Far from a polyphonic ceremony, it is through a kind of cacophony that the feelings and thoughts of those who knew Sancher are conveyed to us."] If there is cacophony in the novel, it consists not of audible voices, but the juxtaposition of contradictory thoughts.

We can now identify the major technical innovation that *Traversée de la mangrove* achieves with respect to literary polyphony: two separate narrative planes extend throughout the duration of the novel, to which the reader has unequal access. The first of these planes constitutes the interior world of the characters' thoughts, which the reader is invited to share; the second comprises of all the external, voiced aspects of the wake, from which the reader is held apart. The reader, while privy to the thoughts of the characters, is excluded to what goes on in the physical space of the wake: the jokes, the stories, and so on. This is the author's very clever way of maintaining opacity, of denying the reader access into the most obvious dimension of the wake, while creating the impression of inclusiveness.

Critics have invariably noted that the novel narrates the thoughts of female characters in the first person, while those of male figures are bracketed off in quotation marks, and narrated in the third person.[40] Crosta (1992, 147) suggests this oscillation demonstrates "the implicit author's intention to differentiate and problematize the narrative voices of her characters." When asked to comment on this, Condé was characteristically opaque: "This decision had no real conscious theoretical underpinnings, as the narratives simply came to me that way in my imagination" (Pfaff, 1996, 73).[41] Each shift in narrative voice, however, effectively places the reader in a different position, from imaginary interlocutor to voyeur. As Jorge Luis Borges suggests: "Such interventions suggest that if the characters of a fictional work can be readers or spectators, we, their readers or spectators, can be fictional characters" (Genette, 1966, 238). The reader becomes an active participant in the novel, on par with the characters, much as Bakhtin imagines the polyphonic author.

Significantly, the silent status of the narratives allows the novel to break out of the model of temporal linearity. *Traversée de la mangrove* belongs to those texts where the time of narration is written into the text. The novel emphasizes the time in which it unfolds. As night passes into day, the characters become impatient, they look forward to returning home and to shedding their Sunday clothes. The text relates each narration in succession, moving around the circle to include each member of the community as though each spoke in turn. However, as the narratives are not spoken but silent internalized thoughts, they can easily play out simultaneously. It thus becomes impossible to situate the characters' thoughts with respect to time.

All the "narrations" could conceivably unfold simultaneously, throughout the entire span of the wake, even though they are related successively in the text. This is certainly one of the most audacious innovations of the novel: Condé presents each element in succession, but in such a way as to suggest their simultaneity and synchronicity. To put it differently, the twenty narratives follow one after the other in the text because of the constraints of writing, but nothing prevents them from actually unfolding concurrently in the imagined universe of the wake because they are not spoken, but interior monologues.

Conclusions: Condé's Polyphony

The widespread use of the term "polyphony" to describe literary texts—and in particular, works by African or francophone authors—has led to problematic assumptions, in part because the notion of *phonè* or voice, while seductive, is misleading. In *Traversée de la mangrove,* Maryse Condé creates what appears to be a quintessentially polyphonic form, the traditional Guadeloupean wake, and subverts it by threading together silent reflections in lieu of what many have read as vocal narrations. Critics have generally celebrated the orality of the novel. Closer examination, however, reveals instead its portrayal of the breakdown of communication within a community. The characters neither publicly voice their reflections, nor hear one another. The seemingly vibrant interchange provoked by Sancher's death is an illusion. Like meta-diegetic music in a film, it is only accessible to the reader. At the same time, Condé ironically denies the reader access to much of what actually transpires at Sancher's wake, providing only intermittent glimpses of the jokes, the efforts of the storyteller, and the psalms. The novel thus maintains opacity and keeps the reader at a distance, all the while conveying the illusion of intimacy.

In final analysis, although Bakhtin and Kundera are helpful in situating Condé's deployment of polyphony in *Traversée de la mangrove,* both models come up short. In a Bakhtinian sense, Condé stages a corrosive confrontation of ideologies, whether political, literary, or aesthetic, on every level of the text. The twenty narratives represent a broad spectrum of ethnicities, genders, social classes, professions, and ages, and Condé goes even further to show how each individual voice is itself internally riven by irony, shifts in perspective, and inconsistencies. According to Kundera's model, Condé uses innovative compositional techniques to achieve the simultaneity and equality of the respective parts, which each contribute to a coherent—although perhaps not indivisible—"whole." The successive internal monologues revolve around the same mysterious figure of Sancher, but each tells a story that exceeds Sancher, as each storyteller revisits his or her own life trajectory in light of the stranger's death. Although laid out in sequence in the text, the various interventions—since they are internal and unspoken—could well unfold simultaneously. They hardly serve to advance the plot since the "events" of the novel have already taken place prior to the beginning of narration. What propels the reading, then, is the desire to piece together the mystery of Sancher's death, a puzzle for which there is no single answer and which can only be seen through the prism of variegated perspectives.

Beyond the models proposed by Bakhtin and Kundera, Condé's treatment of polyphony draws on the Caribbean literary tradition. This is most evident in her reworking of key tropes from Césaire, Glissant, and Chamoiseau and in her engagement in the particularly fraught debate in Caribbean letters over the writer's responsibility to the people, and the extent to which the writer can serve as a mouthpiece for others. From Césaire, who argued that the duty of the poet is to speak for those who have no voice; to Glissant who affirmed the ethical impossibility of the poet to speak in place of those to whom a voice has been denied; to Chamoiseau who suggests that a writer can serve as a scribe, ethnologist or "word marker" and thus preserve the voices of the Caribbean community; Condé provides her own distinctive response. What a writer ultimately seeks in the commotion of diverse perspectives is her own voice: necessarily fractured, borrowed, hybrid, composite, provisional, written, and *silent*. If it has become increasingly common for transnational authors to deploy multiple narrators or to interweave several simultaneous storylines— Nancy Huston's *Les variations Goldberg* [1981, *The Goldberg Variations*], a text considered in Chapter 3; Leila Sebbar's *Shérazade: 17 ans, brune, frisée, les yeux verts* [1982, *Sherazade: Missing, aged 17, dark curly hair, green eyes*]; Abdourahman Waberi's *Transit* (2003); and Nicole Krauss's *The History of Love* (2005) are just a few examples from among recent novels from contexts as diverse as Quebec, Algeria, Djibouti, and the United States—*Traversée de la mangrove* stands out in the degree to which Condé explores both the horizontal and vertical axes of polyphony. The novel offers a magnificent illusion of community and exchange across its different constituent voices, even while exposing the illusion for what it is.

There are compelling ethical stakes in recognizing the silence and social fragmentation in Condé's novel. Whereas critics do not read Huston or

Krauss as having given voice to marginalized subjectivities, they routinely make such claims about Condé—and Waberi, Sebbar, and other authors from the Global South—which indicates a highly problematic tendency in the way polyphony has been deployed in criticism. Revisiting the question of polyphony in Condé's *Traversée de la mangrove* pointedly reveals the tensions between voice and voicing, as well as the irreducible divide between "orality" and literature, which no degree of literary virtuosity can efface.

CHAPTER TWO

Edward Said and Assia Djebar

Counterpoint and the Practice of Comparative Literature

> The basic humanistic mission today, whether in music, literature, or any of the arts or the humanities, has to do with the preservation of difference without, at the same time, sinking in to the desire to dominate.
>
> —*Edward Said*

> Processes of companionship and conviviality [...] are not pre-existent givens but are elaborated between heterogeneous living beings in such a way that they create a tissue of shifting relations, in which the melody of one part intervenes as a motif in the melody of another (the bee and the flower). [...] Relations of counterpoint must be invented everywhere, and are the very condition of evolution.
>
> —*Gilles Deleuze*

In a lecture at the American University of Beirut on July 1, 1999, Edward Said argued passionately for the reimagining of Israeli and Palestinian history. To illustrate how these conflicting experiences inextricably overlap and intersect, Said drew on the metaphor of musical counterpoint. He urged both Palestinians and Israelis to engage one another *contrapuntally*, to recognize and embrace the connections and contradictions between their respective histories and claims to the land.[1] Considering the overwhelmingly anti-Israeli sentiments of his audience, it took courage and vision to advance such an argument.[2] Moreover, that Said should have drawn specifically on musical counterpoint to propose an alternative strategy to the polarized hatred in the Middle East—and that he should have done so in an environment where appreciation and knowledge of Western classical music is increasingly rarefied—is remarkable. It testifies to Said's efforts to extend counterpoint as a viable political rhetoric and analytic tool both within academia and beyond.

In the years since this memorable lecture, the possibilities for contrapuntal exchange between Israel and Palestine have further deteriorated, and the idea of a bi-national, one-state solution has all but vanished from the political vocabulary. If Palestinians still occasionally endorse it, most Israelis today dismiss the idea of a bi-national shared state as absolutely unviable. The separation barrier crosses the landscape as a concrete reminder of intractable conflict and the anxieties it has produced on both sides. And yet Said's insistence on attending to the counterpoint of multiple, intersecting narratives in history continues to impact scholarship across the humanities and holds particular relevance for scholars of comparative literature.[3]

The work of Algerian author Assia Djebar stands out as an important attempt to produce a more nuanced, contrapuntal approach to the past. Born in 1936 in what was then French Algeria and educated at the Ecole normale supérieure, Djebar is part of a generation of writers who came of age just prior to Algerian independence, and whose intellectual formation was shaped by a plurality of influences: Western, Arab, and Berber. Her fiction recognizes the instrumental role that women played in the Algerian war for independence from France from 1954 to 1962, as well as in resisting French occupation throughout the nineteenth century. On a broader level, Djebar's work seeks to renegotiate the relationship between France and Algeria, to establish grounds for mutual recognition and reconciliation despite the legacy of violence and inequality. In pursuing this work, Djebar anticipates Michael Rothberg's notion of multidirectional memory, in that she exposes the ways in which the major historical experiences of the twentieth century are imbricated in one another. Djebar advocates an approach to history and memory that is neither competitive nor exclusive, but involves openness to the other. At the same time, she is deeply invested in questions of language and form. Djebar (1999, 150) describes her approach to writing as "une alternance entre mon besoin d'architecture et mon aspiration à la musique" ["an alternation between my need for architecture and my aspiration toward music"].[4] Djebar's work thus provides an ideal case study for examining the possibilities of counterpoint as a formal device and ethical stance in the transnational novel.[5]

This chapter submits Said's notion of contrapuntal analysis to critical examination, before considering how such an approach can inform a comparative and transnational reading of Djebar's ambitious novel, *Les nuits de Strasbourg* (1997). As we will see, the novel implements counterpoint on multiple levels to develop a more complex and ethical approach to history, to interrogate canon formation, and to address the tensions between individual and collective memory. On one level, the novel juxtaposes the tumultuous history of Algeria to that of Alsace, so as to highlight connections between the two regions, and particularly their similar experiences of foreign occupation. Thus, it illustrates how the German occupation of Alsace in the 1870s actually led many Alsatian refugees to settle in Algeria, where they became *colons*; subsequently, successive European conflicts led to the conscription of Algerians into the French army; after World War II, waves of Algerian immigrants came to Alsace to serve as cheap, manual labor. On a second level, *Les nuits de Strasbourg* brings "minor" texts into dialogue with major canonical works through epigraphs and intertextual allusions, shifting the hierarchical relations between major and minor, as well as between center and periphery. Third, the novel uses crosscultural relationships to stage contrapuntal exchanges between different individuals. Finally, it contributes to a broader dialogue between several contemporaneous Franco-Algerian works that use the Antigone myth to assess the claims of memory and mourning: Leila Sebbar's *La Seine était rouge* [1999, *The Seine was Red: Paris, October 1961*] and Jacques Derrida's *De l'hospitalité* [1997, *Of Hospitality*].

Counterpoint and Democracy

Edward Said introduced the term "counterpoint" in *Culture and Imperialism,* some fifteen years after publishing *Orientalism* (1978), his groundbreaking critique of Western scholarship on the Middle East. Said defines counterpoint as a rigorously comparative perspective that enables us "to think through and interpret together experiences that are discrepant, each with its particular agenda and pace of development, its own internal formations, its internal coherence and system of external relationships, all of them co-existing and interacting with others" (1993, 37). He promoted counterpoint as a critical strategy capable of addressing the entanglements (or complex "alignments") that characterize the transnational condition:

> Gone are the binary oppositions dear to the nationalist and imperialist enterprise. [...] The old authority cannot be simply replaced by the new authority, but the alignments made across borders, types, nations, and essences are rapidly coming into view, and it is those new alignments that now provoke and challenge the fundamentally static notions of *identity* that have been at the core of cultural thought during the era of imperialism. (1993, xviii)

In Said's view, a contrapuntal approach does not seek an overarching resolution, teleology, or synthesis, but instead focuses on the dynamic interplay of contradictions. As such, it represents a decisive departure from the Hegelian dialectic.[6] Rather than simply overturning the established canons and hierarchies, Said proposes counterpoint as a way "to assimilate to canons these other contrapuntal lines" (Marranca and Said, 1991, 36). Through counterpoint, he seeks to bring previously marginalized perspectives into dialogue with dominant voices and, ultimately, to replace a system of hierarchical relations with one of equal exchange.

Following Said's lead, many postcolonial critics have appropriated the term "counterpoint," but few attend to its historical and musical specificity.[7] A highly trained pianist and former music critic for *Nation* magazine, Said deploys the term "counterpoint" with keen awareness of its musical significance. Although his use of counterpoint clearly relates to the work of Mikhail Bakhtin, who half a century earlier deployed the metaphor of polyphony to describe Dostoevsky's multivoiced poetics, Said never publicly engages with Bakhtin's work, nor does he attempt to articulate the differences between his notion of counterpoint and Bakhtin's theory of polyphony.[8]

In order to understand how Said's notion of counterpoint relates to—and departs from—polyphony (explored at length in the preceding chapter), it is essential to establish a clear theoretical distinction between the two terms. This is no simple task, because the terms are often used interchangeably. Both counterpoint and polyphony refer to the musical art of combining two or more simultaneous and independent lines, but polyphony is a more general term, while counterpoint is associated with specific historical developments in music. Polyphony is a broad stylistic and historical classification—the opposite, for instance, of monophony and homophony—while counterpoint connotes theoretical rigor and a systematic method of compositional instruction. The theory and practice of counterpoint developed during the Renaissance and Baroque periods of the Western musical tradition, and extends through the twentieth century, notably in the music of Schoenberg. Although the term originally comes from the Latin for point against point or note against note, in musical practice the horizontal development of each voice is just as important as the vertical juxtaposition between voices. The relationship of the part to the whole is thus complex and highly regulated. Each voice must be fully realized on its own and able to stand independently. All voices are considered of equal importance; no voice dominates, except momentarily. Finally, each voice must satisfy certain rules in order to combine with the others.

Counterpoint offers a useful model for literature because of these very qualities: it is dynamic, in the sense that it describes a relation between voices in movement; regulated, according to conventionally agreed-upon sets of rules; and egalitarian, in that voices are equal and only temporarily assume a dominant position. This notion of alternation is critical to our understanding of democracy. In his essays on democracy, Jacques Derrida (2003) proposes the rotation of a wheel as a metaphor for democratic governance, since every position is held only momentarily and in turn. Likewise, in contrapuntal music, each voice only briefly assumes a dominant role, before allowing another to rise to the fore. As a theoretical tool, counterpoint provides a mode of conceiving relations between different parts within a whole. It is not overtly political, emerging instead out of music theory and practice. Moreover, counterpoint, unlike polyphony, has long had a rhetorical dimension.[9]

In the preceding chapter, we saw how the term "polyphony" accounts for the interplay of multiple narrative voices or plotlines in a novel. Polyphony touches on narratological questions and problems of representation: who speaks within a text; which voices are privileged or withheld; how do the structures of address and audience within the text reflect patterns of social inequality; to what extent can we speak of "voices" that "sound" in a text? Counterpoint similarly brings historical and political issues to the fore, but does so chiefly by juxtaposing different histories and texts, and attending to the new relationships that emerge between narratives and subject positions.

Said is by no means the first to have taken note of the democratic possibilities in counterpoint, but the specific political and intellectual contexts to which he applies them—the Palestinian–Israeli conflict, and more broadly, postcolonial criticism—are radically new. Musicologist Karen Painter (2001,

210), for instance, has shown that counterpoint was similarly aligned "with political ideals" in early twentieth-century Vienna; critics of Mahler's Seventh Symphony attacked the "limitless individualization and democratization of voices," as well as their stark juxtaposition and superimposition. And yet, a crucial question remains to be asked: in what sense can counterpoint embody such qualities beyond the realm of music, and more importantly, outside Western Europe?

Several initial problems stand out. Firstly, counterpoint, unlike polyphony, is not universal. While many musical traditions throughout the world have polyphonic qualities, counterpoint is distinctly European and of a particular moment in the history of European music.[10] Secondly, the development of counterpoint was closely linked to the Christian faith. The finest examples of contrapuntal music, including Bach's chorales, were sacred works written for the Church. Finally, although polyphony can easily arise spontaneously, counterpoint is an extremely written art because of the tight regulations governing it.[11] One of the more interesting aspects of Said's contrapuntal theory is precisely that such a difficult and thoroughly written art should be accorded such a radical, democratic, and healing potential.

On the other hand, the very idea of counterpoint, like that of polyphony, is linked to the human voice. Counterpoint grew out of medieval vocal music, in which each component line had to be "singable," or accessible to the human voice. Each line had to fall within a certain range and avoid excessively large leaps across intervals. Behind each contrapuntal line lies the trace or memory of the human voice. The associations that Said emphasizes between democracy, humanism, and counterpoint make sense when one considers counterpoint's roots in the vocal tradition. In fact, composer Pierre Boulez even uses the term "responsibility" to characterize counterpoint, because the constituent voices have a responsibility to attend to one another and respect the needs of the collective (de Groot, 2005, 221).

It is crucial to note that Said affirms the democratic aesthetic of counterpoint in opposition not to polyphony, but to the hierarchical structures that came to characterize Enlightenment classical music. When the sonata form took hold in the eighteenth century, a clear hierarchy between musical parts emerged, musical phrases shortened, and the tonic became the dominating source of order. In *Orientalism*, Said writes persuasively about how the European Enlightenment constructed a system of knowledge that used, reduced, and asserted control over the non-European other. When he refers to the sonata form in *Musical Elaborations,* he associates it with domination, tyrannical authority, and oppression. "The model for the sonata form is [...] pedagogic and dramatic. [...] It is the demonstration of authoritative control in which a thematic statement and its subsequent development are worked through rigorously by the composer in the space between two strongly marked poles" (Said, 1991, 100). He finds in counterpoint, by contrast, an alternative, more utopian model, one that often allows for exploration, reciprocity, and tolerance.

According to Said, counterpoint is one of the primary features that distinguish Western from Arab music. In a much-cited anecdote, he recalls the first time he saw the Egyptian singer Umm Kalthoum in concert, and admits he found it difficult to relate to her music precisely because it lacked the "counterpoint" of Western music. Having internalized the Western "ethic of productivity and of overcoming obstacles," he found Kalthoum's music to be mind-dulling. It seemed to lull the listener into listless melancholy with its monophony, its constant "byways, details, and digressions," and its lack of developmental tension. As an adult, he eventually came to appreciate the "exfoliating variations" of her music, and as a result, began to listen differently to Western music as well, developing a new interest in the late works of Beethoven, Richard Strauss, and Olivier Messiaen that evolve likewise through variation (de Groot, 2005, 220).[12]

Counterpoint, the sonata form, and non-Western music are thus imbricated in Said's thought in complex ways. Said values the pluralistic, dialogic nature of Western counterpoint, in explicit contrast to the hierarchical, linear structure of sonata form. It is this appreciation of counterpoint that causes him to hear—and initially to dismiss—Arabic music as monophonic. When he later comes to admire the open-ended and circular art of variation and ornamentation in Kalthoum's songs as an alternative to the driven nature of sonata form, he then seeks out these very elements in the classical repertoire, locating them in pieces slightly outside the canon. Both variation and counterpoint become important tropes in Said's critical writings not only on music, but also on history and literature, where he continues his interrogation of established canons. Thus, while musicologists have argued that Said's work on music ignores important recent developments in ethnomusicology—a case put forth most forcefully by Kofi Agawu (1992) in a review of *Music Elaborations* entitled "Wrong Notes"—his thoughts on music nonetheless inform much of his intellectual project.[13] As one critic has noted, Said conceived of counterpoint along three key axes: "as a musical practice, as his personal guide to relate divergent musical and cultural backgrounds, and as a metaphor for humanistic emancipation" (de Groot, 2005, 221).

Said deploys counterpoint in view of showing how writing and culture both participated in colonial politics. He thus reads the works of canonical writers such as Joseph Conrad, Albert Camus, Jane Austen, and others to expose the presence of imperial *and* counter-imperial discourses. In these readings, he undermines "static notions" of history and power by bringing multiple perspectives—within and among texts—into contrapuntal relation.[14] Ultimately, Said shows all cultural forms to be "hybrid, mixed, impure" (1993, 13), and holds the critic responsible for drawing out the relations among these different strands. This approach continues to resonate with critics across different contexts. For instance, Jonathan Arac (1998, 57) adopts Said's contrapuntal methodology to address Mark Twain's *Huckleberry Finn,* in order to evaluate the novel's contradictory attitudes to race and emancipation, and navigate the controversies the work continues to generate in public school systems. Arac observes that while "the counter in counterpoint is a term of opposition, [...] contrapuntal criticism is loving; it joins." Counterpoint has clear affinities with recent critical methodologies inspired by Edouard Glissant's poetics of relation, including Michael Rothberg's (2009) multidirectional memory, and Françoise Lionnet's and Shu-mei Shih's (2005) notion of minor transnationalism and relational comparativism.

Examining Djebar's work in this context is especially productive because, of all Algerian writers today, she is the most acutely aware of her entanglement in both the European and Algerian traditions. Her literary project reflects a constant effort to redefine the relations between fiction and autobiography; between history and oral testimony; and between the music, art, and philosophy of the West and of North Africa. Because her writing places emphasis on theoretical and formal questions, she is not always the most accessible of authors. She has often been critiqued as elitist and alienated from the Algerian public. She occupies what some see as a privileged position because she lives in voluntary exile in New York and Paris, has won favor in the French academy, and successfully marketed herself for American, German, and Italian readers.[15] Several Algerian publishers and writers have voiced frustration at Djebar's popularity abroad, regretting the relative paucity of interest in the work of those authors who remained in Algeria and whom they view as better positioned to understand and represent Algerians.[16] Djebar undeniably cuts a controversial figure. But it is precisely her complex status and her commitment to structuring these multiple poles that make Djebar's fiction so compelling, and that bring it meaningfully into relation with Said's theoretical work. Said, too, was very conscious of his position as an exile, and of the privilege and responsibility that came with his academic role. He also could be seen as elitist.

Yet, unlike Said who had a rigorously classical formation, Djebar's musical experience cuts across several cultural traditions. She was exposed to Berber, Andalucían, Arab, and European classical music from an early age. As she reveals in a recent autofictional novel, *Nulle part dans la maison de mon père* [2007, *No Place in My Father's House*], she studied piano throughout her youth despite her evident lack of talent. Her mother liked to sing traditional Andalucían melodies and hoped her daughter would learn to accompany her on the piano. Unfortunately, Djebar never acquired the skill to improvise in the Andalucían style, in part because her teacher insisted on adhering rigidly to a classical Western curriculum. Later, at boarding school, Djebar participated in at least one comic operetta, an experience she relished because the rehearsals gave her the opportunity to interact with students from a nearby boys' school.

The autobiographical link to music that receives the most weighty treatment in Djebar's work, notably in *Vaste est la prison* [1995, *So Vast the Prison*], involves the loss of her mother's prized collection of musical manuscripts of Berber songs during the Algerian War for Independence. In searching the family home, French soldiers mistook the manuscripts for political tracts and destroyed them, squandering the ancestral inheritance of a long line of Berber women who had treasured this music and passed it on to their daughters. Djebar recounts the loss of this traditional music in conjunction with the disappearance of an ancient Berber alphabet of which women were the custodians.[17] She thus emphasizes the connections between traditional music, orality, and writing, and establishes them as the privileged domain of Algerian women.

Djebar's interest in multiple musical traditions comes across in the diverse variety of musical references that surface throughout her fiction. She deploys the musical indication, "Quasi una fantasia," from Ludwig van Beethoven's Sonata for Piano as a title for the third section of her autobiographical novel, *L'amour, la fantasia* [*Fantasia: An Algerian Cavalcade*], gesturing at the improvised, free character of the writing that follows. In a radical move, she then juxtaposes Beethoven's notion of fantasia to the traditional fantasias performed by North African cavalry prior to engaging in battle.[18] The author dedicates two of her works, the film *La Nouba des femmes du Mont Chenoua* [*c*.1977, *Nouba of the Women of Mount Chenoua*] and the novel *La disparition de la langue française* [2003, *The Disappearance of the French Language*], to Hungarian composer Bela Bartók, in recognition of his journey to the Biskra region of Algeria in 1913 in order to collect and document traditional music. She also frequently includes ethnomusicologists as characters in her fiction, such as Sarah in *Femmes d'Alger dans leur appartement* [1980, *Women of Algiers in Their Apartment*] and Isma in *Vaste est la prison*. More recently, Djebar collaborated in adapting *Loin de Médine* [1991, *Far from Medina*] for the operatic stage, participating in a new genre of postcolonial opera. The work recounts the stories of notable women poets and warriors in the formative years of Islam, celebrating instances of female leadership in response to a patriarchal tradition that has sought to efface women's political agency.

Djebar's effort to accommodate multiple perspectives and voices through increasingly elaborate narrative forms has led critics explicitly to call her writing contrapuntal (Lionnet, 2011) *and* polyphonic (Rice, 2006). Interestingly, Djebar herself has commented on the unfortunate lack of polyphony in North African music, which she sees as all the more regrettable in light of research that suggests that the extent of polyphony in a culture's music indicates the democratic potential of that society.[19] By structuring various forms of contrapuntal exchange into her fiction, Djebar takes steps to remedy this absence. While creating counterpoint in fiction does not amount to establishing it in the public sphere, novels provide a way of imagining and modeling the kinds of discourse that can take place, and thus play a vital role in making political change happen. As Rothberg (2009) argues in his study of multidirectional memory, novels (and films, for that matter) serve a critical function in building relations across different communities by envisioning new possibilities for recognition and ultimately, empathy.[20]

In the midst of the violent civil conflict between Islamic factions and the Algerian government in the 1990s, Djebar found herself in exile in the United States and Paris, and concurrently produced three very unusual texts that relate in different ways to the political crisis. The first, *Le blanc de l'Algérie* [*Algerian White*], is a raw, personal testimony that protests the assassinations of Algerian intellectuals by Islamists. The text holds the FLN governing party accountable for stunting the development of democracy, distorting Algerian history, and exacerbating deep, unresolved divisions between Algerians. Djebar sees in the Algerian civil war of the 1990s the return of repressed traumas from the Algerian War for Independence, citing the practice of targeted assassinations and terror that the FLN used after the war to consolidate their own legitimacy and eliminate opposition. The second work she completed during this time, *Oran, langue morte* [*The Tongue's Blood Does Not Run Dry*], is a collection of short stories that convey the devastating impact of Islamism and civil war on Algerian women. The third, *Les nuits de Strasbourg*, is the focal text of this chapter. It deploys a contrapuntal approach to history, offering a nuanced and complex analysis of the relationship between Algeria and France. The novel interweaves narratives of World War II, the Algerian War for Independence, and the unification of Europe in the late 1980s, to problematize binary distinctions between victim and oppressor, colonized and colonizer, East and West. It thus explores the connections between memories of colonialism and of the Holocaust in contemporary Europe.

Les nuits de Strasbourg marks a significant departure from Djebar's previous work on several levels. It is the first of her novels to be set entirely in Europe and one of her most erotic pieces of writing. The novel uses the principle of contrapuntal dialogue to stage vibrant, difficult exchanges between individuals whose backgrounds and historical experiences are fraught with conflict. These dialogues forge new possibilities for understanding, and combat the culture of "competitive victimhood" (Rothberg, 2009).

Like many of Djebar's novels, *Les nuits de Strasbourg* follows a tripartite logic, consisting of a prologue, body, and epilogue. But unlike the affirmative, symmetrical structure that characterizes sonata form—A, B, A', where A stands for the exposition of the theme, B its development, and A' its subsequent recapit-ulation—the novel concludes not in affirmation, but rather in disintegration, as indicated most graphically by the epilogue's title, "Neige, ou le poudroiement" ["Snow, or Powdering"]. This movement is mirrored on a temporal level: the prologue covers a span of nine months in 1939; the main section encompasses nine days in March of 1989; the epilogue unfolds some time in September later that same year. The sections thus progressively diminish in scope from nine months, to nine days, to an indefinite moment in time. Each part of the novel further subdivides into numbered subsections, underscoring Djebar's preoccu-pation with form. This structural complexity is a signature of her work, and recalls the clocklike architecture of the text many consider to be the founding work of modern Algerian fiction, Kateb's *Nedjma* (1956).

The prologue of *Les nuits de Strasbourg*, "La Ville" ["The City"], documents the massive evacuation of civilians from Strasbourg in September 1939 in anticipation of the German invasion that followed much later, on June 15, 1940. The central part of the novel, "Neuf nuits... cinquante ans après" ["Nine Nights... Fifty Years Later"], imagines the romance between Thelja, a young Algerian art historian, and her French lover, François. Thelja comes to Strasbourg for nine days to consult medieval manuscripts in local archives. During her stay, she renews contact with Eve, a Jewish-Algerian friend who recently moved to Strasbourg. She also explores the history of the region, and uncovers surprising parallels between the Alsatian settlement of Algeria, on one hand, and Algerian immigration to the region of Alsace, on the other. Each night, she and François have long, intimate conversations that inevitably turn around the turbulent history of Alsace and Algeria, and lead them to discover unexpected connections between their experiences.

Djebar places the Franco-Algerian love affair between François and Thelja in counterpoint to several other crosscultural relationships, notably that of Hans (a German) and Eve (a Jewish-Algerian photographer). On Thelja's penultimate day in Strasbourg, Jacqueline, the artistic director of a local theater company is raped and murdered by Ali, her former lover and the son of Algerian immigrants. This crime of passion is painfully reminiscent of the bloody political assassinations and honor killings in Algeria, and interrupts the protagonists' obsessive preoccupation with the past, compelling them to rally together as a community. The brutal murder provides the first suggestion of a remainder of violence that can neither be integrated nor recuperated in the novel's elegant contrapuntal scheme.

The second intimation of the limits of counterpoint comes in the novel's epilogue with Thelja's suicide.[21] Her suicide is indicative of the immense pressures facing Algerian women intellectuals in the late 1980s and 1990s: Thelja is alone in France to conduct academic research; she is estranged from her husband and separated from her child according to the provisions of the Muslim family code that grants fathers custody at the expense of mothers. Her inability to come to terms with her own past as well as with the collective past indicates what Michael O'Riley (2004, 117) describes as a "postcolonial haunting," wherein the disruptive trace of the colonial past surfaces in the postcolonial rewriting of history as an absence or as a testimonial silhouette. Indeed, Thelja obsessively imagines the shadowy figures of nineteenth-century poets walking the streets of Strasbourg. At the same time, her encounters with the city's residents reveal the emotional scars of annexation and World War II. While Thelja actively seeks out knowledge about these different pasts, the stories she encounters overwhelm her. For instance, she chooses to visit the archives on Algerian immigration to Strasbourg, where she finds historical documentation of the hardships Algerian immigrant workers endured: "Me replonger, et à Strasbourg, dans mes lieux d'enfance grâce aux traces d'exils multiples et presque effacés: migrations multiples qui étaient certes celles de la faim, de la sueur, et, à cette époque, de la peur…" (Djebar, 1997a, 401). ["To return, in Strasbourg of all places, to the sites of my childhood, thanks to the barely visible traces of multiple exiles: migrations that were surely those of hunger, sweat, and at the time, fear."] This neglected historical record moves her to empathy, and reminds her of her own history of loss. Thelja engages with multiple, conflicting strands of history throughout her time in Strasbourg, and becomes consumed by the *devoir de mémoire,* the obligation to remember.

Strasbourg is thus the repository of multiple transnational and transhistorical traumas that are voiced and shared by the protagonists. By dealing with these overlapping experiences, the novel addresses an issue of great importance to contemporary multicultural societies, namely "the relationship between different social groups' histories of victimization, the relationship that groups establish between their past and their present circumstances" (Walter Benn Michaels, qtd in Rothberg, 2009, 2). What happens when different histories confront each other in the public sphere? Does the remembrance of one history necessarily erase others from view? Thelja's suicide suggests that dwelling too much on these multiple histories of trauma can be destructive. Her inability to let go of the past anticipates Derrida's (1997) figuration of Antigone as an exemplary instance of interminable mourning, as we will examine more closely at the end of this chapter.

De-territorializing the Novel

In a lecture at the House of World Cultures in Berlin in November 1998, Djebar (1999, 239) presented *Les nuits de Strasbourg* as a radically new project. Whereas her previous literary production had focused entirely on Algeria, she set her new novel in Strasbourg, bringing her imagination and passion for history to bear on the European context. Although this geographical shift was undoubtedly also motivated by Djebar's material circumstances— the author had just won a prestigious writer's grant from the municipality of Strasbourg that funded her residency in the city for three months—it produced an additional layer of complexity in her writing.[22] Algeria remains an ever-present concern, but now becomes an inner layer within a dynamic palimpsest of multiple terms.[23] Algerian memory and experience intersect with the European context.[24] Moreover, by setting the novel in Strasbourg instead of in Paris, Djebar destabilizes the traditional notion of the metropolis, casting it slightly off-center.[25] The novel is not simply about French–Algerian relations, but about internal divisions within Europe as well.

By choosing Strasbourg as her subject, Djebar claims the authority to write an "Occidentalist" novel.[26] The author's act of subversion is even more complex, however, than she admits. Rather than a simple inversion of the Orientalist novel, the work confounds binary positions. In true contrapuntal style, Djebar completely intermeshes the Orient and the Occident to stage "transnational" histories, exposing "the processes of collusion and contention, of appropriation and transformation, that link Algeria and France—Algerians and Franco-Algerians" (Silverstein, 2004, 6).

The novel illustrates how both Alsatians and Algerians experienced successive waves of occupation, forced military service for a foreign power, and linguistic oppression. Thelja's father was tortured and killed by the French in the Algerian War; she is thus surprised to learn that her lover François, who came of age just as French soldiers were deployed in Algeria to crush the Independence movement, similarly lost his father in a Russian prison camp. Thelja's visits to the archives in Strasbourg reveal the direct impact that the German annexation of Alsace and Lorraine in 1871 at the end of the Franco-Prussian war had on the colonial settlement of Algeria: many of the region's francophone refugees settled in Algeria where they became members of the pied noir community.[27] Algerian labor was integral to mining Alsace's rich mineral resources in the early twentieth century. The novel highlights the connections between these histories of immigration, foreign domination and exile, in order to create a contrapuntal dialogue between Algeria and Alsace.

This contrapuntal treatment of Algerian and Alsatian history represents an implicit challenge to the way Algerian national history has been produced and disseminated. Djebar has been outspoken in her criticism of the monolithic nationalist agenda of the Algerian state. In *Le blanc de l'Algérie* [1995, *Algerian White*], for instance, she denounces the Algerian government's refusal to recognize the plurality of Algerian society, its forced insistence on the Arabicization of intellectual and public life, its marginalization of both the French and Berber languages, and continued repression of women. In resistance to such narratives, the text represents the vibrant plurality of Algerian society and particularly foregrounds the Berber heritage. As early as 1993, Djebar delivered an essay version of *Le blanc de l'Algérie* in front of the Strasbourg Parliament of Writers, indicting fellow authors "for keeping silent with regard to the civil carnage in Algeria, its declared open season on intellectuals," a stance that confirmed "her entry into permanent exile" (Zimra, 2004, 152).

In *Les nuits de Strasbourg*, Djebar strategically deploys the device of the chiasmus to reveal unexpected connections between Alsace and Algeria, and to undermine binary narratives of the past. A chiasmic relationship links Alsace to Algeria throughout the novel, to the point that they eventually merge to form a fused entity, "Alsagérie."[28] The two regions exchange their defining attributes: on one hand, abandoned Strasbourg is repeatedly described as a desert; on the other, the name of the Algerian protagonist, Thelja, comes from the Arabic word for snow, *thalj*. Thelja received her name from her mother as a bitter reminder of the circumstances surrounding her conception. Her mother fell pregnant while visiting her husband in the maquis during the Algerian War for Independence. Her feet froze on the return journey and her husband died shortly afterwards. By naming her daughter Thelja, or snow, she memorialized her own suffering and loss, imparting it as a legacy to the next generation. This history of loss accompanies Thelja through life, but it also facilitates her ability to empathize with others. In one of the early exchanges between Thelja and François, she translates her name into French. As she does so, she is able to voice the story of her father, a narrative that resonates with François who also lost his father in a Russian prison camp in World War II. Although born on opposite sides of the Franco-Algerian conflict and belonging to different generations, both are victims of violence and loss. Moreover, throughout the course of the novel, abandoned Strasbourg comes to resemble the deserts of Algeria, while Thelja, the Algerian protagonist, despite her dark features and ardent nature, evokes the snow of the Alsatian winter.[29] This kind of chiasmic writing brings different positions closer together, provoking mutual recognition. It calls to mind the musical technique of contrary motion, whereby different voices in a composition approach one another from opposite directions and exchange positions.

Authorial Signatures: From Intransigence to Reconciliation

Djebar's writing took an increasingly autobiographical turn in 1985 with the publication of *L'amour, la fantasia*, the first installment of a series she called the Algerian Quartet. The quartet features four novels that interweave autobiographical narratives contrapuntally between significant episodes of

Algerian history; its subsequent installments consist of *Ombre sultane*, *Vaste est la prison*, and *Nulle part dans la maison de mon père*. By contrast, the author presents *Les nuits de Strasbourg* as a very different project. It represents her attempt to withdraw into a purely fictional world, distant from the daily reports of massacres of civilians in Algerian villages. Nonetheless, the novel's retreat into "pure fiction" does not go very far. The novel takes on the traumatic legacies of war and occupation. Just as many of Djebar's works draw on oral histories she collected in Algeria in the 1970s, *Les nuits de Strasbourg* is informed by the author's encounters and conversations in Strasbourg as writer in residence (Djebar, 1999, 240). In addition, the central protagonist is an Algerian woman who, like Djebar herself, conducts historical research, is well versed in the writers and poets of both the European and the Oriental traditions, and whose marriage has fallen apart.

Against Frantz Fanon's claim that Algerian women should remain veiled in order to deny the European desiring gaze, the novel explicitly "unveils" the Algerian female body and represents female desire, including that of a pregnant woman.[30] The love scenes are extremely interesting on the level of language, as the protagonists experiment with different modes of translation to convey their experiences to one another across linguistic, religious, and cultural differences. In these scenes, the movements of the body become yet another register of communication that transcends linguistic divisions. The narrator describes the dance-like movements of the body as *"arabesques,"* borrowing from the vocabulary of ballet, but also bringing to the surface Thelja's dialectal Arabic from beneath the veneer of written French (Djebar, 1997a, 226).

Djebar embeds her signature into the text in two key places. The history of her pseudonym has been amply documented: born Fatima Zohra-Imalhayene, she hurriedly chose the pen-name of Assia Djebar in 1956 when her first novel was about to be published, in an attempt to conceal her identity and avoid calling attention to herself and bringing shame to her father.[31] "Djebar" (usually transcribed *djebbar*, but the author was under such pressure to choose a name that she misspelled it with only one "b" and thus it remains) comes from the traditional praise-names for Allah in classical Arabic, and signifies uncompromising and unyielding. "Assia," on the other hand, is a healer, one who accompanies and consoles. In *Les nuits de Strasbourg*, Djebar links the intransigence associated with her name to Antigone.[32] A youth theater group made up of young, second-generation Algerian immigrants from the Strasbourg *banlieue* is preparing a new production of Sophocles's

Antigone. Their director refers to Antigone as *l'intransigeante,* and asserts that her primary role is to bear witness: "la mort d'Antigone, dans sa tombe, est là pour éclairer la vérité de toutes ces morts en marche" (Djebar, 1997a, 210). ["Antigone's death, in her tomb, is there to illuminate the truth of all these walking dead."][33] This interpretation of Antigone as an intransigent witness recalls the component of intransigence in Djebar's authorial name and the importance of testimony and resistance in her work. As a novelist, filmmaker, and historian, she has sought to write Algerian women into history by collecting oral testimonies in rural villages during the 1970s and then inscribing their voices into film and fiction.[34]

This same passage also allows the author to comment on the responsibility of the historian. The nineteenth-century French historian Jules Michelet identified the figure of the historian with Oedipus. Michelet was the "first self-consciously to write on behalf of the dead," insisting "with poignant authority, that he could say what they 'really' meant and 'really' wanted, since they themselves did not understand" (Anderson, 1983, 198).[35] Djebar challenges this patriarchal model by asserting an affiliation to Antigone, a figure who has come to occupy increasing importance in contemporary feminist political thought and in Franco-Algerian writing.[36] Whereas Michelet regarded it as the historian's duty to speak for the dead, Djebar is acutely aware of the danger of speaking "for" and in the place of others. At the very opening of *Femmes d'Alger dans leur appartement,* for instance, Djebar (1980, 9) writes: "Ne pas prétendre 'parler pour,' ou pis, 'parler sur,' à peine parler près de, et si possible tout contre: première des solidarités à assumer pour les quelques femmes arabes qui obtiennent ou acquièrent la liberté de mouvement, du corps et de l'esprit." ["Don't claim to 'speak for,' or worse, 'to speak about,' barely speak near to, and if possible right up against: the first act of solidarity to be taken on by those Arab women who obtain or acquire the freedom of movement, of body and mind."]

The idea of intransigence returns later in the novel, again in connection to Djebar's name and political convictions. Thelja recounts the tragic love story of a Franco-Algerian couple who fell in love during the Algerian War for Independence. The heroine of her story is a twenty-year old Algerian woman who executed multiple terrorist operations throughout the war by passing alternatively as a European or as a native: disguised as a European, she planted bombs; in her traditional veil, she transported weapons. The French authorities ultimately captured and imprisoned her. During the course of her interrogation, she seduced the chief officer and the two began a passionate affair. The romance shook the French officer's convictions and allegiances, leading him to take on suicidal missions, during the course of which he was soon killed. In retelling the story to her own French lover, Thelja admits she has never quite forgiven this resistance heroine for falling for a French man: "si longtemps après, je fus troublée, moi, *l'intransigeante*, par ce détail: elle aima son bourreau, 'elle se laissa séduire un moment par lui!'" (Djebar, 1997a, 221–22). ["for such a long time afterwards, I was troubled—me, always so stubborn—by this detail: 'she loved her torturer, she let herself be seduced by him for a moment!'"] Such compromising behavior on the part of a venerated national heroine reinforced her own patriotic interdiction against any romantic involvement with the French, something she visibly tries to overcome throughout the novel. Djebar aligns herself with Thelja through the phrase "moi, *l'intransigeante*" ["me, the intransigent one"], underscoring her autobiographical affinity to her protagonist. The anecdote, however, is especially significant to Djebar's contrapuntal project as it introduces a nuanced, humanized image of both the resistance heroine and the French officer, blurring the binary of blame and responsibility. Djebar suggests that desire is a sort of Achilles' heel, one place where empathy and understanding can emerge even between two bitterly opposed subjects.[37] In this signatory passage, Djebar critiques strict intransigence to advocate a more nuanced, tolerant approach. The passage highlights the productive tensions inherent in the author's pen name, reconciling the intransigent militancy of *Djebar* and the restorative and creative potential implied in *Assia*.

Revisiting History and Remapping the Canon

Epigraphs constitute another key contrapuntal strategy in *Les nuits de Strasbourg*, as they bring multiple authors and narratives into dialogue, ultimately shifting the boundaries of the canon and highlighting new relations between texts. According to Gérard Genette's seminal study, epigraphs occupy a special status within a text: they are simultaneously outside and of the text; on the border of the text, but in the closest possible proximity to the text itself. Genette assigns four functions to the epigraph: to provide a commentary on the title, a commentary on the text itself, a legitimization of the text through reference to a canonical author, and a way for an author to situate a text in a specific literary tradition. Anne Donadey (2001, 65–68) argues that Djebar's use of epigraphs introduces an additional dimension, because the author manipulates her epigraphs to subvert the tradition they represent, thus performing a "reverse commentary" on the canonical texts themselves. Epigraphs in postcolonial writing thus take on a fifth function in that they critique and challenge hegemonic texts. Djebar's epigraphs often seem to work in yet another way: they expand the very boundaries of what is considered canonical. In this sense, Djebar uses epigraphs contrapuntally to bring the work of writers from the periphery into relation with more dominant, metropolitan authors, as well as to reveal the connections among minor writers working in different contexts. The epigraphs in *Les nuits de Strasbourg* exclusively privilege works by women authors: Iranian poet Forough Farrokhzad (1935–67), medieval French scholar Héloïse (twelfth century), and Spanish philosopher Maria Zambrano (1904–91). They work to situate the novel within a rich history of women's writing across diverse historical and national contexts.

The prologue depicts the displacement and loss experienced by the people of Strasbourg during World War II when, fearing imminent invasion, the municipal government evacuated all of its 150,000 civilians in September 1939. As it turns out, German forces only took Strasbourg in June of the following year, at which point the city had already been empty for months. Djebar (1999, 235–36) found that histories of the period neglected this strange episode and thus determined to address it herself: "[L]e vide de 1939, je le remplis avec des histoires d'amour en 1989, cinquante ans après" ["I fill the emptiness of 1939 with love stories from 1989, fifty years later"].[38] Ironically, although the prologue begins with the anticipation of invasion and the evacuation of civilians, it then skips over the eight intervening months to conclude with the belated German invasion on June 15, 1940. The text thus passes over the very period Djebar claimed she wanted to document. The art of this omission is striking: the text circumscribes its object, speaking around it, designating the vacant space. The love stories intended to fill the void are displaced fifty years into the future, to 1989. Instead of putting one history in the place of another, the author prolongs the memory of loss.

The prologue's account of the German invasion of Strasbourg echoes a much-cited scene from the author's earlier historical novel, *L'amour, la fantasia*, which depicts the French invasion of Algiers in 1830 as a violent sexual conquest. But whereas the narrator of *L'amour, la fantasia* presents the initial moment of encounter as a spectacle of operatic proportions—with Algerian women all over the city ascending to rooftop patios to see the spectacle of French ships assembled in the bay, and a plethora of European artists and scribes looking out from aboard the ships, eager to record their first impressions of the North African city—Strasbourg is deserted. No one remains to witness the impending invasion. The pilots of the German warplanes overhead are alone in contemplating the "desert" below: here again, Strasbourg and Algeria exchange qualities as the Alsatian city takes on the qualities of the North African desert. The only eyes to return the invaders' gaze are those of statues, soon to be "déboulonnées, concassées, transportées à la remise, déportées" ["unbolted, crushed, transported to the depot, deported"] (Djebar, 1997a, 17). As statues have empty cavities in the place of eyes, the image further underscores the haunting absence of witnesses. The text never directly mentions the deportation of Jews, but alludes to it through powerful metonymic images: the deportation of statues and the ghostly music of a radio left behind by a Jewish family who forgot to turn it off in their haste.

As Djebar wrote *Les nuits de Strasbourg* in the mid-1990s, the novel's spectacular, technical description of the German air force's assaults on Strasbourg inevitably calls to mind the highly mediatized images of coalition air power. In fact, the novel emphasizes the trauma and loss the inhabitants of Strasbourg experience as if to challenge the sterile language used by the media when reporting on Operation Iraqi Shield. Terms such as "surgical strikes" or "laser-guided missiles" negate their impact on the civilian population. Djebar's narrator explicitly laments the devastation wrought by airstrikes on the cultural heritage of Strasbourg at multiple points in the city's history. She recalls that more than 2,500 rare manuscripts were destroyed in the Prussian firebombing of 1870, an incident which aroused the indignation of Victor Hugo and other intellectuals throughout Europe (Djebar, 1997a, 102). In a sense, the text is also prescient of the second Iraq War in the fall of 2004, during which the author was to vocally condemn the "coalition's" disregard for the historical and artistic heritage of Iraq, much of which was reportedly destroyed or looted in the aftermath of the air strikes.[39]

Divisive Pasts, Contrapuntal Futures: "Neuf Nuits" (1989)

Crosscultural love relationships function throughout the novel as "performative encounters," which Mireille Rosello (2005, 1) defines as "a type of encounter that coincides with the creation of new subject positions, rather than treating preexisting (preimagined) identities as the reason for, and justification of, the protocol of the encounter—whether it is one of violence or trust, respect or hostility." As Rosello argues, "the violence of some historical contexts makes any initial encounter with another subject almost impossible. No first encounter can take place when the history, language, religion, and culture exert such pressures upon the protagonists of the encounter that their desire to speak or be silent is trapped by preexisting, prewritten dialogues and scenarios."[40] Although Rosello does not specifically employ the term counterpoint, these performative encounters are exemplary instances of contrapuntal exchange, in that the opposition of different voices produces some new unanticipated harmony. The central narrative in *Les nuits de Strasbourg* stages multiple crosscultural relationships, most importantly that between Thelja and François. Through Thelja's first-person narration, we see how her liaison with a Frenchman allows her to engage and work through her continued resentment over France's role in Algeria. In *Les nuits de Strasbourg*, Djebar proposes a model of encounter that depends on the presence of bodies in dialogue, so that inevitable lapses in understanding can be mitigated by the body, through physical love, touch, laughter, and the music of a voice.

The title of the main section of the novel, "Neuf nuits" ["Nine Nights"], initiates a contrapuntal dialogue between two very different literary traditions. On one hand, it evokes the canonical Persian text, the *Mille et une nuits*, in which a sultan's bride, Scheherazade, tells story upon story in order to forestall her execution. On the other, it recalls a line from an erotic poem by René Char, "L'amante" [1992, "The Lover"], in which the speaker imagines the "nights of wild novelty" he spent in the arms of his lover. Eve later recites the full text of Char's poem to Hans, and explicitly mentions Char's active role in the French Resistance during World War II (Djebar, 1997a, 167–68). Through these references to Char, Djebar reminds us that she similarly took up the pen in the spirit of resistance, although Algerian audiences at first did not recognize this. They initially dismissed her as insufficiently political, and judged her early novels, *La soif* [1957, *The Mischief*] and *Les impatients* [1958, *The Impatient Ones*], as frivolous and unengaged at a time when the Algerian struggle for independence was rapidly gaining momentum. On the contrary, Djebar asserts that the writing of her first novel was unequivocally an act of political resistance (Adler and Djebar, 2006). While still a student at the Ecole normale supérieure, she participated in the Algerian students' strike in Paris and refused to take her exams in 1957. Freed from the task of preparing for her exams, she produced the entire manuscript of *La soif* in two months of frenzied writing.

Medieval allusions are also extremely prevalent in *Les nuits de Strasbourg*, and here again, canonical works like *The Letters of Abélard and Héloïse*, *Tristan and Isolde*, and the *Serment de Strasbourg* come into dialogue with lesser known manuscripts, such as *Le Jardin des délices* [*The Garden of Delights*] by the Abbess Herrade de Landsberg, which forms the subject of Thelja's current research. These medieval works occupy a special position in the history of the French language; they constitute the inaugural texts through which writers established the authority of the French vernacular as a vehicle for writing independent of Latin, and began to construct a secular literary tradition in French. Djebar in turn experiments with ways to "extra-territorialize" her writing, bringing dialectical Arabic, Berber, Alsatian, and physicality into the text to newly challenge and reinvigorate the French language.

In a similar vein, the novel deploys images that resonate across both the Eastern and Western literary traditions, although they evoke different associations in each context. For instance, the narrator deploys classical expressions such as the trope of night's hair (Djebar, 1997a, 49) or dawn's golden fingers (119), which then merge with Arabic images. The *doigts de l'Aurore* [fingers of Dawn] evoke the name of the most prized dates from Algeria, the *deglet en nour*, literally "fingers of light" (88). Thelja describes the cultivation of these dates as a courtship ritual, a voluptuous task given to the most agile men of the oasis, who shimmy up and down the palms to take the male seeds and fertilize the female trees (87). The narrator describes childhood memory as a "*lait de palme*" ["palm milk"] that surges up spontaneously, ready to overflow (86). These images recall the evocative palm trees in twentieth-century European poetry: Valéry's majestic "Palme," James Merrill's "Lost in Translation," and the palm at the end of the mind in Wallace Stevens's "Of Mere Being." Later in the text, Djebar uses the image of the palm again to describe the laugh lines around François's eyes, fanning out like palm trees (228). Djebar performs such subtle modulations throughout the novel, describing the process of linguistic and metaphorical exchange as a "*tangage*," or oscillation (282).[41]

The author strategically uses only first names throughout the novel in order to undermine static notions of identity and history. The absence of surnames frees the protagonists of the historical weight of the father, and enables them to forge new relationships across ethnic and national boundaries.[42] The symbolic significance of names is evident in Thelja's initial unwillingness to pronounce François's name because it contains the syllable "France," which reminds her of France's colonial domination over Algeria and the bitter struggle for independence in which she lost her father. Her eventual act of naming François signifies reconciliation and recognition of his history: "François, et je vous appelle, je vous hèle, et répétant votre prénom, j'accepte en vous toute votre histoire, ce que j'en sais" (344). ["François, in naming you, I call out to you, and repeating your first name, I accept in you all your history, what I know of it."] In their successive encounters, Thelja and François work towards mutual recognition and understanding. On their final night together, they playfully combine Alsace and Algérie to form new entities with hybrid French and Arabic sonorities, "Alsagérie" and "El zadj erie" (372). They thus reconfigure histories of violence and conflict to create a fragile space of plurality.

And yet, despite moments of rapprochement, historical and cultural conflicts are never completely resolved in the novel, despite the protagonists' best efforts to engage one another. One of the most problematic scenes of the novel arises when Eve and Hans argue over the upbringing of their (still unborn) child, whom Eve plans to circumcise according to Jewish tradition, despite Hans's objections that the act is barbaric. In order to make amends, the couple decides to reenact the *Serment de Strasbourg*, the medieval political oath between Germany and France. After performing the oath in each other's language, Eve claims: "toute guerre entre nous est finie" (238) ["all warfare between us is finished"]. The notion that this medieval oath will provide "closure" is highly utopian and deceptive because the *Serment de Strasbourg* did not prevent further conflicts between Germany and France. Moreover, the fact that Eve remains unwilling to enter German territory, despite the toll it will take on the new family she and Hans are founding together, undermines her claim that she has put the past behind her. The couple's enactment of the ancient pledge remains, nonetheless, an attempt to recognize the other on his or her terms. In light of the turbulent history of Franco-German conflict and the immense trauma and loss caused by the Holocaust, this movement toward the other will continuously have to be renewed. While their bi-national child merges their two distinct historical trajectories, his or her upbringing will constantly require them to negotiate the tensions between "the individual, embodied, and loved side *and* the collective, social, and constructed side of [their] relations to the past" (Rothberg, 2009, 4).

Thelja's suicide is also deeply problematic. As she jumps to her death from the Strasbourg cathedral, she cries out into an empty sky. The novel closes on a haunting description of Thelja's scream as a "cri dans le bleu immerge" ["call immersed in blue"]. This call issues from the highest spire in Europe, the site of one of Europe's most historically contested frontiers, now the capital of a newly unified Europe and a city of refuge for exiled writers. Thelja's cry anticipates that of Zoulikha, the heroine of the Algerian resistance movement who appears in Djebar's later novel *La femme sans sépulture* (2006), and whose voice continues to sound well after her murder at the hands of French soldiers. It also recalls the unforgettable figure of Atika from Djebar's short story "La femme en morceaux" ["The woman in pieces"], a young teacher who is brutally murdered by Islamist militants in front of her students and whose voice continues well after her head is severed, just as Orpheus's head went on singing as it floated down the river. In each of these cases, female voices command our attention and engagement, and refuse to be silenced. Their political agency, however, remains questionable, particularly in the case of Thelja, whose final cry leaves open many possible readings.

Mireille Calle-Gruber (2001, 12) reads this final scene as emblematic of Djebar's writing in general. Thelja's wrenching cry transports us momentarily out of ourselves, just as Djebar's fiction does in a larger sense: "Les architectures littéraires d'Assia Djebar empruntent à la musique cette faculté qu'elle a de nous tirer vers le haut. De nous faire [...] plus grands que nous. Et l'on note qu'elles portent jusqu'au bout d'elles-mêmes, jusqu'à la béance sur quoi tous les livres s'interrompent, cri, prière, apostrophe, plainte, conjuration, cri jeté, 'un cri dans le bleu immergé'..." ["The literary architectures of Assia Djebar borrow from music the faculty of elevating us. Of making us [...] greater than ourselves. And they go to the very limit, to the gaping abyss that interrupts all books, cry, prayer, apostrophe, incantation, complaint, shout, *a cry immersed in blue.*"] While poetic, this reading evacuates politics and agency by not attending to what Thelja's scream seeks to express: is it her empathetic response to the diverse, overlapping traumas that she has encountered in Alsace and Algeria, or her protest of the seemingly endless cycle of violence and victimhood?

Throughout *Les nuits de Strasbourg,* the contrapuntal intermeshing of conflicting histories and experiences works to complicate the exclusionary narratives and binary oppositions that have characterized relations between France and North Africa, as well as between France and Germany, Jews and Muslims. The novel takes on the kind of difficult work which Said argued is the responsibility of intellectuals and artists: "Overlapping yet irreconcilable experiences demand from the intellectual the courage to say that *that* is what is before us" (Said, 2012, 39). While never equating the diverse historical traumas that figure in the novel—the Algerian war, the murder and displacement of Jews during the Holocaust, the successive occupations of Alsace, Soviet prisoner-of-war camps, the dispossession of North African Jews after 1948—Djebar brings them into relation with one other and explores the possibilities for, and impediments to, reciprocal recognition and healing.

Antigone: Counterpoint and the Canon

We now turn to examine a final thread in the contrapuntal texture of *Les nuits de Strasbourg*: the recurring references to Sophocles's *Antigone*. Djebar evokes Antigone not only in the novel, but also in essays, lectures, and interviews throughout the 1990s. In an interview with Laure Adler, Djebar explained that her interest in Antigone dates back to her school days when, denied the opportunity to learn Classical Arabic, she studied Greek and read Sophocles' tragedies in the original. Antigone's courageous public stance made a deep impression on her, particularly since Algerian women were still largely confined to the domestic sphere (Adler and Djebar, 2006). Elements of the Antigone myth surface repeatedly in *Les nuits de Strasbourg*: the play itself is under production, and several unburied or displaced corpses haunt the text, prolonging mourning and resisting closure. Neither Thelja nor François ever recovered their fathers' bodies, and consequently, neither was unable to hold a proper burial. In another passage, we learn that Jewish graves in Constantine, Algeria have been unearthed and displaced to clear the land for real estate development. Catherine Dana (2004, 113–25) suggests that Djebar's interest in Antigone participates in a wider phenomenon. Antigone came to have renewed significance for Algerian writers in the wake of the violent civil conflict of the 1990s, when the disappearance and murder of thousands of civilians was compounded by the Algerian government's subsequent failure to provide information or to bring perpetrators to justice. As the Algerian state passed successive amnesty laws, imposing silence at the expense of justice and accountability, writers felt compelled to take on the role of witness.

Djebar makes a particular effort to consider contemporary versions of Antigone by authors working outside the main metropolitan centers of literary production: Swedish poet Gunnar Ekelöf, Belgian psychoanalyst Henry Bauchau, and Spanish philosopher Maria Zambrano.[43] She thus brings a quintessentially contrapuntal dimension to the Antigone myth, showing how this highly canonical figure has inspired multiple rewritings, by minor as well as major authors. Bauchau, Ekelöf and Zambrano all imagine Antigone's voice from within the tomb, recalling Djebar's efforts to give voice to the rural Algerian men, women and children who were buried alive in caves in the mid-nineteenth century during the French conquest of Algeria. In a haunting section of *L'amour, la fantasia*, the author commemorates the martyrdom of these Algerian tribes whom the French army literally entombed, sealing up the entrances to the caves to which they had retreated and then using fire and smoke to suffocate them as part of a ruthless campaign to crush tribal resistance.[44]

Significantly, Djebar's interest in Antigone is echoed in two other Franco-Algerian works published between 1997 and 1999: Sebbar's novel *La Seine était rouge* and Derrida's philosophical essay on hospitality, *De l'hospitalité*. This simultaneous turn to Antigone is remarkable as it is unlikely that these writers were aware of one another's projects. Djebar claims, for instance, that she has never read Derrida.[45] While Dana sees the presence of Antigone in Franco-Algerian writing of the 1990s as a reflection of the crisis in memory and accountability brought on by the civil war in Algeria,[46] Sebbar's novel demonstrates that it is also linked to France's belated recognition of its own violent colonial history.

Sebbar brings Antigone into *La Seine était rouge* to commemorate the October 17, 1961 massacres of Algerian demonstrators by the Parisian police. Her interest in the massacres reflects a new willingness in France to confront the colonial past. Signs of this shift include the long overdue official recognition by the French Senate that the "events in Algeria" from 1954 to 1962 had in fact constituted a war for independence, and that the French army had routinely used torture in Algeria. It also involved the public admission by the mayor of Paris, Bertrand Delanoë, that the police had brutally attacked peaceful Algerian demonstrators in Paris and other provincial cities in 1961. Under Delanoë's leadership, a commemorative plaque was placed on the Pont de Saint-Michel in the heart of Paris.

Sebbar's title lends a graphic and shameful image to the massacres, bearing witness to the attempts of the Parisian police to hide the consequences of their disproportionate brutality by disposing of murdered demonstrators in the river Seine. The novel's protagonists are young second-generation North African immigrants who come to learn of the massacres through the media coverage of Maurice Papon's trial in 1998. Although Papon was brought to trial for his participation in the deportation of French children to Nazi death camps under Vichy, his criminal responsibility as prefect of the Paris Police during the October 1961 massacres also came under scrutiny. Although he was never held legally accountable for the incident, a government report released in 1999 acknowledged that he had given the mandate for inappropriately brutal tactics to suppress what by all accounts were peaceful demonstrations, resulting in the deaths of at least forty-eight Algerians at the hands of the police (the unofficial figure is significantly higher).

Upon learning of the massacres, the protagonists of Sebbar's novel collect testimonies from witnesses of the October 1961 massacres, and then create documentary film, graffiti, and theatre to raise awareness in their communities. Omer projects a new version of the play *Antigone*, in a symbolic attept to restore dignity to those who were dumped into the river: "C'est l'histoire d'une fille qui creuse la tombe de ses frères la nuit, sur la colline, elle s'acharne, la terre est dure, des soldats surveillent les corps, des frères jumeaux, exécutés. L'armée a exposé les cadavres sur la place du village..." (Sebbar, 1999, 125). ["It's the story of a girl who digs the grave of her brothers at night on a hillside; she struggles at it, the earth is hard, soldiers guard the bodies of her twin brothers who were executed. The army exposed their corpses in the village square..."]

Both *Les nuits de Strasbourg* and *La Seine était rouge* imagine new productions of *Antigone*, but neither play actually comes to fruition. *La Seine était rouge* ends just as Omer offers Amal the title role in his still unwritten play. It is uncertain whether she will accept the part of Antigone, or whether she will insist on commemorating this history on her own terms. In *Les nuits de Strasbourg*, the murder of the play's director, Jacqueline, just before opening night prevents the play from being performed as planned. The actress who was to play the title role surprises the assembled audience by abandoning the script and improvising an impassioned monologue. Still wearing the costume of Antigone, she affirms the integral place of North Africans in Strasbourg's history. Ultimately, Djebar and Sebbar both evoke the story of Antigone in order to address the experience of North African immigrants in France—to expose the violence of this history *and* to insist on its centrality to French twentieth-century history. The fact that the play is deferred or interrupted in each novel suggests the need for new forms of mourning and remembrance.

Taking a different approach, Derrida (2000, 93) positions Antigone as the exemplary figure of the foreigner. In his reading, Antigone has been exiled on three counts: first, when she willingly leaves her native city of Thebes alongside Oedipus, offering herself as her father's companion and guide in exile; second, when she gives up her maternal language; and finally, when the state refuses her access to her father's grave in order to guarantee the future prosperity of Thebes.[47] In Derrida's (2000, 111) terms, Antigone is "without a tomb, without a determinable place, without monument, without a localizable and circumscribed place of mourning, without a stopping point [arrêt]," and thus obliged to mourn mourning itself. By situating a canonical heroine such as Antigone in the place of the marginalized foreigner and refugee, Derrida deconstructs the binary relationship between the West and the "other."

At the same time, Antigone's impossible mourning resonates all too well for Algerians: the devastating violence of the War for Independence and the Civil War of the 1990s displaced many Algerians internally and sent thousands into exile.[48] Historians of Algeria have identified the ghettoization of memory as a major obstacle to working through the turbulent history of France and Algeria, deploring the fractured way in which each community holds on to their own particular narrative of the past, making national reconciliation difficult (Stora and Harbi, 2005). In Les nuits de Strasbourg, the protagonists use dialogue to knit together the fractures between their different histories. Sebbar's protagonists deeply resent the fact that their parents and grandparents never told them about the massacres of 1961; they never saw their elders grieve, and feel obliged to mourn in their place. They engage the entire community in the process. While contrapuntal narratives such as these represent an important effort to bring disparate perspectives into dialogue, Djebar and Sebbar both emphasize the importance of collective projects, particularly theater and documentary film, as strategies to encourage mourning and healing in the public sphere.

Several Franco-Algerian artists have subsequently taken up related projects. In 2002, the young Beur novelist, Faïza Guène, produced a seventeen-minute documentary on the massacres of October 17, 1961. Like the projects imagined in Sebbar's novel, Guène's film features oral testimonies by workers, demonstrators, journalists, photographers, and organizers who witnessed the police violence against demonstrators.[49] As Guène remarks, "Mes parents, ils ont connu la guerre en Algérie, Octobre 1961 à Paris. Ils ne veulent pas faire de bruit. Mais nous, on est né ici, on ne se tait pas" ["My parents experienced the Algerian War and October 1961 in Paris. They don't want to make any noise. But we were born here and we will not keep quiet"].[50] At the Théâtre du Grabuge[51] in Lyon, Franco-Algerian director Geraldine Bénichou took a more poetic route, to produce an intriguing, dramatic adaptation of Henri Bauchau's novel, Le cri d'Antigone [Antigone's Scream] in 2004. The play features two female performers, Magali Bonat in the role of Antigone, and Kabyle singer Salah Gaoua, and intersperses Arabic and Kabyle songs between Antigone's verses to stage a contrapuntal, feminine protest. The production toured throughout France and Algeria between 2004 and 2006, bringing issues of mourning, memory, and accountability into the public forum on both sides of the Mediterranean.

Conclusions

Djebar clearly shares Said's commitment to challenging the canon, bringing to the fore different, marginalized voices, and confronting the complications and connections between the most disparate historical narratives. Several critics, however, have questioned not only whether Djebar truly establishes equality between the voices in her fiction, and furthermore, whether equality is a desirable quality in postcolonial writing given the need to correct a long history of domination and effacement. Al-Nakib (2005, 272) destabilizes the very notion of equality by arguing that counterpoint profoundly reconfigures the terms of every relationship and undermines the very notion of hierarchy: "French is undeniably the colonizer's language; however, in counterpoint with an Arabic that has denied women use of the first-person pronoun, it embodies the possibility of freedom even as it remains a tool of oppression." In *Les nuits de Strasbourg*, it is impossible to assess the equality of voices at any given moment. There is no permanently dominant perspective, nor a permanently subordinate one, but always an oscillation as different subject positions interact, contaminate, deterritorialize, and transform one another. It is precisely this performative, interactive, non-hierarchical dynamic that makes counterpoint a valuable conceptual model for thinking about reconciliation. Musicologists have attributed the impact of counterpoint to the fact that "hearing counterpoint entail[s] being in the music, perceiving the relations between the strands, in effect being surrounded by the music [...] Counterpoint allow[s] no safe distance from the compositional materials" (Painter, 2001, 203). Likewise, *Les nuits de Strasbourg* presents multiple conflicting experiences together with all their contradictions *and* entanglements.

To return to Said's plea for a contrapuntal reevaluation of Israeli and Palestinian history, it is not a question of which history should be privileged, or whether the two histories carry "equal" claims. On the contrary, Said argues that the two histories must be considered as inseparably interrelated to one another. In *Les nuits de Strasbourg*, Djebar takes on the traumatic legacy of colonialism and violence on a transnational scale. Staging encounters between historically divergent experiences within the cosmopolitan city of Strasbourg, the novel undermines any one group's monopoly on victimhood, and models a contrapuntal engagement with others. Through its audacious formal experimentation, temporal displacements, revisionist approach to history, and contrapuntal commitments, the novel places significant demands on the reader. To "hear" all the voices in such a multilayered text—and to attend to what their interaction and juxtaposition produces anew—requires an active and compassionate approach to reading, the kind of worldly, secular criticism that Said modeled on musical counterpoint.

If Said's own contrapuntal readings remain caught up in the binary structure of relations between the center and the periphery, it falls upon writers and critics today to think counterpuntally on multiple planes and in multiple directions. As a methodology, counterpoint allows us bring new perspectives into dialogue and to uncover new understandings of how diverse histories are imbricated in one another, as Djebar illustrates in writing Alsace and Algeria into relation. As such, counterpoint provides an important tool for the ethical and worldly practice of comparative literature.

CHAPTER THREE

Glenn Gould and the Birth of the Author

Variation and Performance in Nancy Huston's
Les variations Goldberg

More than two decades after Canadian pianist Glenn Gould burst onto the music scene in 1955 with revolutionary performances of Johann Sebastian Bach's Goldberg Variations, the young writer Nancy Huston made her literary debut with a novel called *Les variations Goldberg/The Goldberg Variations* (1981).[1] The story unfolds on a mid-summer evening, as Liliane Kulainn performs Bach's Goldberg variations for friends at her Parisian apartment. As she plays, Liliane imagines the thoughts of the people in the audience, authoring thirty potential responses to her performance.

The novel itself is a remarkable performance on several levels: firstly, Huston chooses to write in French, a language she adopted as an adult. Second, the novel's form mirrors its content.[2] It appropriates the structure of Bach's Goldberg Variations—thirty variations framed by an aria on either end—in order to stage a performance and its critical reception. The author paints a portrait of contemporary Parisian society while presenting wide-ranging perspectives on music and performance. Significantly, she brings music performance into relation with ongoing literary debates over the nature of voice, the role of the author, and the practice of interpretation.

Huston, like Samuel Beckett, writes interchangeably in French and English, and translates her own works.[3] Born in Calgary, Canada in 1953, and raised first in Alberta and then Boston, her childhood was marked by the traumatic departure of her mother when she was only six years old. Huston embarked for Paris as a twenty-year-old college student and fell in love. Although she initially intended to spend just the academic year in France, she stayed on to write her Masters thesis under the supervision of Roland Barthes, and developed a keen sensitivity to the ideology of language and style. According to Huston, Barthes often fantasized about writing fiction, but was too caught up in technical questions.[4] She began work on her first novel shortly after her mentor's death and never looked back, producing a dozen novels, three works of theater, and multiple collections of essays.[5] Her fiction has earned France's top literary prizes, including the Prix Femina (in 2006 for *Lignes de faille/ Fault Lines*) and the Goncourt des lycéens (in 1996 for *L'empreinte de l'ange/ The Mark of the Angel*), and garnered prestigious—if controversial—awards in Britain and Canada as well.[6] Despite her success as a bestselling author on both sides of the Atlantic and high profile in French literary circles,[7] Huston's work only began to receive commensurate scholarly attention in the past decade, primarily from critics interested in questions of bilingualism, self-translation, and the relationship between music and literature.[8]

Because she is not a native French speaker, Huston's name invariably comes up as an instance of how writers from outside France have come to shape the direction of French literature.[9] Yet, although a francophone writer by virtue of her use of French, Huston's position with regard to the language differs considerably from that of writers from former French colonies. She chose to adopt French out of a personal affinity for the language, and has often described it as emotionally neutral territory—a claim few francophone Caribbean or African writers would make, coming from contexts where French has served (and in many cases, continues to serve) as a vehicle of political, linguistic, or cultural oppression.[10] In the early stages of her career, Huston collaborated with Algerian writer Leila Sebbar on a series of letters, *Les lettres parisiennes: autopsie de l'exil,* in which both authors reflect on their relation to the French language as outsiders. Huston claims that writing (and living) in French enabled her to approach language differently, to hear things she might otherwise not have noticed. As she writes to Sebbar, "Je ne *subis* pas l'écart, je le cherche" ["I am not *subjected* to difference; I seek it out"] (Proulx, 2000, 84). This productive distance—or dissonance—informs her writing, most visibly in her exploration of the gaps between languages, and between music and literature. Several of her works call on the metaphor of dis-tempered and dissonant instruments to convey a sense of difference and displacement. Huston (2003, 55) sees her interest in performance as an inevitable consequence of living between languages: "A person who decides voluntarily, as an adult, unconstrained by outside circumstances, to leave her native land and adopt a hitherto unfamiliar language and culture must face the fact that for the rest of her life she will be involved with *theater, imitation, make-believe.*"

Huston's novels push the boundaries of literary form and confront existential and historical questions with unflinching intensity and nuance.[11] Nearly all of her works use music, whether as a figure for the arts in general, as a way of integrating multiple perspectives and temporalities, or as a formal device. The relation of her work to music can at times be transparent, as in the case of *Les variations Goldberg*, or more implicit, as we will see in later novels.[12] Huston's experimental approach to form, of which music is one dimension, suggests a debt to the New Novelists, especially to Nathalie Sarraute whose *Les fruits d'or* [*The Golden Fruits*] eschews a traditional plot and instead anticipates how the novel itself will be received by critics and the public.[13] *Les variations Goldberg* similarly focuses on reception.

Few critics have grappled substantively with *Les variations Goldberg*, perhaps because the author herself has dismissed the novel as overly facile, as too much of an intellectual game (Barca, 2009). Nonetheless, Werner Wolf (1999, 352), one of the most active scholars in the field of interdisciplinary criticism, cites the novel as an impressive instance of postmodern intermedial writing because its formal structure conforms so closely to a musical model.[14] Wolf argues that the novel's experimental form presents challenges for the reader that match those we experience when grappling with a difficult piece of music; both endeavors reward us with the sensual pleasure that comes from having achieved something through concentrated effort. For Wolf, then, Huston uses music to enhance the sensuality (and corporality) of the literary experience, drawing on a Barthesian understanding of music as linked to the body. Frédérique Arroyas (2007) situates Huston's interest in open-ended Baroque forms in relation to the wider Baroque revival in the mid twentieth-century, a turn which reflects the leftist social movements of the 1960s and the widespread impatience with bourgeois values and fixed ideas.[15] According to Arroyas, Huston desacralizes music by calling attention to the material conditions of its production, bringing amateur voices into a conversation often dominated by experts, showing how music has traditionally privileged male voices at the expense of women, and exploring the expressive eccentricity of particular Baroque instruments: the mistuned violin and the tempered harpsichord.

Surprisingly, in reading Huston's *Les variations Goldberg*, nearly all critics have missed its overt relation to Gould—and this is the thread we take up here.[16] Huston chose for her entry into fiction the very work on which Gould began his astonishing career. Unlike the many other literary adaptations of the Goldberg Variations, the novel explicitly addresses the problem of performance, an area where Gould made an indelible mark. Its pivotal variation, Variation XV or "Roche" (Rock), features a celebrated public intellectual Bernald Thorer who abruptly interrupts a vibrant career and decides to stop writing, despite the protests of students, colleagues, and readers—a move that recalls Gould's withdrawal from the concert stage in 1962 in order to focus exclusively on recording.[17] Gould's influence is even more evident in the recorded adaptation of the novel, *Pérégrinations Goldberg/Goldberg Wanderings*, that Huston produced in 2000 in collaboration with harpsichordist Freddy Eichelberger, guitarist Philippe de Schepper, and serpent (Baroque tuba) player, Michel Godard.[18] In the recording, Huston reads the arias and select variations against an eclectic musical score that includes fragments of the Goldberg Variations on harpsichord, a Frescobaldi song,[19] and several original compositions.[20] The range of vocal timbres, intonation, and accents that she calls upon in these readings emphasizes the musicality of speech. The overall effect of *Pérégrinations Goldberg* is very similar to the "contrapuntal radio" recordings Gould produced between 1967 and 1977, particularly *The Idea of North* (1967), a haunting piece for five voices that evokes the experience of living in northern Canada. Gould treats the voices like five independent contrapuntal lines, setting them against each other above the ostinato sound tapestry of a train and Sibelius's Symphony No. 5.[21]

The fact that both Gould and Huston returned to the Goldberg Variations multiple times over the course of their careers illustrates the pull Bach's work exerted over both artists. Gould first recorded the Goldberg Variations at the outset of his career, and felt compelled to return to them in 1981 to offer a new reading of the work. Huston similarly revisited the variations several times: first to produce her own English translation of the novel in 1996, and then to create the *Pérégrinations Goldberg* four years later.

This chapter sets out to examine Huston's use of variation form in *Les variations Goldberg* and to read the novel both as a response to Gould and as an intervention in contemporary debates on performance, authority and democracy. The first section considers the subversive theatricality of the novel; the second part offers a close look at variation form and the issues it poses for literary adaptation; we then examine the role of musical strategies across Huston's later fiction; the final section illustrates the influence of Gould's revolutionary ideas on Huston's understanding of both performance and authorship.

The *Mise-en-Scène*

Perhaps the most striking aspect of Huston's debut novel is the way the narrative is situated spatially and temporally within a performance. Yet, instead of remaining grounded in the physical confines of the theater, the narrative moves into the expansive territory of the imagination, leaving bounded, everyday time for the subjective, flexible time opened by music.[22] Each variation presents the thoughts of a different individual in the audience. In an unexpected twist, however, these different subjectivities are then subsumed into the imagination of a single narrator, the performer, who claims she has invented them all. The novel thus gives readers the illusion of access into the thoughts of thirty characters, only later to reveal that we have been "played" by the performer. The concert becomes a scene of writing, the performer an author.

The deliberate attention accorded to the *mise-en-scène* of the concert evokes the commitment of early music practitioners to use period instruments and recreate the "authentic" conditions for which Baroque music was intended: following the indication on the score, Liliane performs the Goldberg Variations on a double-manual harpsichord.[23] She selects an intimate setting illuminated by candlelight. On closer examination, however, it becomes clear that this staging is determined not by the search for authenticity, but on the contrary, by repeated instances of wordplay. Liliane gives a literal reading to the expression "chamber" music, positioning the instrument inside her bedroom: it is a "concert de chambre dans une chambre" ["a chamber music concert in a bed chamber"] (Huston, 1981, 32). This move exemplifies Huston's playful approach to language, and particularly, her interest in puns and untranslatable expressions. Similarly, the expression "sur leur trente-et-un" ["dressed to the nines"] is literally realized in the thirty-one people assembled for the concert, and in the thirty variations and aria that comprise Bach's work. Liliane enhances the sense of occasion by setting out a lavish reception to follow the concert, with hors d'oeuvres and champagne laid out on the balcony. The hors d'oeuvres off-stage serve as a playful riposte to the musical oeuvre on stage, signaling to the audience that they will be expected to participate in the obligatory exchange of critical judgments and small talk once the concert comes to a close. The novel thus examines both the performance and *reception* of a musical work. The prevalence of wordplay here and throughout the novel defamiliarizes language, and introduces a tone of irreverence that undermines notions of "authenticity."

An exaggerated theatricality permeates other aspects of the *mise-en-scène* as well. Liliane's cousin greets the guests at the door in a maid's uniform, playing the part of a servant, prompting reflections on social class and privilege. The musician herself is in a long black dress that dramatically sets off her pale complexion. This theatricality unsettles the audience, who begin to wonder what role they are to play. In what sense are they too part of the spectacle? What, alongside Bach, is being performed? To what degree is the performance a parody? From the harpsichord's unorthodox position in the bedroom to the costumed maid, the concert compels the audience to interrogate their own positioning *vis à vis* the musical experience and one another. The staging thus raises questions concerning the value of attending a concert. How does live performance impact the performer, the individual audience member, and the community, and to what extent does it transform the relations among those present?

As one character informs us, the staging of the concert is intentionally designed to disorient the audience and provoke them to dream and reflect (127). Liliane holds the concert on June 24, the night of Saint John, in an allusion to Shakespeare's *A Midsummer Night's Dream*. The novel thus reaches not only towards music, but also towards the theater.[24] In *A Midsummer Night's Dream*, moreover, the fanciful play-within-the-play undermines established power structures by bringing the political and magical orders into contact, so that the evocative universe of dreams, fairies, and forest creatures contaminates that of the court and law. The performance in the novel similarly destabilizes the social order. The concert's *mise-en-scène* and the performer's explicit reflections on her role introduce a Brechtian effect of alienation, revealing the ideological and institutional codes that govern how classical music is produced and consumed.[25] The performer consciously agrees to execute the music from beginning to end, adhering as closely as possible to the score. Once she commits a note to sound, she cannot take it back or revise it. The audience, in turn, maintains an attentive silence throughout the concert and applauds only at appropriate moments. Beneath this respectful veneer, however, the novel exposes the underlying violence that structures even the most refined cultural performance. The audience prepares to critique not only Liliane's interpretation and technical skill, but also, because she is a woman, her physique, style, marital status, and sexuality. She suspects that their pleasure comes, not from the music, but from the sadistic prospect of witnessing her extreme vulnerability. Like spectators at a bullfight, they want to see her test her physical limits, recalling

Edmund Burke's notion of the sublime as "[w]hatever is fitted in any sort to excite the ideas of pain, and danger, [...] is productive of the strongest emotion which the mind is capable of feeling" (Burke 1759, 1958, 113, qtd in Sisman, 1993, 13). As Liliane observes, "Les gens s'assemblent, plus ou moins sur leur trente-et-un, pour assister au déroulement d'un rituel. Corrida en *sol* majeur. Mais qu'espèrent-ils y ressentir? Et qu'est-ce que j'y ressens? Quant à moi, rien. C'est même la condition" (Huston, 1981, 15). ["People gather, more or less in their Sunday best, to watch the ritual unfold. Corrida in g minor. But what do they hope to feel in it? And what do I feel? As for me, nothing. It's the very condition."]

Liliane circumvents this oppressive structure by diverting her attention outwards to the audience.[26] Thus, in each successive variation, she puts herself in the place of a different individual in the audience, anticipating their thoughts and reactions. The performer makes the audience the object of *her* scrutiny, and forestalls its criticism by producing it herself. Again, this strategy recalls Sarraute's *Les fruits d'or* which similarly anticipates and parodies every possible response, except that Huston inserts an additional layer of critical distance into her text. Whereas Sarraute imagines and preempts the reception of the very novel she is writing (and we, by extension, are reading), so much so that the entire text is given over to critical response, Huston's novel recounts a musical performance and simultaneously weaves audience response into the fabric of the performance itself.

Liliane's ability to invent the thoughts of her audience while playing the Goldberg Variations challenges one of the most persistent myths associated with musical activity: that music grants fullness of presence. Instead, it generates states of absence and excess. Moreover, at the opening of the narrative, Liliane recounts a dream in which she finds herself in a room with a perfectly square keyboard. The instrument's strings are all equal in length and its keys produce the exact same note, "la même perfection" (Huston, 1981, 17): "mi." She sits down at the keyboard and plays through the entire concert repertoire, converting passionate flurries of notes and chords into pure, undifferentiated expression, an endless repetition of identical "mis." The dream conveys the desire for a transparent expression of the self, as the "mi" clearly stands in for "me,"[27] but music fails to provide this immediacy. Even within the dream, Liliane remains exterior to the experience, listening to herself as if from the outside, not at one with the music.

The novel confronts us with an instance of amateur performance, one motivated by pleasure and leisure, rather than by economic necessity.[28] While

Liliane is a highly accomplished player, she earns her living as an interpreter at UNESCO, which facilitates the comparison that Huston explicitly draws between performance and translation, and plays on the French use of the word "interprète" for musician. Both music performance and translation position the practitioner as a mediator between a source text and an audience, but music performance involves temporal constraints and a level of precision that interpretation generally does not require. Liliane observes that when she translates for a UN congress, she can vary her words so long as it does not alter the speaker's meaning. She can take her time, correct herself, even stumble:

> Ici et là, c'est l'expression de quelqu'un d'autre qui passe à travers mon corps. Ici et là je suis l'interprète et surtout pas le créateur. Seulement, ce sont des mots qui entrent par mes oreilles, subissent un traitement dans mon cerveau et ressortent par ma bouche dans une autre langue, je peux hésiter, corriger, balbutier et même faire de erreurs de syntaxe sans que le contenu soit altéré. Ici, le contenu c'est la forme—chaque faute infléchit, gauchit un peu le sens même du message—, et donc, le jugement porte sur chaque seconde. (Huston, 1981, 14)

> [Here and there, someone else's expression goes through my body. Here and there I am the interpreter and above all, not the creator. Only, words enter my ears, undergo a treatment in my brain, and exit through my mouth in another language, I can hesitate, correct, mumble, and even make syntactical errors without altering the content. Here, the content *is* the form—every mistake inflects, destroys a little the sense of the message itself—, and thus, every second is critical.]

Liliane understands performance as much more unforgiving than translation. When translating an oral text, the message is not always dependent on the form.[29] By contrast, the form and the message are indistinguishable in music. This provides a key to understanding how Huston conceives of music: music exemplifies the perfect integration of form and content to which she aspires. Only the beginning and end of the novel truly achieve this marriage of form and content. The first words of the text are "Maintenant, c'est commencé" ["Now it has started"] while its final statement is: "oui, c'est la fin maintenant" ["yes, this is the end now"]. Both constitute exemplary performative statements, as they accomplish—or perform—exactly what they announce. The deictic utterance "now" brings the performance to completion, and with it, the writing and reading of the novel. This simple word makes three distinct temporalities—and the three corresponding creative acts of writing, performing, reading—coincide as one.

On Variation Form and Literary Adaptation

Thus far we have focused primarily on the *mise-en-scène* and the relationship between performance, language, and theatricality in the novel. We shift here to more formal considerations, to evaluate how the novel deploys the musical form of theme and variations. Variation form occupies an ambivalent status in music history and criticism, partly because it was commonly used as a pedagogical exercise for beginning composers who were assigned the task of writing variations on a given melody or harmonic sequence. Variations typically involve borrowed material. In as much as novice composers would hone their craft by writing variations on an assigned theme, Huston's first attempt at writing fiction borrows its theme and structure from Bach. Other commonly cited weaknesses of variation form include its tendency to involve excessive repetition, and to privilege embellishment and virtuosity over substance. Sets of variations are often paratactic and lack organic inevitability because they consist of items in a linear series. According to Elaine Sisman, the most satisfying sets of variations—those of Bach, certainly, and later Haydn and his successors—are organized in ways that "seek the advantages of repetition while [...] also mitigating it."[30]

While this is not the place for an extended analysis of the history of variation form, it is important to call attention to the considerable interest the form has sparked in literary and cultural studies, especially among postcolonial critics who embrace repetition and variation as alternatives to dominant forms of European discourse. Antonio Benítez-Rojo makes repetition the signature trope of a Caribbean aesthetic in *The Repeating Island* (1997). Edward Said (1991, 98) embraces the possibilities offered by variation form, and holds it up as an open-ended mode of inquiry that facilitates non-hierarchical relationships. He cites the work of Egyptian singer Umm Kalthoum as an exemplary instance of variation form, whose style comprises of "exfoliating variation, in which repetition, a sort of meditative fixation on one or two small patterns, and an almost total absence of development tension were the key elements." He argues that the point of her performance was "to

luxuriate in all sorts of byways, to linger over details and changes in text, to
digress and then digress from digression." This exploratory aesthetic seemed
to offer a complete departure from the contrapuntal and goal-driven Western
classical repertoire he had previously encountered, although he later locates a
similar aesthetic in Beethoven's late works, in Richard Strauss, and in Bach's
Goldberg Variations. Said (1983, 113–14) expressed particular appreciation for
"the quiet triumph that occurs at the end of the Goldberg Variations, as the
theme returns in its exact first form to close off the aberrant variations it has
generated."[31]

Indeed, Bach's Goldberg Variations represent an exceptionally sophisticated instance of variation form, because of their rigorous, symmetrical
organization and the fact that the variations proceed not from a common
melodic theme, but from the varied treatment of a given harmonic
progression. The work consists of thirty-two sections (an aria, thirty
variations, and an aria), and the opening aria itself contains exactly
thirty-two bars. Each variation consists of two halves that are both played
twice" (Williams, 2001, 44). The thirty variations fall into two grand-scale
schemes: they can be seen as ten sets of three, each culminating in a canon,
or alternatively, as two sets of fifteen. The sixteenth variation, a French
overture, occupies a central position, and introduces the increasingly
virtuosic style that characterizes the second part of the work. As Charles
Rosen notes, the Goldberg Variations resemble "an encyclopedia: a survey
of the world of secular music. [...] [Bach] absorbs and transforms the
popular styles of his time."[32]

Huston deliberately focuses on major formal aspects of the Goldberg
Variations—their underlying harmonic structure, stylistic diversity, *da
capo* form, and mathematical design—and adopts innovative strategies
to reproduce these features in the novel. For instance, the novel
achieves the effect of a constant harmonic progression by positioning Liliane
as the source of all of the constituent voices in the text. Although thirty
characters successively occupy the position of speaker, they ultimately flow
from Liliane's dominating voice. This constitutes an audacious experiment
with the flexibility of narrative voice, the extent to which fiction can create
"other" subjectivities—*and* erase them. As the author later reminisced,
"Je dis 'je' à la place de trente personnes différentes! En effet, je voudrais
pouvoir être tout le monde" (Argand, 2001). ["I say 'I' from the position
of thirty different people! In effect, I'd like the ability to be everyone."]
The text unfurls these voices like an accordion or arpeggiated chord, only

to later fold them all into one.[33] Significantly, the novel features a woman performer, who serves as the generative source of this heteroglossia and the site of creative authority.

The thirty speakers in the text represent a wide spectrum of ages, professions, socioeconomic classes, and national backgrounds, including a French-Canadian, an African American, and an Irishman, and the text plays up these differences by exploring the different dialects of each. The title of each chapter/variation indicates its general theme or mood, in keeping with the musical convention whereby the title of a movement dictates its tempo and character. The chapter titles, however, are more abstract and varied than those typically deployed in classical music. They include "Ombrage" (Shadow), "Vents" (Winds), "Filiation," "Insomnia," "Joual" (the French-Canadian dialect), "Profit," "Fatigue," and so on. Key motifs circulate throughout all of the variations—time, sexuality, memory, and desire—lending a thematic coherence to the work as a whole. The intense mathematical structure of Bach's work comes into play on a thematic level, as several variations involve mathematical figures and measurements. For instance, Variation XXVII, 'Mesure' (Measure), features an eighteen-year-old narrator, Nathalie Fournier, who is obsessed with numbers and counting. Embroiled in a power struggle with her mother—she wants a career in music but her mother is bent on persuading her otherwise—she struggles to remember whether there are thirty or thirty-one variations in the piece, and spends the duration of the concert reducing her existence to a series of mathematical calculations: the number of days in a calendar month, the length of a typical menstrual cycle, how many cherries and lettuce leaves she consumed, when she will turn twenty, thirty, and so on.

The *aria da capo* form of the Goldberg Variations poses a particular challenge for literary adaptation. Bach's work opens with an aria, a *sarabande*, which returns at the end in what is known as an *aria da capo*. The indication *da capo* ("from the head") instructs the performer to go back and repeat the beginning until reaching the sign *"fine"* ("end"). The *aria da capo* form was especially popular in seventeenth- and eighteenth-century operas, and posed a major difficulty to librettists. Although repetition is satisfying on a musical level, it inevitably hinders the emotional development of characters by preventing the plot from moving forward. The form remained a point of contention between composers and librettists until the late eighteenth century when Christoph Willibald Gluck reformed opera by abolishing the *da capo* aria on the grounds that it was excessively artificial and compromised the dramatic action. In Bach's work, the aria and *aria da capo* are identical to one another, lending the work a circular symmetry.[34] In Huston's subsequent literary adaptation of the work, this circularity poses a unique challenge.

Significantly, Huston opts not to reproduce strict *da capo* form in the novel. Apart from the fact that the novel begins and ends on the same word "maintenant" ("now"), the initial and final arias are very different, which emphasizes Huston's understanding of performance—and writing—as transformative. Liliane's situation changes significantly over the course of the concert. In the opening aria, she is anxious about how the concert will unfold; in the final aria, she is relieved at having reached the end, inspired by what she has learned in the process, and ready to claim her role as the "author" of the preceding monologues. In a sense, this turns out to be a very clever way of bringing the idea of *da capo* form into play, as a pun, since all the constituent voices of the text emerge from Liliane's imagination—from her head. Thus, once again, Huston takes a figurative expression and makes it literal.[35]

A similar wordplay marks Huston's treatment of the musical notion of invention. The chapters of the novel—like Bach's musical inventions, short vocal or instrumental piece(s) whose defining characteristics are "novelty of form" and "original ideas"[36]—take on highly original and fragmentary forms, often trailing off in mid-sentence. Taking this kind of linguistic exploration one step further, Huston destabilizes the French expression "assister à un concert." The verb "assister" means either to attend or to help, depending on context; generally, in the case of a concert, it simply means to attend. Liliane merges these two meanings to claim that the audience's attendance has "helped" her gain a new understanding of the Goldberg Variations, of performance, and of herself. This brings the audience into the signifying process, while enhancing the reciprocity between performer and audience.

It is worth reflecting on the differences between the *da capo* form of Huston's novel and the circular forms of major modernist novels of the early twentieth century. Both Proust's *A la recherche du temps perdu* [*In Search of Time Past*] and Sartre's *La Nausée* [*Nausea*] leave off with their narrators having finally come to understand *how* fiction works and on the cusp of writing a novel. Marcel and Roquentin announce something to the effect of, "Now that I know how to write, I just hope to have the time." In each case, the text in the reader's hands could well stand in for the one that each of these narrators aims to write. By contrast, Huston's text aspires to the condition of performance and embraces the premise that each performance is a singular, unrepeatable event. As the narrator argues, any subsequent encounter

with the Goldberg Variations would produce an entirely different text. This
implies that there is no single, authoritative reading of the work—an idea that
is reinforced by the fact that Huston herself returned to adapt the work in 1996
for her English translation and again in 2000 for the recorded version, just as
Gould also returned to refine his interpretation of the piece in 1981. Instead
of anticipating a future writing as if none has already occurred, Huston's
narrator (like that of Sarraute's *Les fruits d'or*) acknowledges the performance
she has just completed *and* the audience's role, as if to say, "I accomplished
what I set out to do; I might do it again—differently, of course; I appreciate
your accompanying me and helping me through this performance." The
reciprocity she brings to performance also makes space for the reader who,
like the audience at the concert, becomes an active agent in the signifying
process.

While the novel engages with diverse aspects of performance—performance
as a function of language, following J. L. Austin's notion that language does
what it says (as we saw in several examples in the preceding discussion);
musical performance, marked by an awareness of current debates triggered
both by Gould and by early music practitioners; and gender performance,
anticipating Judith Butler's demonstration that sexuality is not natural, but
articulated and performed[37]—it also makes the case that writing itself is a
mode of performance. One speaker regards writing as much more forgiving
than musical performance because it is produced away from the public eye,
whereas music performance unfolds in the present ("dans le temps") and
every single instant is subject to critical judgment (Huston, 1981, 95). Another
character fantasizes about abolishing this distance between writing and the
public, by imagining a text that would record the act of writing. Such a text
would include blank spaces every time the writer hesitated, which the reader
could then choose to fill or leave empty:

> Si par exemple il lui fallait dix seconds pour écrire une ligne, alors un
> minute d'hésitation vaudrait six lignes de blanc. Ainsi de suite. Des
> pages entières seraient blanches, et comme ça les lecteurs verraient que
> l'inspiration de l'écrivain ne coulait jamais de source. En plus il pourrait
> écrire eux-mêmes dans les blancs tout ce qu'ils voudraient... (45)

> [If for example it took her ten seconds to write a line, one minute's
> hesitation would be worth six blank lines. And so on and so forth. Entire
> pages would be white, and in this way readers would see that a writer's

inspiration never flows smoothly. In addition, they themselves could write whatever they wish in the blank spaces...]

The novel subsequently enacts this idea by introducing ten lines of blank space into the paragraph, calling attention to the performative aspect of writing.

The relationship between writing and performance crystalizes around the figure of Bernald Thorer, a highly successful public intellectual who inexplicably renounces his academic career, abandoning both writing and public lectures. When a journal editor asks him for a reaction to the Cambodian killing fields, he refuses to turn out the eloquent moral outrage expected of him and instead produces an unintelligible statement, leaving the editor at a loss as to whether to read the text as a bad joke, or as evidence of a mental breakdown: "Il n'y avait presque rien écrit dessus, à peine quelques mots: 'c'est horrible', 'non', 'c'est ----', des mots illisibles, et même des sortes d'onomatopées genre band dessinée: 'Aaaargh'" (135). ["There was barely anything written on it, hardly a few words, 'it's horrible,' 'no,' 'it's -----,' illegible words and even the kind of onomatopoeias one finds in comics: 'Aaaargh.'"] Bernald later participates in a televised roundtable discussion, during the course of which he falls embarrassingly silent when asked to comment on whether or not the world is veering towards catastrophe. Finally, he breaks down into uncontrolled laughter in the French national library,[38] introducing physical excess and disorder into the very edifice where reason and order are held most sacrosanct. In choosing suddenly to abandon his activities as a public intellectual, Bernald resembles Gould, who similarly left off performance at the height of his performing career. Whereas Gould saw the body as a threat to the integrity of his performance, however, Bernald uses the body to contest the ideological production of meaning. Bernald's physical and non-verbal "performances" indicate his refusal to participate in practices that sanction a political violence and intellectual hypocrisy he finds abhorrent.

Musical Form in Huston's Literary Production

It is Huston's practice to give her fictional works a specific generic designation in addition to their titles: these range from the more conventional *roman* (novel) in the case of *Dolce agonia*, *Plainsong*, *Instruments of Darkness*, and *Mark of the Angel* to the more inventive "polyphonie" for *Prodige/Prodigy*. *Les variations Goldberg* stand out as the only text Huston labels as a romance.

Unlike the masculine *roman*, the French word for romance is feminine, which underscores the feminine aesthetic at play in the text, particularly in its nonlinear structure, engagement with the body, and interest in how a woman's performance is marked as different.[39] By affiliating her first novel to the category of romance, Huston calls attention to her use of French, the Romance language par excellence. On a formal level, romance conveys an improvisational and experimental approach to form, while gesturing to the tradition of medieval literary romances that feature a hero who undergoes a series of ordeals, to emerge with newfound self-knowledge—as Liliane does at the keyboard.

Music thus occupies a central and highly visible role in *Les variations Goldberg*: the concert functions as the narrative device that gathers a diverse cast of characters in a unified space and time, while Bach's work organizes these voices around a unifying focal topic. Musical devices take on similar importance in Huston's later novels as well, although often in less explicit ways. *Instruments des ténèbres/Instruments of Darkness* (1996) engages with another cornerstone work of the Baroque instrumental repertoire, Heinrich Biber's Resurrection Sonata, one of the Rosary Sonatas for solo violin (also known as the Mystery Sonatas). The novel uses Biber to interweave two distinct plotlines, both of which feature female protagonists who experience trauma and recovery. The first of these plotlines is the journal of Nadia, a New York-based author, who documents her efforts to complete a novel while coping with her father's alcoholism, her mother's acute dementia, and her own history of repeated abortions and failed relationships. The second narrative thread consists of the novel that Nadia is writing: the story of Barb, a young woman in seventeenth-century France who loses her mother at birth, endures abuse and rape as a domestic servant, commits infanticide against her own child, and ultimately becomes a healer. Nadia calls her journal the *Scordatura Notebook* in reference to the musical technique that Biber deploys involving the tuning of an instrument's strings to irregular pitches. It is a gesture of homage to her mother, a former concert violinist who made Biber's sonata into one of her signature pieces. Nadia's commitment to writing and creative work contrasts with her mother's lack of choice a generation earlier; her mother was forced to sacrifice her musical career to raise children. Weighed down by serial pregnancies and caught in an abusive marriage, she developed debilitating dementia—Nadia is determined not to fall into the same trap.

Just as *Les variations Goldberg* borrows the variation form of Bach's work, *Instruments of Darkness* follows the twelve different stages of the Virgin

Mary's life as evoked in Biber's Resurrection Sonata.[40] Within this narrative arc, the text shuttles back and forth between the protagonist's journal and the novel she is writing, between present-day Manhattan and seventeenth-century rural France. Ironically, although Nadia laments that all writing is maddeningly linear,[41] the structure of the text is everything but linear due to its constant spatial and temporal disruptions.[42] But despite the narrative fragmentation, the novel follows the sonata's redemptive structure: both Nadia and Barb ultimately recover a sense of self and purpose through writing (in the case of Nadia) and the practice of women's traditional medicine (for Barb). It becomes clear that the instruments of darkness evoked in the title are not only the mistuned violin, but also feminine writing and traditional forms of healing.

   Scordatura, the principal musical metaphor in *Instruments of Darkness*, was a favorite technique of Biber's. Changing the tuning of the violin opens up new harmonic possibilities and engages the virtuosic capabilities of the composer—somewhat like writing in a foreign language. The irregular tuning defamiliarizes the instrument by creating an unsettling visual and audial disconnect between the notes written on the score and the sounds the instrument produces.[43] When performing a composition that involves *scordatura*, a musician reads and plays the note "mi," but the instrument produces a different sound (Lindley, 2012). Huston's novel invites us to consider fiction itself as a form of *scordatura* as it submits language to an alternative "tuning": in any first-person narrative, the word "me" is understood as belonging neither to the reader nor to the author, but to another who exists only within the space of the text.

   An even more productive way to understand *scordatura*—and music itself—in the context of Huston's writing is in relation to bilingualism. It is illuminating to consider the musical aspects of her work in relation to the questions of translation, self-translation, displacement, and deterritorialization. At the outset of her career, Huston chose to write in French in order to make language unfamiliar and strange. Over the years, as she became more adept at writing in French and made her life in Paris, English, too, took on an aspect of strangeness. She later wrote, "The acquisition of a second tongue destroys the 'naturalness' of the first; from then on, nothing can be self-evident in any tongue; nothing belongs to you wholly and irrefutably; nothing will ever 'go without saying' again" (Huston, 2003, 62). In writing *Instruments of Darkness*, Huston experimented at producing a novel simultaneously in both languages; she wrote alternatively in French or English, translating as she went along. This process of crafting a text in one language, and instantaneously carrying it across into the other, achieves an unsettling, shifting effect of deterritorialization, similar to what *scordatura* produces in music.[44] The presence of the other language initiates the dismantling of figurative expressions that occurs throughout Huston's work, as we saw earlier in *Les variations Goldberg* in such expressions as "musique de chambre," "sur leur trente-et-un," "assister à un concert," "interprète," and "*da capo.*"

The relationship between bilingualism and music can be seen in yet another light if we consider Huston's bilingual writing as a "minorization" of both French and English. Deleuze and Guattari make a distinction between major and minor literatures, calling on categories that invoke not only the political concept of the majority (as the site of agency and power), but also the *musical* modes of major and minor. They use the metaphor of stuttering to convey what great writers do to language: they "make the language itself stutter," by creating within language "a sort of foreign language, which is not a different language, nor a rediscovered patois, but a becoming-other of the language, a minorization of that major language, a delirium that carries it away, a sorcerer's line that escapes the dominant system" (Bogue, 2004, 70). This link between minorization, music and sorcery is important, as it captures what is at stake in the connections between writing, performance, and witchcraft that Huston lays out in *Instruments of Darkness*, in opposition to a tradition that has suppressed women's voices and discouraged or devalued their creative pursuits.

It is important to note that Huston brings a comparable complexity of form into later novels that are not as explicitly musical, but nonetheless adapt musical ideas to resolve distinct narratological challenges. All of her novels deploy multiple voices, feature narrative fragmentation, and are obsessed with time. *Dolce agonia* exemplifies these concerns, and is staged around the successive courses of a traditional Thanksgiving feast. The ritual of the meal fulfills a similar function as the concert in *Les variations Goldberg*—and the wake in Maryse Condé's *Traversée de la mangrove*, discussed in Chapter One. The celebratory meal brings together multiple protagonists, and provides an organizing structure: the novel begins with the preparation of the food, and proceeds through the arrival of the guests and the various courses of the meal, to culminate in their departure. The host, Sean, a specialist in Irish poetry (who subsequently appears in another of Huston's novels, *Virevolte*), has recently learned he has terminal lung-cancer, but has yet to tell any of the friends, colleagues, and former lovers who have gathered to celebrate the holiday with him. Beneath the flow of conversation, all those present struggle with loss and mortality. Huston knits together the different sections of the text by using God as a narrator, an irreverent but effective strategy. This fully omniscient voice announces how and when each of the characters will die, giving the meal the somber aspect of "the last supper" as we learn the fate of each character in the intervals between each course.

A more recent novel, *Fault Lines/Lignes de faille* (2006), provides an example of how Huston brings structural aspects of the musical fugue into her writing. The text deploys four narrators who enter one after another at different temporal intervals to tell the history of a family over the course of four generations. The novel begins in the present and proceeds backwards into time, unpeeling the layers of family history and catching each successive narrator at the age of six.[45] The interventions of these four six-year-olds, spaced at distinct intervals, evoke the entries in imitation that characterize a fugue or canon. The word fugue comes from the Latin *fuga*, a term related both to *fugere*, "to flee," and *fugare*, "to chase," and both notions come into play in the text as the protagonists seek to uncover their family's past, but flee from its implications. The opening of the novel presents all four narrators together: six-year-old Sol, an over-indulged child who secretly pours over graphic photos of the Abu Ghraib scandal and of Iraqi war casualties on the Internet; his father, Randall, who produces robot-controlled weapons for the US Army and has a palpable hatred of Arabs; his grandmother, Sadie, a well-known historian of the Holocaust; and his great-grandmother, Krystina Erra, a celebrated singer who specializes in songs without words, a style she developed in response to her traumatic childhood. She was raised by a German family and nurtured on German folksongs only to discover she had been kidnapped from Ukrainian parents as a baby as part of the sinister Nazi Lebensborn project designed to promote the Aryan race. The German folksongs she had come to love were suddenly no longer innocent, but part and parcel of a program of cultural and ideological indoctrination; at the same time, because she could not simply unlearn them, she created her own distinctive repertoire of wordless song.

According to the logic of a fugue, the first narrator, six-year-old Sol in California in 2004, announces the "subject"; the narrative cuts to his father Randall as a six-year-old in Haifa in 1982 who "answers" the subject in similar terms; the third section is narrated by Sadie, in Canada in 1962; and the final part presents Krystina in Germany in 1945–46. By moving backwards in time in such a disjointed manner, Huston catches her characters in the awkward and painful act of becoming; this fugal technique of narration creates empathetic connections between the different generations that bridge the histories that divide them. If the novel's formal relation to music is more implicit than that of *Les variations Goldberg*, it similarly borrows and transforms a musical form (the fugue) to reveal the connections between the musical, the linguistic, the historical, and the political.

Gould and the Death of the Author

Huston's treatment of performance in the *Les variations Goldberg* reflects the enormous impact of Glenn Gould. The pianist's withdrawal from the concert stage is widely understood in relation to his intense anxiety about the body and the need to control his physical environment, but also reflects an important ethical dimension. Gould was famous for his mistrust of the body: he claimed that live concerts put the "'naked fact of your humanity' too much on display; and likewise the audience's humanity." He was known to wear gloves, soak his hands in warm water, travel with the same old chair for use in performances, take innumerable pills, and follow a carefully scripted physical regimen before any appearance in order to achieve maximum control over the physical variables of his performances. He hated perspiring in public, and was equally repulsed at being exposed to the audience's perspiring bodies. Because he saw live performance as intolerably open to accident and contingency, studio recordings offered a "way of putting distance between human biology and art, none of the audience's bodily infirmities communicated to him, none of his to them" (Mansell, 1985, 61).

Gould's shift to recordings, however, was also largely motivated by ethical convictions about current practices in the music industry concerning how music is produced and consumed. He believed that recordings would extend the repertoire, make music more widely available, shape more informed listeners, and allow the public more control over their listening experience. He argued that recordings had already helped to revive interest in Renaissance and Baroque repertoire, in part because they brought music into people's homes, into the kinds of intimate spaces similar to those for which much of this repertoire was intended. Recordings also created a disciplined and knowledgeable basis to guide musicians in approaching early music, because they facilitated the comparison of different editions and interpretative practices. They offered artists more control in crafting interpretations, and also held out the promise of democratizing music: Gould's biographer Kenneth

Bazzana (2010, 266) explicitly highlights the ethical underpinning of Gould's retreat from the stage: "[R]ecording, like everything else, was ultimately about ethics. His powerful artistic ego notwithstanding, he approved of the 'democratic' and 'anonymous' nature of recordings, which is a collaborative process undertaken in private settings, out of the public eye and away from the constraints of real time and unburdened by 'personality' in the way that a concert performance is." Thus, Gould saw recordings as "democratizing" *and* as a way to escape the vagaries and "distracting theatricality" of performance.

Gould's first recording featured, of course, the Goldberg Variations. When the twenty-two-year-old pianist approached the management at Columbia Records in 1955 with the project of using the Goldberg Variations for his debut album, they advised him that such a monumental and esoteric work was inappropriate for such a young artist at the beginning of his career. Gould insisted, and in hindsight, his unorthodox choice could not have been more auspicious; it is still impossible to mention the variations without Gould coming to mind. His 1955 and 1981 recordings of the work outsold other classical albums and remain benchmarks for subsequent interpretations, and are widely praised for bringing out the contrapuntal voices more than any other recording of the work. Gould described the variations as

> thirty remarkable views of an entirely unremarkable ground bass theme, views which like snapshots randomly filed range back and forth over the decades, revealing at one moment the sturdy contrapuntal craft of Bach's maturity, at another the indulgent exhibitionism of his youth, and at all the best moments, the passionate aestheticism of his old age. (Monsaigneon, 1981)

Interestingly, Huston also chooses to render the variations as multigenerational perspectives, pairing each variation with a character from various moments in Liliane's life: "people she loves and has loved."

Gould's advocacy of recording constituted a powerful—and controversial—statement about the production and reception of music, particularly since he openly embraced the technique of splicing, which allowed an artist to cobble together a recording by using segments from multiple takes. His critics argued that splicing was "dishonest and dehumanizing," as it "sabotage[d] some unified architectural conception that [they presumed] the performer possesses." Gould claimed the opposite, that splicing frees artists to realize a unified conception of a musical work, and accords them a fuller and more determining role as performer *and* editor. In other words, the artist arrives at an interpretation through the process of recording and editing. Gould insisted that recording "eliminates those conditions of chance and accident upon which [...] certain of the more unsavory traditions of Western music are founded," and transforms a solitary act of interpretation into a collaborative effort, as the performer works with a team of technicians and editors (Gould, 1966). This represents a radical departure from the Romantic view of the artist as the sole authority behind a musical interpretation.

In Gould's view, it was entirely natural for classical music to evolve in the direction of increased collaboration and shared responsibility for interpretation, as a similar shift had already occurred in the film industry. "It would be impossible for the listener (of a recording) to establish at which point the authority of the performer gave way to that of the producer and the tape editor, just as even the most observant cinema-goer cannot ever be sure whether a particular sequence of shots derives from circumstances occasioned by the actor's performance, from the exigencies of the cutting-room, or from the director's a priori scheme." The concept of authorship becomes much more complex. Moreover, Gould saw recording as enhancing the agency and involvement of the listening public:

> This listener is no longer passively analytical; he is an associate whose tastes, preferences, and inclinations even now alter peripherally the experiences to which he gives his attention, and upon whose fuller participation the future of the art of music waits. He is also, of course, a threat, a potential usurper of power, an uninvited guest at the banquet of the arts, one whose presence threatens the familiar hierarchical setting of the musical establishment.

Until now, critics have not acknowledged how Gould's emphasis on the active involvement of the listener anticipates the role Barthes assigns the reader in "The Death of the Author" (1967). Barthes unseats the author as the traditional locus of authority in a text in order to clear the way for the reader to participate in the production of meaning. Two years earlier, however, Gould had already argued for an ethics of participation in music, asserting that "[r]ecording compels the performer to relinquish some control in favor of the listener, a state of affairs, by the way, which I happen to find both encouraging and charming, not to mention aesthetically appropriate and morally right." Literary theorists—and Barthes in particular—seem to have taken their cue from debates already circulating in music concerning the status of the audience.

While Gould embraced the more casual, engaged and intimate relationship that recording fosters between listeners and music, these changes are the object of critique in Said's essays on musical performance. Gould considered it a good thing that the performance of music had "ceased to be an *occasion*, requiring an excuse and tuxedo, and accorded, when encountered, an almost religious devotion; music has become a pervasive influence in our lives, and as our dependence upon it has increased, our reverence for it has, in a certain sense, declined." Said countered that recordings degrade how people listen. Before the advent of recording, amateurs would gather together to play music themselves, and would often adapt symphonic or operatic scores to the keyboard. Recordings alienated listeners from the means of producing music, and conditioned the public to expect an artificial perfection that is in the reach of very few highly specialized musicians. Because digital recordings enable people to compare different interpretations of a piece by sampling recordings side by side, listening to music was transformed from a sensual pleasure, to an exercise in judgment. Said saw classical music as more available, but in many ways, less accessible, less participatory: it has been accorded the most "menial roles, serving as a mood regulator, a filler of feared emptiness, an identity marker..." (de Groot, 2005, 220). Ironically, in contrast to Gould's ruthless perfectionism, Said, Barthes, and Huston all champion amateur playing—although clumsy, amateur playing is truly participatory and democratic. These concerns form the subject of animated debate throughout Huston's variations, and the novel's innovative structure itself restores a participatory element to the concert and reading experience.

Ultimately, Huston's novel affirms the idea that something happens— emerges, develops, and transforms—in every performance, be it musical, theatrical, or textual. As the end of her performance (and the novel) approaches, Liliane reflects on what the concert will have achieved:

> Tous, nous serons soulagés. Nous aurons accompli notre devoir. Nous aurons fait quelque chose de notre soirée. Nous pourrons dire qu'au lieu de lire un livre ou d'aller voir un film, nous avons écouté un concert. Ou donné, selon le cas. Nous aurons eu la patience et la civilité de tenir jusqu'à la fin. Nous aurons entendu toutes les variations, dans leur ordre invariable. Personne n'aura pleuré, personne n'aura éclaté de rire,

personne n'aura proféré d'obscénités à haute voix. Nous pourrons nous en féliciter. (Huston, 1981, 245)

[We'll all be relieved. We will have fulfilled our duty. We will have done something with our evening. We will be able to say that instead of reading a book or going to a movie, we have listened to a concert. Or given one, depending on the case. We will have had the patience and civility to hold out until the end. We will have heard all the variations in their unchanging order. No one cried, no one burst out laughing, no one swore. We can congratulate ourselves.]

The passage makes little difference between giving or attending a concert, instead portraying both as interchangeable and necessary parts of a ritual distinct from other social activities. But the question remains: *does* live performance achieve something that recording cannot? What happens when we witness something together in the same time and space? Does instrumental performance, like the theater, provoke consciousness of the social order and one's place within it in such a way as to allow for change? Becker, Hernández, and Werth (2012, 3–4) argue that "the individuals who witness a performance constitute themselves as a theatrical audience or 'public' not simply by watching or listening to the real actions of the performers before them, but rather by transforming these actions into a representation through their individual interpretative acts and through the requisite consonance between these acts." But can a novel that addresses performance and interpretation reproduce anything of the experience of a live performance, "its capacity to generate a human connection through sensorial intensity, social intimacy, and the joint physical presence of bodies on and offstage?"

The novel tests this possibility. Its fragmented form reproduces *and* parodies the mode of reading advocated by post-structuralist critics who seek to privilege an audience's situated engagement with a text instead of authorial intention. The novel creates the illusion of audience response by presenting thirty varied responses, while also reinforcing the authority of the performer/writer. Like a palimpsest in which the incompletely effaced original writing remains visible, a reader can imagine the music of the Goldberg Variations as a concurrent narrative thread—all the more so because, as several audience members observe, Liliane's interpretation is faithful to a fault, and does not take the liberty of a single *rubato*. Bach's Goldberg Variations structure the novel and serve as a catalyst for the unfurling of contradictory views on music, political crises, the lost opportunities of May 1968, the evolving role of women as artists, and of course, language and literary form.

Rewriting Genealogies and Shifting Boundaries

Huston's *Les variations Goldberg* represents a striking instance of musicalized fiction, laying the groundwork for the sophisticated and sustained engagement with music that marks the author's later works. As Huston's virtuosic debut, the novel displays a formal and linguistic bravura that matches Gould's first recording of the Goldberg Variations. More significantly, it exposes the indebtedness of literary debates over the role of the author to similar discussions in music, establishing Gould as an important precursor to Barthes and Foucault.

Why return to the novel today, and more pointedly, why do so in the context of transnational writing? What does Huston's writing have to say to the other novels considered here? Unlike the other works under discussion, Huston's novel represents an in-depth engagement with a *specific* work of music and the history of its performance practice, while at the same time using variation and performance to open up new literary and ethical questions as well. The next chapter examines how J. M. Coetzee engages with opera in order to think about the role of the novel in contemporary Africa and the ethical demands of representing others—or rather, *of not presuming to represent* others. Huston deploys music in order to push representation to its limits, expanding and collapsing subjects. For Huston, performance and writing offer the possibility of creating and transforming the world as we know it. While she exposes the ideological, historical, political, and linguistic forces that shape every performance, she also configures it as a space of play. Gould argued that recording offers a more thoughtful and collaborative platform to create music than the concert stage, and foresaw the end of live performances; Huston, by contrast, recognizes performance as a dynamic site of ritual, play, risk, and reciprocity, and attempts to harness its magic and bring it into the novel. Some thirty years later, the novel retains the experimental excitement of using Bach's variations to interrogate boundaries—between literature and music, between languages, between performer and audience, and between writer and reader.

CHAPTER FOUR

Opera and the Limits of Representation in J. M. Coetzee's *Disgrace*

I am still interested in how the voice moves the body,
moves in the body.

—J. M. Coetzee

This final chapter turns to J. M. Coetzee's *Disgrace* (1999), a novel that commands a place in any discussion of musical forms in transnational literature through its provocative engagement with opera. The author's first novel to be staged in post-apartheid South Africa, *Disgrace* calls on music to paint what one critic has called "an anxious, comfortless portrait" of a nation undergoing radical changes (Cooper, 2005, 22). The protagonist, David Lurie, a middle-aged literature professor at the University of Cape Town, falls into "disgrace" when his efforts to seduce an attractive young student misfire and he finds himself charged with sexual harassment. In his highly publicized university hearing, Lurie shows no remorse and stubbornly champions his right to act on desire. The adjudicating committee considers the case as part of a long history of racial oppression in South Africa, particularly because the student in question, Melanie Isaacs, is a woman of color. In keeping with the spirit of the national Truth and Reconciliation process, they demand his apology; his refusal to comply costs him his teaching post. In the wake of the scandal, Lurie withdraws to his daughter Lucy's modest farmstead in the Eastern Cape. Lucy's country lifestyle is the antithesis of his academic life in Cape Town. There, Lurie assists with daily chores while trying to make progress on his current project, an opera about the Romantic poet—and ruthless womanizer—Lord Byron. Ironically, although he has never written music before, Lurie expects it to come more naturally and be more satisfying than academic prose. Needless to say, it is a ridiculous presumption on Lurie's part and the opera does not come together as he had hoped. This chapter argues that the failed opera nonetheless fulfills an important function in the novel. It illustrates the problems of representing others and provokes an evaluation of the place of the English-language novel and other forms of artistic expression in democratic South Africa.

Published five years after the country's first democratic elections, the novel offers an unusual twist on the bildungsroman. It presents a narrative of self-education and emerging social consciousness, but does so through an older protagonist whose arrogance and sense of entitlement alienate readers.[1] Like the protagonists of many late twentieth-century novels, this central figure is a writer, but one who produces literary criticism and opera, not fiction. Lurie's moral development commences after a brutal encounter with racial and sexual violence. Three armed Black men invade Lucy's home, beat him, douse him in alcohol and set him alight. Leaving him locked in the lavatory, they gang rape Lucy and shoot the dogs in her care. The incident has far-reaching consequences for both father and daughter. Pregnant from the assault, Lucy agrees to become a second wife to her former farmhand and neighbor, Petrus, in exchange for his protection. She also announces she will keep the baby, whom she regards as a product of South Africa's racialized history and whose racially mixed heritage offers an unassailable tie to the land she loves.[2] For Lurie, the attack is a deeply unsettling experience of impotence and victimization. He must come to terms with his incapacity to protect his daughter and his failure to obtain the justice he expects. In its aftermath, he finally reassesses his own behavior towards women and questions the notions of justice, lyricism, beauty, and grace that he had hitherto taken for granted.

The incident provokes Lurie to revise the opera project in dramatic ways. The fact that he cannot know what exactly happened to Lucy—she remains resolutely silent about her experience, at least as far as he is concerned—forces him to acknowledge that women have stories of their own. For the first time, he questions whether he can tell those stories, and if so, on what terms.[3] This points to the key issue at stake in the novel: can literature and art represent without dominating, or does all representation inherently overpower the subject and efface difference? Does music hold the potential to represent differently?

The following discussion aims to shed light on the critical role of opera in *Disgrace*, while also seeking to bring Coetzee's work into broader dialogue with transnational writing. The opera provides a vehicle through which to consider one of the core ethical challenges of writing, namely the task of representing others without overpowering their subjectivities. It also calls attention to the relationship between aesthetic forms and the project of nation-building. Across his fiction, Coetzee asks whether forms such as the English-language novel, opera, and lyric poetry can still speak to the postcolonial present. *Disgrace* thus extends an inquiry begun in earlier novels like *Age of Iron* (1990), which similarly evokes the devaluation of the humanities and the arts in contemporary Africa; it also anticipates the later novels, *Elizabeth Costello* (2003) and *Diary of a Bad Year* (2008), where Coetzee offers a cynical picture of a world given over to global capitalism in which artistic production is stripped of value.

Although Coetzee is thoroughly versed in the British literary tradition from Shakespeare, Byron, and Wordsworth to Pound and Eliot, he also engages extensively with French theory and fiction, and has in turn influenced contemporary writing in French. As is well known, the author completed his doctoral work at the University of Texas Austin on Beckett, the Irish modernist who wrote in French as a means of displacing English, a language he associated with Great Britain's political oppression of Ireland. Writing in French also allowed Beckett to achieve a more transparent relationship to language itself, a path the Canadian author Nancy Huston later emulates, as we saw in Chapter 3. Coetzee's affinity to French philosophy is evident in *Disgrace* as David Lurie liberally cites Jean-Jacques Rousseau's views on the origins of language at the very opening of the novel, and ventures to compose an opera as did Rousseau. In the other direction, Coetzee's fiction has inspired authors who write in French, including Maryse Condé, who appropriates elements of *Disgrace* in her own novel about South Africa, *Histoire de la femme cannibal* [2003, *Story of the Cannibal Woman*]. Surprisingly, however, no critic has considered Coetzee's work in relation to the French philosophical tradition, or to postcolonial writing in French.[4]

In the years since its publication, *Disgrace* has generated a rich critical response, including readings by Derek Attridge, Rita Barnard, David Attwell, Mark Sanders, Graham Huggan, Rosemary Jolly, Sam Durrant, Mike Marais, Gayatri Spivak, Zoë Wicomb, and others. The novel's musical content, however, has not been sufficiently addressed. The opera is incongruous on so many levels in the context of the novel. Not only does its subject matter—the dissolute ways of an English poet and the desires of an Italian countess—have seemingly little bearing on contemporary South Africa, but the genre of opera itself has historically been associated with elitism and the European colonial project—certainly an odd detour for a novel set in a newly democratic African nation. Opera performances typically offer a striking display of narrative and representational power. They are often extravagant productions, in that they deploy a team of set designers, musicians, singers, and so on, requiring a budget that exceeds that of most other genres, with the exception of film. Lurie's complete lack of experience in opera and misguided assumption that he will nonetheless be able to produce both the music and libretto himself, lend a touch of ironic comedy and implausibility to the text. He cuts a ridiculous figure: a solitary, bruised man with operatic aspirations, picking away at tunes on a child's banjo with a stray dog at his heels. Why does Lurie turn to music at this stage in his career? Why an *opera* about Byron in Italy, instead of a piece of theater or another book of criticism? Why does the author choose to portray Lurie as so inept and ridiculously presumptuous, almost to the point of undermining the narrative's credibility? How are we to understand the opera's diminishing progression and eventual abandonment? Moreover, on a meta-textual level, what do the repeated references to opera achieve within the novel? To what extent do the novel's references to music add to or disrupt the narrative?

In view of addressing these issues, it is helpful to consider the status of music in *Disgrace* against other major twentieth-century "musical" novels. Most of these novels draw on actual composers and existing compositions for inspiration, or include a score. For instance, as we saw in Chapter 3, Nancy Huston appropriates J. S. Bach's Goldberg Variations for her novel *Les variations Goldberg* (1981), closely following the structure of Bach's composition; Marcel Proust models the iconic Vinteuil Sonata of *A la recherche du temps perdu* on the music of César Franck, Richard Wagner, and Camille Saint-Saens (Adelson, 1942, 228–33); Thomas Mann addresses the music of Arnold Schoenberg in *Doktor Faustus* (1947); Assia Djebar dialogues with specific sonatas by Beethoven in *L'amour, la fantasia* (1985); and Vikram Seth evokes Bach, Schubert, and Beethoven in *An Equal Music* (1999). Beckett embeds original musical scores into his novel *Watt* (1953). In *Disgrace*, the opera narrative engages with historical material about Byron, but its music is entirely fictional. Coetzee offers no external referents to anchor that music. Because our only means of imagining it is through the vague descriptions offered by the protagonist, the music is all the more alienating. The opera thus takes on a performative function in the text, as it confronts the reader with a knot of opacity and unreadability at the same time as the protagonist himself is coming to terms with the irreducible difference of others.

The opera that Lurie is writing, *Byron in Italy,* recounts the romance between the celebrated lyric poet and a young Italian noblewoman, the countess Teresa Giuccioli.[5] It was one of Byron's last love affairs; he lured Teresa away from her husband, only to leave her shortly afterwards. Although Lurie first conceived it as a chamber opera between "a passionate young woman and a once passionate but now less than passionate older man,"[6] the attack leads Lurie to reimagine Teresa in middle age. In this revised scenario, Byron himself is long since dead, and Teresa lives alone with her ailing father and mourns the loss of her youth and her famous lover. Lurie introduces changes to the score as well. He had initially planned a lush orchestration, "a complex, restless music [...] sung in English that tugs continually toward an imagined Italian" (Coetzee, 1999, 18), but decides on a stark, minimalist score that includes banjo, cello, flute, and bassoon, and eventually, possibly a dog.[7] He had intended to borrow melodies from others, but decides to write the music himself. He also puts aside the letters and historical documents he has been consulting and plumbs his own imagination for the libretto. Ultimately, however, Lurie realizes he will never complete the project. The opera will never be staged, and it will certainly not facilitate his triumphant return to society; instead, it reflects his alienation and disempowerment. Moreover, the increasingly limited status Byron comes to occupy in the opera as a ghostly off-stage voice, incapable of answering his young daughter's cries, provides an image for Lurie's own sense of failure as a father and his growing social marginalization. It also problematizes the place of English-language literature (a tradition Byron clearly represents) and white male privilege in the emerging post-apartheid South Africa.

The opera has perplexed critics, firstly because it is such a strange turn for a contemporary African novel to take, and secondly because it fails miserably. Many readers have understood the opera's failure as an indication that Lurie has begun to confront the issues brought to the fore by his daughter's rape. His newfound interest in Teresa's experience indeed suggests that he has come to explore subjectivities other than his own. By creatively investing himself in the character of Teresa, Lurie is seen to possess a newfound respect for female subjectivity. Such a reading is problematic, however, because Lurie's attempt to speak for Teresa demonstrates, on the contrary, his failure to concede limits to knowledge and to make space for another's alterity. His usurpation of Teresa's voice makes it clear that he has not heeded his daughter's admonition to allow the other to speak for herself, "You tell what happened to you; I tell what happened to me" (Coetzee, 1999, 99). Furthermore, Lurie relegates the feminine to the position of the "other," which blinds him to the otherness of male characters (Petrus, the boy, Bill Shaw, and even, to some extent, Byron).

Critics have also tended to read the opera as a classic instance of *mise-en-abyme*, as a text within a text. Typical of embedded narratives, the opera repeats numerous thematic elements of the larger narrative, namely rape, abandonment, betrayal, the drama of aging, and the problems of desire. There is, however, a shift in genre between the novel and the opera embedded within it that merits our attention, especially since *mise-en-abymes* generally repeat the same genre. In both Shakespeare's *Hamlet* and *A Midsummer Night's Dream,* for instance, we encounter a play within a play. Similarly, in the *Arabian Nights*, we find stories enfolded within the larger frame story. The move from literature to music in *Disgrace* is of a different order and entails a rupture whose consequences we must consider. Furthermore, since Coetzee supplies only the thinnest narrative descriptions of its music, the opera remains oddly mute. Much like Lucy's narrative of rape, we can neither access the score, nor hear its music.[8] Through its very inaccessibility, the opera powerfully illustrates the ethical imperative presented by the other.[9]

In one of the most thought-provoking essays on Coetzee's work to emerge in the 1990s, Benita Parry (1998, 152) disputes Attridge's assessment of Coetzee's fiction "as a continued and strenuous effort in figuring alterity as a force out there disrupting European discourse," not by entering into dialogue but by "interrupting or disturbing the discursive patterns in which we are at home." Parry takes Coetzee to task for assigning a narrative muteness to women and black South Africans. Among the many examples of silenced subjects across Coetzee's early novels are the barbarian girl in *Waiting for the Barbarians*, Michael K. in *The Life and Times of Michael K*, and Friday in *Foe*. The silencing of these subjects is extremely problematic, Parry argues, because it intimates the author's "narrative disinclination to orchestrate a polyphonic score, the silenced remaining instead incommensurable, unknowable, unable to make themselves heard in the sealed linguistic code exercised by the narrating self, and thus incapable of disturbing the dominant discourse."[10]

Parry's critique speaks to *Disgrace* as well. Set in post-apartheid South Africa, *Disgrace* stages multiple reversals of power. On one hand, through Lurie, we witness the pathetic decline of a white South African male. On the other, the black neighbor Petrus acquires land, builds a house, and by the end of the novel, comes to stand as Lucy's protector and even spouse, incorporating her by contractual arrangement into his household. Yet while a good portion of the novel is devoted to Petrus—to his rise as a landowner and influential force in the region, and also to an analysis of his speech— many other subjects remain speechless.[11] Pollox, the disturbed child who participates in the assault, has no voice. In the scene near the end of the novel where Lurie finally faces him down, the boy inarticulately shrieks, "Ya ya ya ya," and barely manages to heave out the words, "I will kill you" (Coetzee, 1999, 207).[12] Lucy never recounts her experience of rape; her inscrutable, opaque silence bars our access to what constitutes the center of violence in the novel.[13] Lurie's emphasis on the problem of finding Teresa's voice only calls attention to the way the novel itself elides these other voices, and to the broader problem of literary representation. Durrant (2004, 27) rightly suggests that there is an important link between silence and ethics in South African literature. He reads Coetzee's fiction as staging the inability to identify with the other. While other major South African novelists including Nadine Gordimer operate under a "liberal humanist assumption that the novelistic act of empathy can transcend difference," Coetzee cautions us that "to transcend the other's alterity is to efface that alterity [...] the act of empathy is to imagine the other as the same."

The fact that Lurie "gives up" the opera holds particular significance. As several critics have noted, acts of "giving up" occur throughout the novel. Lurie not only leaves off the opera project, but also "gives up" his favorite dog in the kennel and allows it to be put to sleep, although he has come to love its limp and to rely on its soulful accompaniment to his banjo playing. He gives up seduction as well. As Sanders argues in a magnificent critique of the novel, the author deliberately avoids using the perfective tense throughout the text in order to deny any sense of completion or resolution. In all of these instances, the act of giving up implies not only failure and abandonment, but also sacrifice and renunciation. This is critical in a novel bent on reevaluating what constitutes grace in a secular universe, and what it might take to achieve it. The question of grace and redemption can be seen in relation to South Africa's transition, as a response to the way the post-apartheid National Unity Government chose to address the legacy of apartheid through a process of Truth and Reconciliation. The novel calls into question the institutional practice of granting forgiveness and absolution, by asking whether it is enough to confess in order to restore justice, or whether some larger self-sacrifice is called for, something that would give evidence of real atonement and transformation.[14] Lurie works at the opera over the course of months, only to "give it up," which emphasizes the importance of the process and the journey, rather than the end product or destination. In this sense, grace—like disgrace—is not a place one can arrive at, but a process without term.

Music in Coetzee's Earlier Writings

Before delving into a more detailed reading of music in *Disgrace,* it is important to consider how Coetzee uses music in key passages in earlier works to provoke reflection on universality and difference. The first such passage occurs in *Age of Iron* (1990), a novel written just before the end of apartheid.[15] Mrs Curren, a retired scholar of classical literature, is dying of cancer and has notified no one, not even her daughter in America. A tramp by the name of Mr Vercueil[16] has taken residence in her driveway, and after an unsuccessful attempt to evict him, she comes to accept and even depend on his presence. In the scene in question, Mrs Curren plays the piano, keenly aware that Vercueil is listening at the window:

> I played some of the old pieces: preludes from the Well-Tempered Clavier, Chopin preludes, Brahms waltzes. [...] Then at last I went back to Bach, and played clumsily, over and over again, the first fugue from Book One. The sound was muddy, the lines blurred, but every now and again, for a few minutes, the real thing emerged, the real music, the music that does not die, confident, serene. I was playing for myself. But at some point a board creaked or a shadow passed across the curtain and I knew he was outside listening.
>
> So I played Bach for him, as well as I could. When the last bar was played, I closed the music and sat with my hands in my lap contemplating the oval portrait with its heavy jowls, its sleek smile, its puffy eyes. Pure spirit, I thought, yet in how unlikely a temple! Where does that spirit find itself now? In the echoes of my fumbling performance receding into the ether? In my heart, where the music still dances? Has it made its way into the heart too of the man in the sagging trousers eavesdropping at the window? Have our two hearts, our organs of love, been tied for this brief while by a cord of sound? (Coetzee, 1990, 24)

Music functions here as a connective tissue, creating "a cord of sound" that crosses space and time to link Mrs Curren, her uninvited guest, *and* Bach.

The text draws poetically on the euphonic resonance between cord, chord, and the Latin *cor*, or heart. The ability of music to abolish borders and establish a connection between such incongruous subjects stands in powerful contrast to the political and racial borders in apartheid South Africa.[17] While sanctions and visa requirements make travel impossible, music offers an outlet for escape, transgression, and ultimately survival. The text echoes an earlier passage, where Mrs Curren reflects on her approaching death as a kind of emancipation from the authority of the state: "the one border they cannot close, I thought: the border upward, between the Republic of South Africa and the empire of the sky. Where I am due to travel. Where no passport is called for" (Coetzee, 1990, 23).

The communion that Bach's music seems to bring about between Curren and Vercueil, however, is tenuous. Although they experience the music side by side, neither has access to the other's experience, nor do they necessarily hear music the same way. Because of her illness, Curren seeks solace in the idea that Bach's music is universal and immortal. She needs to believe in the idea of "music that does not die, confident, serene." The presence of the other listener, the tramp, makes her uneasy about the veracity of her own experience of the music. Her faith in the immortality and universality of the classic begins to waver. The passage underscores this through its interrogative tone, "*Has* it made its way into the heart too of the man in the sagging trousers eavesdropping at the window? *Have* our two hearts, our organs of love, been tied for this brief while by a cord of sound?" (Coetzee, 1990, 24). Coetzee's repeated insistence on the "*real* thing," "the *real* music" and "*pure* spirit" further undermines the notion of authenticity, by calling attention to how every musical experience is impure, because it is inevitably mediated by education and socioeconomic class. The passage thus stages a reevaluation of what we consider "classics."

In a lecture on T. S. Eliot, delivered the same year as the *Age of Iron*, Coetzee again uses music to question the basis of the classic.[18] The lecture is striking due to its tone of autobiographical intimacy. Coetzee (2001, 8–9) recounts how, sitting in the garden at age fifteen, he heard a recording of Bach's Well-Tempered Clavier emanating from the neighbor's house. The music transfixed him, leaving him breathless. "[E]verything changed. A moment of revelation which I will not call Eliotic—that would insult the moments of revelation celebrated in Eliot's poetry—but of the greatest significance in my life nonetheless: for the first time I was undergoing the impact of the *classic*." In revisiting this formative experience of music, Coetzee attempts to understand the mechanism of his enchantment. What exactly had moved him: the inherent qualities of Bach's music, or rather, what the music stood for? In other words, was his reaction involuntary, or at some level, was he already in the process of affiliating himself to European high culture in order to leave behind his own social position in South Africa, and to forge a path to becoming an internationally celebrated author? The two alternatives are entangled to the point where he cannot readily answer his own question.

Coetzee further inflects the notions of canon and classic by exposing how classics are always "constructed." To this end, he evokes the changing reception of Bach's music. Bach did not initially have universal appeal; instead, appreciation of Bach was confined to small circles of connoisseurs and scholars until the mid-nineteenth century when Felix Mendelssohn led a popular revival of Bach. As Coetzee reminds us, this revival was itself highly problematic, because it was mediated by highly stylized Romantic performance practices. The process by which Bach was incorporated into the canon thus illustrates how "all canons rest on exclusion; the voice they give to some can be heard only by virtue of the silence they impose on others. But it is not just a silencing by exclusion, it is a silencing by inclusion as well: any voice we can hear is by that very fact purged of its uniqueness and alterity" (Attridge, 1996, 181). At the very crux of the lecture, Coetzee (2001, 16) defines the classic as that which survives in the face of criticism. Thus, "the interrogation of the classic, no matter how hostile, is part of the history of the classic, inevitable and even to be welcomed. Criticism, and indeed criticism of the most skeptical kind, may be what the classic uses to define itself and ensure its survival."[19]

The emphasis Coetzee places on music in his fiction and critical essays is intriguing for a writer who claims to have had no musical education and little childhood exposure to music. The author's longstanding interest in Beckett in part explains why music functions as such a privileged trope in his work, as Beckett's fiction and theater are intensely musical.[20] In his doctoral thesis, "The English Fiction of Samuel Beckett: An Essay in Stylistic Analysis," Coetzee reads *Watt* as a novel that aspires to the condition of music, in which words, emptied of content, constitute a "lulling rhythm" (1969, 163). Yet music is hardly a "lulling rhythm" in *Disgrace,* but an otherness that constantly unsettles the narrative.

The role music plays in *Age of Iron* prefigures *Disgrace.* The word "disgrace" itself recurs numerous times throughout *Age of Iron,* further linking these two works.[21] In *Age of Iron,* Mrs Curren decries the collective shame produced by apartheid, "the disgrace of the life one lives under them: to open a newspaper, to switch on the television, like kneeling and being urinated on. Under them: under their meaty bellies, their full bladders" (Coetzee, 1990, 9). She goes so far as to call South Africa "a pit of disgrace": "Why should I be expected to rise above my times? Is it my doing that my times have been so shameful? Why should it be left to me, old and sick and full of pain, to lift myself unaided out of this pit of disgrace? I want to rage against the men who have created these times…" (Coetzee, 1990, 116–17). By contrast, *Disgrace* moves from the register of collective guilt that characterized the apartheid era to questions of individual responsibility. Lurie's apology to Mr Isaacs (the father of Melanie Isaacs, the student with whom he had a brief affair) in *Disgrace* deliberately echoes *Age of Iron,* but it is an individual, not the nation, who has fallen: "I am sunk into a state of disgrace from which it will not be easy to lift myself" (Coetzee, 1999, 173).

While both *Disgrace* and *Age of Iron* place music in relation to shame and marginalization, elsewhere in Coetzee's literary production, music is a source of national pride, albeit one that can prove destructive. The narrator of *Diary of a Bad Year* (2008), for instance, contrasts Sibelius's Fifth Symphony to the institution of torture at Guantanamo as two extremes of human achievement: "What would it have been like, I wondered, to be a Finn in the audience at the first performance of [Sibelius's Fifth Symphony] in Helsinki nearly a century ago… [O]ne would have felt proud, proud that *one of us* could put together such sounds, proud that out of nothing we human beings can make such stuff. Contrast that with one's feelings of shame that we, our people, have made Guantanamo. Musical creation on one hand, a machine for inflicting pain and humiliation on the other: the best and the worst that human beings are capable of" (Coetzee, 2008, 45).[22] The juxtaposition of Sibelius and Guantanamo as high and low points of human achievement is particularly provocative. The argument is often made that Nazi crimes against humanity are all the more appalling because they took place in a nation that had produced such pinnacles of aesthetic and intellectual achievement: Goëthe, Schilling, Beethoven, and so on. Geoffrey Hartman (1994, 135–39) makes the case that the Nazis used the arts to consolidate a narrative of national superiority, "to gild aggressive and transgressive ambitions." By extension, the impressive cultural production of South Africa under apartheid stands in contrast to the violence that was simultaneously being perpetrated against the majority; many South African authors deliberately sought to withhold "aesthetic pleasures" from their work, by embracing a hard-edged realism as did Nadine Gordimer or André Brink, or by producing challenging, barren, experimental texts, the route taken by Breyten Breytenbach and Coetzee.

Yet Coetzee portrays the declining status of classical music and poetry in postcolonial Africa as symptomatic, not just of a turn from Western culture to embrace African heritage, but of the rise of global capitalism and mass consumerism. Coetzee notes a growing hostility directed toward anything that cannot be rationalized, justified, and commercialized on a mass scale. The intimate nature of the chamber opera Lurie sets out to write implicitly challenges this value system. Similarly, the narrator of *Diary of a Bad Year*, a South African writer in exile in Australia like Coetzee himself, grimly observes that "the mass is the norm and the solitary the aberration" (Coetzee, 2008, 170). Writing, composing music, and reading are important modes of resistance, precisely because of their marginality and irreducibility.

Incongruous Comedy

While Coetzee's projection of opera into "the desolate yard of Africa" (Coetzee, 1999, 214) constitutes a highly original narrative gesture, it also veers towards the absurd and the comic. Set in a nineteenth-century Italian palazzo, the opera immediately is completely out of place and out of sync with the times. As we have noted, Lurie has no prior experience as a composer, and his subject matter has little to do with contemporary South Africa. The opera's incongruity in the landscape recalls musicologist Richard Leppert's (2007, 112) broader view of opera itself as "now largely strange and estranged," although he goes on to assert that "this strangeness constitutes its saving grace in late modernity." Carolyn Abbate and Roger Parker (2012, 15) identify strangeness as a fundamental characteristic of opera, as the genre rests on a highly improbable premise: the fact that "most characters sing most of the time." Opera's basic lack of verisimilitude has "tended to guarantee that opera libretti almost never deal with the ordinary, while spoken theatre can thrive on it."

The untimeliness of Lurie's opera contributes to its comic effect.[23] Edward Said (2006, 6) observes that untimeliness is an essential part of comedy: "Comedy [...] seeks its material in untimely behavior, an old man falling in love with a young woman (May in December). [...] It is also comedy as a form that brings about the restoration of timeliness through the *kommos* with which the work usually concludes, the marriage of young lovers." Both *Disgrace* and the opera within it stage the coupling of old men with young women.[24] The opera offers no such restoration of timeliness as it remains unfinished. The novel, on the other hand, concludes with two parallel unions between young "lovers"— the reunification of Melanie with her sinister boyfriend, and the formal marriage between Lucy and Petrus, though neither union brings resolution in the conventional sense since both pairings are highly problematic. Melanie's boyfriend has shown himself to be dangerously possessive and violent, while Lucy's "marriage" is an arrangement for the transfer of land in exchange for protection. The novel thus deliberately emphasizes disjointedness: opera is ill suited for the times; the lyric poets fall flat in the classroom; South Africa "is no country [...] for old men." As Lurie notes, "a curtain seems to have fallen" between this generation and the next (Coetzee, 1999, 190, 210).

The comic untimeliness of the opera uncannily recalls Adorno's observation that classical music itself "has become comic [...] because something so completely useless is carried on with all the visible signs of the strain of serious work. By being alien to solid [*tüchtig*] people, music reveals their alienation from one another, and the consciousness of alienation vents itself in laughter" (Adorno, 2002, 314). When juxtaposed to Bev's pro bono veterinary work with animals in need, Lucy's farmwork, and even Melanie's acting—as the play in which she appears turns out to be a big popular hit, warranting an extended run—Lurie's work on the opera seems "completely useless," an eccentric and anachronistic undertaking of dubious social value. Lurie himself is uncomfortable with the opera, recalling Blanchot's (2003, 196) description of "the artist's embarrassment at still being something in a world in which he nonetheless sees himself as unjustified."

And yet, it is precisely this lack of justification that critics have seized on in reading the novel. Sanders (2002b, 365) suggests that *Disgrace* deliberately calls into question the very notion of value. He sees Lurie as a "figure of silent resistance to the instrumentalization of language and learning implicit in Communications, the subject he now teaches." Lurie contests the reduction of language to "a communication tool [...] in the interests of global capital," and insists on engaging in activities with no quantifiable value. He never justifies his desire to compose an opera, nor does he explain to himself what motivates him to attend to the incineration of the cadavers from the animal clinic, as he does faithfully each week after helping to put down unwanted dogs.[25] In this sense, the novel approaches Stanley Fish's (2008) provocative assertion that "an activity that cannot be justified is an activity that refuses to regard itself as instrumental to some larger good." The closest Lurie comes to explaining his commitment to the dogs is that it upholds his "idea of the world as a

place where one doesn't beat corpses into a convenient shape for processing"
(Coetzee, 1999, 146). The opera similarly upholds the idea of the world as a
place where not everything can be quantified and rationalized.[26] The text
refuses justification for either activity, and thus, as Attridge (2004, 188) has
demonstrated, the acts of accompanying dead dogs to the incinerator and
composing an opera come to be intimately interrelated, although seemingly
at opposite ends of a spectrum: "Both manifest a dedication to the singularity
that exceeds systems and computations: the singularity of every living—and
dead—being, the singularity of the truly inventive work of art."

The opera itself has two rather singular attributes: it includes dead
characters, and possesses animal-like qualities. Because Lurie has displaced
the temporal setting of the narrative to focus on a middle-aged Teresa,
Byron and his daughter Allegra are dead. Both nonetheless play important
roles as ghostly, post mortem voices. This is a strange choice for an author
whose fiction places particular emphasis on the body. Even in his critical
essays, Coetzee (1992, 23) privileges the body, and claims that "Beckett's later
short fictions have never really held my attention. They are, quite literally,
disembodied. [...] The late pieces speak in post-mortem voices. I am not there
yet. I am still interested in how the voice moves the body, moves in the body."
Yet Lurie writes two disembodied voices into his opera: those of Byron and
his little daughter Allegra. Byron's voice wafts up "from somewhere, from
the caverns of the underworld, [...] wavering and disembodied, the voice of
a ghost" (Coetzee, 1999, 183). Allegra's haunting voice comes unsolicited into
Lurie's imagination:

> [T]here emerges from the dark another voice, one he has not heard
> before, has not counted on hearing. From the words he knows it belongs
> to Byron's daughter Allegra; but from where inside him does it come?
> *Why have you left me? Come and fetch me!* calls Allegra. *So hot, so hot, so*
> *hot!* she complains in a rhythm of her own that cuts insistently across
> the voices of the lovers. To the call of the inconvenient five-year-old
> there comes no answer. Unlovely, unloved, neglected by her famous
> father, she has been passed from hand to hand and finally given to the
> nuns to look after. *So hot, so hot!* she whines from the bed in the convent
> where she is dying of la mal'aria. (186)

Her feverish cries recall Freud's account of the dream of the burning child,[27]
and the nightmares Lurie has after his own daughter's rape in which she

calls out to him and he is unable to help her (Coetzee, 1999, 103). Allegra's voice refuses to be silenced, and thus functions as a call to responsibility. The punctuation of mal'aria, furthermore, invites us to read on two levels: it evokes not only the child's illness, but also an aria gone wrong, playing on Lurie's evident lack of skill as a composer.

The presence of these dead characters lends the opera an Orphic dimension, but with an important twist: Teresa, not the poet, takes on the role of Orpheus.[28] Although she once longed for the everlasting fame her liaison with an important poet seemed to promise, she now attempts to retrieve her beloved from the underworld through the forceful passion of song. It is not through Byron that Teresa will live on, but on the contrary, Byron who "lives through Teresa." The opera thus reverses the gendered structure of the Orpheus myth. No longer merely the object of masculine desire, Teresa becomes the opera's chief subject on whom the masculine subject depends. This reversal is significant, given the problematic representation of women across operatic history. At earlier points in the narrative, Lurie alludes to operas such as *Madame Butterfly* and *Rigoletto*, which stage the symbolic demise of women. After the attack, his own opera takes a radically different direction, more in line with the feminist music criticism that Abbate (1991), Mary Ann Smart (2000), Catherine Clément (1988), and others have produced over the last two decades, to expose and contest opera's tendency to silence, destroy and contain the feminine voice.[29]

The other aspect of Lurie's opera that demands attention is its pronounced animal-like qualities. Although descriptions of the opera are sparse, they invariably include references to cold-blooded creatures like serpents, crabs, reptiles, and fish, to animal parts such as tails and scales, and to instruments used to control or capture animals such as lines and reins. For instance, Teresa and Byron's lines coil "wordlessly around and past each other like *serpents*"; "the trio of instrumentalists play the *crablike* motif" (Coetzee, 1999, 185); "the voice [...] strains to soar away from the ludicrous instrument but is continually *reined* back, like a *fish* on a line" (187); "a lone clarinet answers, *tails* off, falls silent" (182).[30] Another key passage evokes a "[m]elody without climax; the whisper of reptile scales on marble staircases; and, throbbing in the background, the baritone of the humiliated husband" (121). The animal-like attributes of the opera are inseparable from Coetzee's ongoing efforts as a public intellectual to defend the claims of all life, animal or human. Attwell argues that Coetzee extends the notion of ethical responsibility further than other thinkers because of the positions he takes on animal rights. Lurie even contemplates the addition of a dog to the opera, wondering whether animals can make music. Can an animal occupy a subject position, he asks, or must it, like the elephants in *Aïda*, remain merely a prop or an object? Is the ability to make music a quality specific only to human beings? Why then does the stray dog accompany his music-making sessions so assiduously, and howl alongside him? Does his primitive banjo plucking have a musical value that exceeds the dog's howl?

To return to the question of subjectivity, Lurie goes to great pains to understand the feminine position in the wake of his daughter's rape. He puts considerable effort into imagining and empathizing with Teresa and reworks the whole opera in an attempt to develop her point of view. This suggests that in Lurie's phallocentric thinking, the "other" is feminine. This is reinforced by his problematic assumption that he can occupy the place of another man with no great difficulty by virtue of their common gender. The opacity of the African characters Petrus and Pollux in the text powerfully undermines this belief. On the whole, Lurie's desire to imagine himself into the place of others raises the question: what does it mean to "be" the man, to "be" Lucy, to "be" Teresa? Beyond constructing a convincing narrative, can anyone really occupy another's place? These questions recall Gary Tomlinson's (1999, 112) broader understanding of operatic song as built on the principles of "mediumship and possession visited upon the singer, whose voice is not hers but some other, more universal voice that seizes, inhabits, and sings through her. And it is possession of the listeners, too, whose individualities are besieged and ultimately dissolved by the great sweep of primordial vocal will." While fiction does not involve the dimension of stage performance that Tomlinson evokes, these issues are fundamental to the work of making and reading fiction *and* point to fiction's limits. As Coetzee suggests in an essay on Faulkner, "Fictional Beings," the whole enterprise of writing fiction is always predicated on an attempt to enter other subjectivities, but even the best writing produces "verbal imitation" or ventriloquism:

> Although it may be argued that stories give access to no one's mind but the storyteller's, the observable fact is that most stories present themselves as being about other people [...] and that most listeners gladly and eagerly give themselves over to the fiction (if fiction it be) that stories are not just about their tellers. [Faulkner] knows that he is not really entering the minds of the four Compson children, merely writing down verbal imitations of their thoughts. Nevertheless it is

convenient to think that the Compson's are "real" and that somehow, magically, he is inhabiting each of them for a while. (Coetzee, 2003b, 133–34)

Another term for this movement towards the other is empathy.

Music and Empathy

In an exemplary passage at the very opening of the novel, Lurie explicitly alludes to Rousseau, bringing to the fore the relation of music to questions of empathy and authenticity. Lurie complains that, although an expert on poetry, he has been transferred to the department of Communications, as part of a wave of post-apartheid institutional changes that have subsumed the Humanities into more practical, vocational programs. He rejects the instrumental view of language endorsed by the Communications department.

> He finds its first premise preposterous: "Human society has created language in order that we may communicate thoughts, feelings, and intentions to each other." His own opinion, which he does not air, is that the origins of speech lie in song, and the origins of song in the need to fill out with sound the overlarge and rather empty human soul. (Coetzee, 1999, 3)[31]

Lurie directly quotes Rousseau (1990, 114), who famously posited the origins of language in song. The passage makes superb use of language: the entire second sentence has an extremely vocalic quality and resonates with the "o" sound, emphasizing language's ties to music. The juxtaposition of "speech" and "lie," and the suggestive dual valence of lie, concisely perform the critique of language that is sustained throughout the novel: that language is insincere, inadequate, empty. Moreover, the use of the verb "air" conspires with the image of sound filling out the vacant cavity of the soul, a post-religious image if ever there was one, to convey sound in terms of spatiality and insubstantiality, and to suggest the frivolous inflation of a balloon. Even as he ridicules the department's understanding of language as a product of human society to facilitate intersubjective communication, Lurie also undermines the communicative function of music, foreshadowing, of course, the fate of his own opera to remain a solitary project, unfinished and unshared.

In Rousseau's account of the genealogy of language, the expressive—and social—function of the voice is critical. In the *Discours sur l'origine et les fondements de l'inégalité*, Rousseau argues that language marks the distance man has come from the state of nature, but its simplest component, the voice, provides an important link to the origin of society. He insists on the vocal cry as the original human expression: spontaneous, universal, and transparent. The cry is vital to establishing the possibility of pity, on which society itself is predicated. As the cry immediately penetrates the other, it incites the movement of imagination that transports us outside ourselves, allowing us to imagine ourselves in the position of the one suffering (Rousseau, 1990, 92). Pity is the "source" of all human virtues: it precedes conventional laws, and it constitutes the social bond that allows man to identify with other sentient beings. For Rousseau, vocal music is more expressive than spoken language because it retains traces of this original transparency and affectivity, and reinforces the social bond by establishing a relation of intersubjectivity between speaker and listener.

In *Disgrace*, music accordingly provides an expressive alternative—or supplement—to a degenerate language. The English language is portrayed consistently as "dead," "unfit" (Coetzee, 1999, 117), and contaminated:

> The language he [Petrus] draws on with such aplomb is, if he only knew it, tired, friable, eaten from the inside as if by termites. Only the monosyllables can still be relied on, and not even all of them. What is to be done? Nothing that he, the one-time teacher of communications, can see. Nothing short of starting all over again with the ABC. By the time the big words come back reconstructed, purified, fit to be trusted once more, he will be long dead. (Coetzee, 1999, 129)[32]

The indifference of Lurie's students to poetry underscores the crisis of the English language.[33] The verses that speak to him "in a flash" fail to move his students. By contrast, music connotes breath and life: "Byron, alone on the stage, draws a breath to sing" (Coetzee, 1999: 162). Teresa "has immortal longings and sings her longings. She will not be dead" (209). The novel sustains a dichotomy between language and music, whereby language represents stiff, arthritic articulation while music evokes promise, passion, and spontaneity.[34] Ironically, of course, despite the Orphic associations invested in it, the music in the novel is ultimately mute and sterile—and certainly not a solid base on which to found intersubjective relations in contemporary Africa. Only

African languages escape this schema and retain life. Lurie observes a griot performing at the neighbor's housewarming party, and marvels at how the griot "is speaking, orating in rounded periods that rise and fall. He has no idea what the man is saying, but every now and then there is a pause and a murmur of agreement from his audience, among whom, young and old, a mood of quiet satisfaction seems to reign."[35] Though the narrator calls attention to the griot's adornment in imperial medals, suggesting his privileged relation to colonial power structures and problematizing his authenticity, the griot's performance holds the attention of a diverse audience—Lurie's opera would never command that kind of popular response, even had he the resources or inclination to complete it. Lurie reads the confluence of young and old around the griot as evidence of his relevance across generations; by contrast, he concludes that "what [is called] 'classical' music is simply no longer cultural currency" (Coetzee, 2008, 129).

Lurie's abrupt turn to opera recalls Rousseau's efforts to write opera. Largely self-taught in music, Rousseau passed himself off as a music teacher and copyist of musical manuscripts to make a living, until he built up the audacity to write his own operas.[36] As I have argued, the opera in *Disgrace* is, at some level, a parodic gesture, in that it positions David Lurie as a belated Rousseau, a man at odds with the world, whose personal ethics provoke uproar, but who continues nonetheless to seek a lyric correspondence with nature—as Rousseau does in the *Reveries of a Solitary Walker*—and to redeem himself through confession.

Lyricism and Failure

Disgrace portrays the devaluation of music and lyric poetry as evidence of the passing of an era and the triumph of rationality and consumer culture. Throughout the novel, the lyric appears in an array of different guises, as "a flash" (Coetzee, 1999, 12), a fire, a capacity for song (171), and an impulse (214). Lyrical language aspires to the intensity, spontaneity, and emotional vibrancy of song. In a study of opera and mimesis, Philippe Lacoue-Labarthe (1994, 9) defines lyricism as the "most spontaneous, germinal seed of all literature, its purest modality." He goes on to define music, through Wagner, as the "one language that is equally intelligible to all [...] a sovereign language, which, resolving ideas into feelings, offers a universal organ of the most private aspect of the artist's intuition: an organ with a limitless capacity [...] Music

sublates the mind which is enslaved to language—in and through feeling."
Lacoue-Labarthe's highly romanticized claims are problematic as they ascribe
a universality, immortality, and immediacy to Western music and poetry.
Though Lurie himself voices similar beliefs, the novel as a whole works to
undermine and complicate such ideas.

Lurie regards poetic language and music as transcendent and alive, in
contrast to prose which he regards as dry and cold. He "is tired of criticism, of
prose measured by the yard. What he wants to write is music" (Coetzee, 1999,
4). In music, however, Lurie is willing to take the sorts of creative liberties in
writing the opera that an academic scholar would never dream of in scholarly
work: "I'll borrow the music, for the most part. I have no qualms about
borrowing" (66). "There will be time to search through the masters—through
Gluck, for instance—lifting melodies, perhaps—who knows?—lifting ideas
too" (182).[37] He later abandons the idea of using "purloined songs" (183) in
favor of writing his own music, but the work fails to take shape despite his
efforts. At the end of the novel, Lurie concedes defeat and leaves the opera
unfinished:

> *Byron in Italy* is going nowhere. There is no action, no development, just
> a long, halting cantilena hurled by Teresa into the empty air, punctuated
> now and then with groans and sighs from Byron offstage. [...] The lyric
> impulse in him may not be dead, but after decades of starvation it can
> crawl forth from its cave only pinched, stunted, deformed. He has not
> the musical resources, the resources of energy, to raise *Byron in Italy* off
> the monotonous track on which it has been running since the start. It
> has become the kind of work a sleepwalker might write. (214)[38]

Lurie's failure as a composer and lyrical subject anticipates one of Coetzee's
later characters, Paul Rayment, the protagonist of *Slow Man*. When fictional
novelist Elizabeth Costello encounters Rayment, she dismisses him as too
plodding, too lacking in passion to inspire her art. Too mired in the real,
he does not have what it would take truly to "take off" as a character. Lurie
similarly plods along. He uses Shakespeare's sonnets and Mozart's Clarinet
Quintet to seduce Melanie, but the borrowed lyrics no longer work: "The
cadence that served so well to oil the serpent's words now only estranges"
(Coetzee, 1999, 16). Later, in his awkward apology to Mr Isaacs, Lurie
confesses: "I lack the lyrical. I manage love too well. Even when I burn I don't
sing, if you understand me. For which I am sorry" (171). He evokes similar

terms to sum up his life at the end of the novel: "Not a bad man but not good either. Not cold but not hot, even at his hottest. Not by the measure of Teresa; or even by the measure of Byron. Lacking in fire—will that be the verdict on him?" (195).

In fact, a pattern of self-conscious "lyrical failure" runs throughout Coetzee's work. The author presents his own literary production in such terms: "I think of my own prose as rather hard and dry; but there remains in me a tug toward sensual elaboration—toward the late Romantic symphony and away from the two-part invention" (Coetzee, 1992, 208). Instead of the full, nineteenth-century symphony with its lush textures of brass, winds, strings— Wagner, Mahler, Brahms—Coetzee sees his work as coming closer to the stripped-down dialogue between instruments that, interestingly, defines the opera in *Disgrace*. In fact, *Disgrace* as a whole resembles a complex two-part invention. The text puts into play a sustained counterpoint between the opera and Lurie's life. The violence of Lucy's rape provides a counterpoint to the more muted violence of Lurie's relations with women. Byron's historical status as a glorious nineteenth-century adventurer and seducer is placed in comic parallel to Lurie's self-image as a declining "Casanova," a belated Rousseau, in post-apartheid South Africa. Through such relentless juxtapositions, the novel resists the lyrical and incessantly produces its own critique.

*   *   *

Opera plays an ambivalent role in *Disgrace*. On one level, the opera can be read as the protagonist's unwillingness to participate in the new South Africa. The opera allows Lurie to retreat into a fictional world where he can manipulate other subjectivities like marionettes, and supplement his stilted prose with music. And yet, the process of working on the composition transforms him. His efforts to extend his sympathies, stretch his imagination, and mine hitherto unused resources, have a humbling and de-centering impact on his life.

In his subsequent novel, *Elizabeth Costello*, Coetzee argues that the work of art is profoundly transformative for whoever engages in it. But as for how such a transformation operates, and whether always for the better, these are questions that both novels leave unanswered. Coetzee seems quite literally to be reworking issues posed by Blanchot in *L'espace littéraire* (1955, 108–9), where to André Gide's claim that writing "modifies the course of our life," Blanchot adds: "Writing changes us. We do not write according to what we are; we are according to what we write. But where does what is written come from? Again from us? From a possibility within ourselves that uncovers and affirms itself through the work of literature alone?"[39]

At the same time, Coetzee works against the image of music as spontaneous plenitude and full presence, by exposing the effort, imitation, and technique that go into its making. While nonetheless fascinated by the powerful sensual and emotional response commanded by Romantic music and lyric poetry, Coetzee shows these forms to be exhausted and implicated in a system of values that have traditionally dispossessed and objectified indigenous subjects, women, and others. Old forms cannot be resurrected. As the narrator states in *Diary of a Bad Year*, "the animating principles of that music are dead and cannot be revived. One cannot compose a nineteenth-century symphony that will not be an instant museum piece" (Coetzee, 2008, 134). And what then of the novel? What forms and principles retain sense and vitality in literature?

Coetzee's novels themselves have become increasingly ironic and self-reflexive, explicitly staging the problems of their own writing and experimenting with new forms. The foray into opera in *Disgrace* represents precisely such experimentation, but even as Coetzee explores the boundaries of the novel, he parodies the previous experiments of his literary precursors. For instance, in the "Aha!" moment in *Disgrace* where Lurie, finally making progress on the opera and marveling at how melodies arrive unsolicited into his head, remarks, "So this is how art works," Coetzee clearly satirizes similar moments in Sartre's *La nausée* and Proust's *A la recherche du temps perdu*. In both texts, narrators suddenly stumble on what they see as the essential key to a musical masterpiece, whether the formal principle that unifies Wagner's music—and by extension, Balzac's *Comédie humaine*—or the immortal, stirring quality of the ragtime tune "Some of These Days." They then resolve to reproduce that very aspect in their own future writing.

In Coetzee's work, however, musical composition is not simply a mirror image for writing, but a different kind of writing that disrupts the text and compels us to think about difference. If during the late nineteenth century, Wagner sought to unite music and lyric poetry in order to take opera to the summit of artistic expression, this totalizing vision of opera would be exhausted and discredited in World War II. In the aftermath of colonialism, the novel has emerged as the privileged genre where difference can be preserved, and where—as we have seen in *Disgrace*—music and literature can commingle without dissolving into one another. Without a score and with only limited narrative descriptions, the opera remains inaccessible, illustrating how other narratives are similarly withheld from the novel. Moreover, the relentless diminishment of the opera from a lush, symphonic piece, to a minimalist chamber ensemble, and finally to nothingness, seems to perform the haunting teleology Blanchot envisions for literature itself, as "going toward itself, toward its essence, which is its disappearance" (Blanchot, 1959, 195). But in keeping with his conviction that criticism is what enables the classic to survive, Coetzee's critical interrogation of opera and lyrical expression prolongs their presence and marks their singular importance.

As Adorno (2002, 674) argued in the context of contemporary music, art "must want to reach people. For even in its most inaccessible form, it is a social entity and is threatened with irrelevance as soon as that thread to the listener is broken off." While deeply engaged in the questions of writing, agency, and authorship, *Disgrace* maintains precisely such a connection to the public by inviting readings on multiple levels. It is also a novel about race in South Africa, a reflection on rape and its aftermath, a meditation on the trauma of witnessing—or rather, of *not* witnessing, and a comment on the power structures and value systems in place in post-apartheid South Africa. Following the thread of music throughout the novel allows us to consider what lies outside the literary text, what it deliberately withholds, and thus to rethink the relationship between ethics and aesthetics.

Conclusion

Quand, le cœur en fête, je fredonne un air, ce n'est
pas toujours une rumba congolaise. Serait-ce alors
trahir? J'exprime aussi une part substantielle de mon
être quand le nègre que je suis sifflote un blues, un
air de jazz, une valse, des phrases d'une symphonie
de Beethoven, d'un opéra de Verdi ou *Les bateliers de
la Volga*. Au-delà du Congo, je me sens africain.[1]

—*Henri Lopes*

Twentieth-century writers have consistently sought to appropriate music's
subversive ability to transcend boundaries and transform relations. In the
early 1960s, Barbadian writer George Lamming argued that Caribbean
musicians had begun to reverse Christopher Columbus's conquest of the
Americas by invading and transforming European sensibilities: music "has
made a most welcome invasion on the English spine. That spine is no different
from my spine: but it needed, perhaps, to be fertilised by a change of rhythm"
(1960, 77). In more recent years, authors have come to look to music as a
means of escaping binary categories. Thus, Congolese author Henri Lopes,
like Maryse Condé and others, radically dislodges music from questions of
national identity in order to affiliate himself with a wide spectrum of music
that encompasses folksong, the blues, Verdi, and Beethoven. This illustrates
the shift from the oppositional and nationalist character of early postcolonial
movements to the more complex, multilayered interrogation of nation and
identity that characterizes the transnational moment.

The effort to rethink national identity and history is a common thread running through the works discussed in this book. Condé insists that a writer defines her own identity and creates her own language, that the imagination is as good an approach to history as any other. Similarly, Nancy Huston dwells on the capacity a writer has to "say I" from countless different perspectives. And yet, in Assia Djebar's view, the Algerian woman writer takes on a particular responsibility with respect to other Algerian women; she defines this as the imperative not to speak for other women or from their place, but rather in a relation of proximity and solidarity. Coetzee cautions that fiction offers *at best* the illusion of embracing different subject positions; it does not fulfill our responsibility to the other as an embodied, situated subject. These authors all deploy innovative narrative forms in their efforts to foreground issues of agency, representation, and voice. As we have seen, these forms draw heavily on the musical models of polyphony, counterpoint, variation, and opera. Music thus provides authors with alternative strategies to introduce reciprocity, plurality, performance, and alterity into their writing.

The novels examined here all question the ideology of the nation— whether its official history in the case of Djebar; its literary manifestos, in the case of Condé; its values, in the case of Coetzee; or its monolingualism and genealogies, in the case of Huston. All of these novels embrace multiple languages: beyond the French or English in which they are written, they open up complex, multilingual worlds—worlds that require the active participation of our imagination. Although Condé writes *Traversée de la mangrove* in French, the text nonetheless asks us to imagine a multilingual soundscape in which Creole plays a significant part, particularly as the story unfolds in a rural village and presents the thoughts of working class people. Multilingualism also pervades *Les nuits de Strasbourg,* as the Algerian protagonist Thelja attempts to share her Arabic vernacular with her French lover. Thelja's conversations with her childhood friend, Eve, imply a back and forth between colloquial Arabic and French, although the written text flattens out this dimension. Huston's *Les variations Goldberg* consciously plays on the different vernaculars of characters, moving between Parisian French, working-class Canadian French dialects, an Irish-inflected English with the introduction of the haunting Irish folksong "Cockles and Mussels," and the French-English Creole of a blues musician from Louisiana. Throughout the text, the underlying presence of the writer's English disrupts the French, by de-familiarizing and deconstructing metaphors and colloquialisms. Finally, Coetzee writes *Disgrace* in an English that is deeply self-conscious and critical, a *maimed*, incomplete English because, as Mark Sanders (2002b) observes, the author avoids the perfective verb tense. The novel puts this impoverished, tired English in relation to African languages, to animal howls, and to music; ironically, of course, the richness of these contrasts comes through the very English that the protagonist claims is inadequate.

The musical strategies these writers deploy constitute an important dimension of their transnationalism. As we have seen, they each draw on musical forms from the European Baroque, mediated by more recent literary and theoretical movements, including Russian formalism, structuralism, and postcolonialism. Of the works discussed here, only Huston's novel and Cortázar's novella represent full-on appropriations of a musical work, taking on Bach's Goldberg Variations and the Musical Offering, respectively. In the other texts, music occupies a surreptitious role, but its effects are no less powerful. The concepts of polyphony and counterpoint not only influence the structure of the novels, *Les nuits de Strasbourg* and *Traversée de la mangrove*, but also allow the authors to stake out alternative responses to political, social, and historical conflict, in the case of Djebar, or to articulate a distinct literary agenda, in the case of Condé. Music exerts a prominent thematic presence in *Disgrace*, while also performing a formal and ethical function. It opens a space to which readers have no direct access, referencing a music that we can only apprehend in the most tenuous of ways. This forces us to recognize what lies outside our own knowledge and purview. The disruption and incongruity that opera introduces into the novel provokes reflection on the history, social relevance, and ethical implications of forms.

In *Borrowed Forms*, I have attempted to map out a more responsible, rigorous, and situated engagement with the music in transnational fiction and theory. On the broadest level, the readings here demonstrate that the literary, the musical and the political are inseparable, and that musical forms have wide-ranging, important applications in literature. One conclusion that emerges from these readings is that we are in need of a more nuanced, critical understanding of polyphony. It is not enough to call a text polyphonic. It is essential to identify and situate the precise narrative techniques that contribute to the illusion of polyphony, and to attend to the specific ethical, political, and aesthetic work that this "polyphony" performs. As I have sought to demonstrate through my reading of Condé, grounding polyphony musically and textually helps to avoid the essentializing and exoticizing commentaries to which narrative strategies in African and Caribbean texts have often been subjected.

Counterpoint offers an elegant conceptual model of how to bring disparate voices into relation. Whereas Said deployed counterpoint largely to challenge colonial hierarchies of power and knowledge, it now falls to critics to extend the methodology more radically to consider relations transnationally and transhistorically, across and among peripheries.[2] As we have seen, contrapuntal criticism complements other critical approaches, particularly Michael Rothberg's multidirectional memory (2009), Mireille Rosello's notion of performative encounters (2005), and also (more implicitly) Sarah Nuttall's theory of entanglement (2009), and Kimberlé Crenshaw's intersectionality (1989); indeed, it can be productive to combine these different approaches.

Reading Huston's *Les variations Goldberg* in relation to Glenn Gould illustrates how debates in music over the value of live performance in the middle of the twentieth-century anticipated literary debates over the creative authority of the author. Acknowledging how such musical debates shaped literary theory opens up many questions for future interdisciplinary scholarship. Finally, the consideration of J. M. Coetzee, an anglophone South African writer, in the broader context of opera studies and French theory, stages the kind of border crossing and interdisciplinarity that transnational criticism demands.

While the work of Condé, Djebar, Huston, and Coetzee spans the entire latter half of the twentieth century and bears witness to the momentous events of Algerian independence, the departmentalization of Guadeloupe and Martinique, the upheavals of May 1968, the fall of Apartheid, the Algerian Civil War, and the reunification of Europe, this inquiry has focused in particular on novels written in the 1980s and 90s. In these works, musical forms provide a means of holding together divergent voices and positions, and maintaining a tension between the national and the transnational, memory and reconciliation, presence and absence, and speech and silence.

As we might expect, younger writers are appropriating popular genres of music as they continually reinvent the novel. One of the most compelling instances of new musical writing is Chris Abani's novel *GraceLand* (2005). Born in Nigeria, writing in Los Angeles, Abani develops a highly original narrative by combining aspects of Nigerian *juju* and *asiko* musical forms (Sereda, 2008, 35) with riffs on Elvis Presley, Bob Marley, and Tina Turner. The novel charts the journey of a young boy, Elvis, from a small Nigerian village to the Lagos slums and onward to "redemption" in the United States. Elvis's trajectory is punctuated by repeated traumas—losing his mother to cancer, witnessing the repeated sexual abuse of his cousin, experiencing rape himself by an uncle, seeing his father slide into alcoholism and overhearing him order a relative's murder, being pulled into drug sales and the traffic of human body parts, and watching the demolition of the Moroko district where he and his friends reside. His need for guidance is met intermittently—and with mixed results—by relatives, beggars and street actors, and, significantly, the lyrics of popular songs overheard on the radio, in street bars, at the movies, and in his head. His name reflects his mother's passion for Elvis Presley, whom he tries to emulate in the street performances he gives to eke out a meager living. These performances allow him to explore and transgress racial and sexual boundaries: makeup and dance put him in touch with a part of himself that Nigerian society rejects as feminine, a side his conservative father has tried to beat out of him. The novel's title, *GraceLand*, refers to Presley's extravagant mansion in Memphis, Tennessee, but also recalls the album Paul Simon produced in collaboration with South African musicians Ladysmith Black Mambazo in 1987, a wildly successful, if controversial release that violated the boycott against apartheid South Africa. The title interrogates the status of the United States as a place of redemption for African refugees. Elvis does not wish to leave Nigeria and resents his compatriots for viewing America as a "Graceland" that will solve all their troubles; eventually, however, he has no alternative but emigration, as he has already been marked out by government thugs and jailed, and would have limited chances of developing himself as an artist if he remained in the country. Following Coetzee's scrutiny of the notion of "grace" and what it entails in a secular world, Abani's title questions the promise of redemption, grace, and refuge that the United States holds in the African imagination.

Music plays a complex role in Abani's novel: in seeming reference to Nigeria's booming film industry, constant musical citations permeate the reading experience like the soundtrack of a film. Thus, in the opening scene of the novel, the competing strains of different kinds of music vie for Elvis's attention against the din of the street:

> The radio played Bob Marley's "Natural Mystic," and he sang along, the tune familiar. "There's a natural mystic blowing through the air / If you listen carefully now you will hear…" His voice trailed off as he realized he did not know all the words and he settled for humming to the song as he listened to the sounds of the city waking up: tin buckets scraping, the sound of babies crying, infants yelling for food and people hurrying but getting nowhere. Next door someone was playing highlife music on a radio that was not tuned properly. The faster-tempoed

highlife music distracted him from Bob Marley, irritating him. He knew the highlife tune well, "Ije Enu" by Celestine Ukwu. Abandoning Bob Marley, he sang along. [...] On the road outside, two women bickered. (Abani, 2004, 4)

Snatches of song titles and lyrics interrupt the narrative thread to convey the fragmented and overloaded sensory experience of the modern city, and the ways in which American (and here, Caribbean) culture permeate the African street. The hybrid mix of references to African, Caribbean, and American popular music marks other Nigerian novels as well, particularly Chimamanda Adichie's *Purple Hibiscus* (2003), where the protagonist's evolving musical tastes mark out her growing consciousness of her African heritage and willingness to embrace it. A relentless frequency of musical citations also characterizes Condé's *Histoire de la femme cannibale*, in which diverse musical quotations—from Bizet's *Carmen* to pop—signal the Guadeloupean protagonist's transnational affiliations, her sense of being in multiple places at once. Song citations play a similar role in Fatou Diome's *Le ventre de l'Atlantique* (2003), where the leading character Salie expresses her layered identity by belting out the lyrics to Senegalese songs while drinking tea and watching television in her Strasbourg apartment.

Popular music, as evoked in the novels above, invariably involves lyrics, unlike the instances of music considered elsewhere in the book, with the notable exception of opera. Thus, while snatches of popular music can interrupt a narrative, they do not necessarily do so as *music*, but as another kind of text, as words. Drawing on Anahid Kassabian's (2001) observations with respect to the effect of popular music in film, allusions to popular songs in novels can forge a powerful connection with readers who are familiar with those songs, as they call on readers' associations in the context of their own lives, and by extension, render the experiences and situations evoked in the text that much more familiar. While the citation of popular music represents an important phenomenon and suggests a fascinating direction for further study, the primary concern of this book has been with music as *form*, as an alternative model of plurality, reciprocity, and relations.

This journey began with Cortázar, whose wittily titled short story "Clone" encapsulates some of the major questions in musico-literary criticism: to what extent can a literary work mimic music? How do we read "musical" fiction? What is the relationship between Baroque forms and the transnational moment? Is the presence of these forms an indication of the continued cultural domination of Western forms, or is this exchange more dynamic? It seems appropriate, therefore, to conclude with a brief consideration of Alejo Carpentier's *Concierto barroco* (1974), both an extravagant illustration of the possibilities that musical forms bring to transnational fiction and a perfect bookend to Cortázar's "Clone."

Like the authors we have examined, Carpentier was both a prolific novelist and an important critic. Born in Cuba in 1904, he lived in Paris and traveled extensively throughout the Caribbean, Europe, Asia, and North Africa. Moreover, like Kundera, he was an accomplished musicologist: he completed an extensive study of music in Cuba in 1946, in which he explored the African influences on Cuban music and culture, and he brought multiple musical strategies into his fiction. Although Carpentier's investment in musical form merits full consideration on its own terms, we leave off here with a fertile but fleeting encounter with *Concierto barocco.*

In Carpentier's novella, music again functions as a means of questioning origins and influences, and provides a more dynamic and inclusive way of approaching history. The novella explodes temporal and spatial limits, moving from Mexico to Venice, from the Baroque to Louis Armstrong. The story recounts the voyage of an unnamed Mexican aristocrat to Europe. Along the way, he stops in Cuba, where he hires the services of an Afro-Cuban page, Filomeno, a freed slave who possesses not only a distinguished genealogy, but also extraordinary musical abilities. The two arrive in Venice in 1709 amidst the frenzy of Carnival celebrations, and encounter Handel, Scarlatti, and Vivaldi. The latter is so taken with the Mexican that he decides to write a New World opera on Montezuma. The New World thus "makes its grand entrance as the scene of dramatic action on the operatic stage" for the first time in history in Vivaldi's exotic opera; the work premiered in 1733, anticipating by two years Jean-Philippe Rameau's *Les Indes Galantes.*[3] As the opera takes shape on the stage, however, the Mexican is outraged to see the grotesque misrepresentation of his history, the erroneous introduction of Oriental tropes like elephants to the New World, and the emasculation of important Mexican figures. Brushing aside his objections, Vivaldi upholds the principle of poetic illusion and asserts his artistic freedom to represent the Americas as he imagines them.

Meanwhile, Filomeno's presence in Venice leads to wild, impromptu music-making sessions at the Ospidale della Pièta, bringing together Afro-Caribbean rhythms, Northern European counterpoint, and Italian virtuosity:

Prendido el frenético allegro de las setenta mujeres [...] Vivaldi arremetió en la sinfonía con fabuloso ímpetu, en juego concertante, mientras Doménico Scarlatti [...] se largó a hacer vertiginosa escalas en el clavicémbalo, en tanto que Jorge Federico Haendel se entregaba a deslumbrantes variaciones que atropellaban todas las normas del bajo continuo. [...] Pero, entre tanto, Filomeno había corrido a las cocinas, trayendo une batería de calderos de cobre, de todos tamaños, a los que empezó a golpear con cucharas, espumaderas, batidoras, rollos de amasar, tizones, palos de plumeros, con tales ocurrencias de ritmos, de síncopas, de acentos encontrados, que, por espacio de treinta y dos compases lo dejaron solo para que improvisara. (Carpentier, 2011, 74).

[Having enkindled the frenetic allegro of the sixty-six young women, Vivaldi attacked the symphony with astonishing abandon in concertante form, as Domenico Scarlatti [...] rippled off vertiginous scales on the harpsichord, and Georg Frideric Handel launched into dazzling variations that violated all the rules of figured bass. [...] But in the meantime, Filomeno had run off to the kitchen and returned with a battery of copper kettles of all sizes that he began to beat upon with spoons, skimmers, rolling pins, stirrers, feather-duster handles, and poers with such prodigies of rhythm, syncopation and complex patterns that he was given a thirty-two bar chorus all to himself. (Carpentier, tr. Zazt, 1988, 79–81)]

This unprecedented jam session between Afro-Cuban, Northern European, and Italian cultural expressions is facilitated, of course, by the radically non-hierarchical space of carnival. What is remarkable in Carpentier's description of this scene is his emphasis on transgression and excess as constitutive of the exchange, even before Filomeno's introduction of Afro-Caribbean rhythms. Once Filomeno enters, he reorients the exchange according to his own terms, so much so that he asserts a thirty-two-bar solo, the standard form in jazz. As eccentric as this may be in a Baroque context, the concerto incorporates it and continues on through a final *da capo* to its decisive final cadence.

While the novella clearly exploits the qualities of invention, accumulation, atemporality, and multiplicity inherent in the Baroque, it also draws on the particular aesthetics of the *concerto*, a form that originated in Venice and that relies on the principles of contrast and opposition, both of which come into play in the scene we have just examined. In the final scene, Filomeno is magically transported to the jazz age, where he witnesses Louis Armstrong in performance. Significantly, he recognizes elements of the Baroque concerto that resurface, displaced and transformed in the jazz performance:

> Y, embocando la trompeta, atacó, como él sólo sabia hacerlo, la melodía de *Go down Moses* antes de pasar a la de *Jonah and the Whale*, alzada por el pabellón de cobre hacia los cielos del teatro [...] que evocó, para Filomeno, de repente, la persona de *Aquel*—el Jorge Federico de aquella noche [...] Y concertábanse ya en nueva ejecución, tras del virtuoso los instrumentos reunidos en el escenario: saxofones, clarinetes, contrabajo, guitarra eléctrica, tambores cubanos, maracas, [...] y el piano de tapa levantada que ni se acordaba de haberse llamado, en otros tiempos, algo así como "un clave bíen temperado." (Carpentier, 1974, 82–83)

> [[Armstrong] attacked, as only he knew how to the melody of "Go down, Moses" before passing to "Jonah and the Whale" elevated by the bell of his horn to the ceiling of the theater [...] evoked for Filomeno the image of *that one*—the George Frederic of *that night* [...] And here the virtuoso was followed in improvisational breaks by instruments on stage: saxophones, clarinets, bass, electric guitar, bongos, maracas, [...] and the piano [...] which itself didn't remember that it had once been called [...] a "well-tempered clavier." (Carpentier, tr. Zazt, 1988, 130–31)]

A "new Baroque concerto," the jazz performance stages a play of opposition between the solo virtuoso and the instruments on stage, between musical convention and invention. As Filomeno listens in rapt attention, Armstrong's trumpet recalls Handel's cornetto, merging two distinct musical experiences.

Benítez-Rojo (1994, 194) argues that Carpentier's fascination with the Baroque is symptomatic of the more general desire of Latin American writers to refer to two sources for legitimation, "both of them unattainable: Nature and the American tradition [...], and European language and episteme." Through the baroque concerto and jazz performance, Carpentier stages the tension between distinct traditions, while also envisioning the possibility of their creative fusion. He thus asserts two extremely important notions: that cultural influences are rhizomatic and flow in multiple directions, and that musical forms are never pure, but rather dynamic structures of relations.[4] The novella portrays Africa and the "New World" as constitutive of Europe.

Thus, when African, Caribbean, Canadian, or Argentinian writers lay claim to "Western" "European" musical forms, these forms are already the product of dynamic, multidirectional, and multilayered cultural exchange. Moreover, when these forms are deterritorialized and deployed in literature, they are transformed once again in the process.

Carpentier's novella thus offers another striking illustration of the vibrant influence of musical forms on twentieth-century transnational literature, and points to the creolized nature of the forms themselves. Like the works examined throughout this book, the novella deploys musical forms to pose questions of representation, history, and agency, and to counter monolithic ideologies with a commitment to pluralism and hybridity. Here again, the turn to music stems from a desire to open up the dimensions of time and space in a text, to challenge and reinvent boundaries, to reconfigure hierarchical relations, and to engage with diverse voices without subsuming them into one single dominant reading.

The challenge for readers, however, is not to be seduced by what transnational writers may wish to do through music. Rather, we must attend closely to what music actually accomplishes in specific contexts, while remaining attuned to the possibilities that music brings to literature.

Notes

Introduction

1 Werner Herzog produced a television film devoted to Gesualdo in 1995, *Tod Stimmen*, or *Death for Five Voices: The Composer Carlo Gesualdo (1560–1613)*.

2 In this sense, "Clone" differs from Aldous Huxley's *Point Counterpoint*, in that Huxley makes explicit his project of incorporating musical forms and effects into the novel. Huxley overtly frames the narrative with Bach's Suite in B minor and Beethoven's String Quartet no. 15 in a minor.

3 Oulipo is short for Ouvroir de Littérature Potentielle (Workshop for Potential Literature), an experimental group founded in 1960 by the poet Raymond Queneau and mathematician François Le Lionnais. Oulipo writers rejected the subconscious as a source of literary creativity, instead using systematic constraints to generate their texts.

4 Of course, both Bakhtin and Derrida have shown how multilingualism and difference inhabit every voice. Bakhtin (1981, 291) holds that "at any given moment of its historical existence, language is heteroglot from top to bottom: it represents the co-existence of socio-ideological contradictions between the present and the past, between differing epochs of the past, between different socio-ideological groups in the present, between tendencies, schools, circles and so forth, all given a bodily form."

5 See Anthea Morrison (1995) for an insightful discussion of voice and voicelessness.

6 Tom Cohen (1996) offers a fascinating assessment of the different ways in which critics on the left and the right have appropriated Bakhtin. He also discusses the relation between Bakhtin's work and that of Paul de Man.

7 Since Bakhtin's work precedes the advent of deconstruction and many of the insights of psychoanalysis and phenomenology, it can seem to offer

a less fraught approach to notions of voice and subjectivity, although in fact, Bakhtin understands every voice as emerging from a specific sociohistorical situation, and asserting its singularity in contestation against homogenizing forces. See Kristeva, 1973.

8   Kassav is a popular Antillean Zouk band.

9   The musician cautions the protagonist: "Regarde ce pays, le nôtre, le tien, à l'encan. Bientôt peut-être, il ne sera plus qu'un souvenir qui s'amenuisera petit à petit dans les mémoires. Moi, ce que j'essaie de faire, c'est de lui garder sa voix. Et toi aussi, tu peux, tu dois faire quelque chose" (Condé, 1987, 333). [Look at this country, ours, yours, being sold off to the highest bidder. Soon perhaps it will be no more than a memory, little by little growing dim in our minds. Me, what I'm trying to do is preserve its voice. And you, too, you can, you must do something.]

10 *Disgrace* also inspired a stage adaptation by Alexander Maxime at the Baxter Theater in Cape Town which premiered in 2012.

11 This book looks particularly at forms that emerged in the Baroque period, but I use the term "classical" here in the broad sense to designate the tradition of Western music that encompasses works from the Renaissance through the twenty-first century.

12 Coetzee's doctoral thesis of 1969 focused on the novels of Samuel Beckett, the Irish writer whose revolutionary act of deterritorialization—writing in French—can be seen as both a political act of resistance against English rule in Ireland and an aesthetic desire to submit writing to difficulty and constraint. Coetzee's engagement with the French tradition—with Rousseau and Beckett—constitutes a similar gesture of deterritorialization. Coetzee also engages with European literature more broadly, and particularly with Wordsworth, Byron, Kafka, Defoe, Tolstoy, and Dostoevsky.

13 My translation. All translations are mine unless otherwise indicated.

14 See Catherine Bédarida, "John Coetzee dans son exil intérieur" in *Le Monde*, October 10, 1997: "Qu'en est-il de quelqu'un né en Afrique du Sud, qui peut-être y réside, qui écrit en anglais, est édité en Angleterre ou aux Etats-Unis, qui est extrêmement lu dans ces pays et traduit en Europe, de telle sorte que pour chaque lecteur qu'il a en Afrique du Sud il en a des centaines ou des milliers par ailleurs, quelqu'un qui se sent peut-être témoin de son pays d'origine pour le monde alors que chez lui il est accusé par les critiques de propager sur son pays une vision d'étranger, ou au moins une vision confortable pour les étrangers ? [...] J'espère avoir démontré que le terme 'écrivain sud-africain' n'est pas aussi transparent qu'il le paraît." My translation.

15 Lionnet made this case compellingly in a talk entitled "New World Exiles

and Ironists from Evariste Parny to Susan Howe and Ananda Devi" at the University of Massachusetts Amherst in April 2011.

16 On these issues, see also Graham Huggan (2008, 1).

17 While the "First World" and the "winners" of globalization may be ready to move beyond the concept of the nation state, the national remains an important category for young and emerging states such as Israel, Palestine, and Kosovo, as well as for regions that still aspire to statehood, like Quebec and the French Antilles.

18 In Quebec, by contrast, the French language represents a mode of resistance against the dominance of English.

19 Writing and reading presuppose education, material means, and the luxuries of solitude and leisure, which are not universally available. According to Sofiane Hadjadj, the editor of the Barzakh editions in Algiers, books are prohibitively expensive in Algeria, restricting both publishing and reading. Personal communication with Hadjadj, Paris, October 6, 2005.

20 J. Michael Dash (1998, 117) evokes the "verbal delirium, the quest for orality" as examples of a "radical, modern poetics that reacts violently to the tragic separation of artist and life, observer and observed in the past."

21 Djebar makes this point in an interview conducted by journalist Anne-Brigitte Kern on Radio France Culture on May 27, 1994: "On parle tellement d'oralité mais il y a une culture écrite, toute une patrimoine d'écriture au Maghreb."

22 See in particular Bakhtin's *Problems in Dostoevsky's Poetics*, Barthes's *Le grain de la voix* and *S/Z*; Deleuze's *Le pli: Leibniz et le Baroque* and *Milles plateaux*; Said's *Culture and Imperialism*, *Musical Elaborations*, and *Of Late Style*.

23 See Mai Al-Nakib's insightful discussion of musical ekphrasis in Djebar's *L'amour la fantasia*. Al-Nakib (2005, 266) uses Deleuze and Guattari's notion of deterritorialization to argue that the turn to music in the novel opens up lines of escape, a way of moving beyond the dominant, rigid orders of being and understanding, whether colonial or patriarchal.

24 I argue for a much more dynamic, hybridized understanding of forms and genealogies.

25 Rousseau, *La Nouvelle Héloïse*, part 1, lettre XLVIII (qtd in Starobinski, 1971, 110–13).

26 Simon Gikandi's (2001, 628–29) caveat is well taken that "while we live in a world defined by cultural and economic flows across formally entrenched national boundaries, the world continues to be divided, in stark terms, between its 'developed' and 'underdeveloped' sectors. It is precisely because of the starkness of this division that the discourse of globalization

seems to be perpetually caught between two competing narratives, one of celebration, the other of crisis."

27 Smyth (2008, 22–23) sees Bakhtin as "the most powerful influence on the development of English literary theory in the late twentieth century."

Chapter 1: From Mikhail Bakhtin to Maryse Condé: the Problems of Literary Polyphony

  1 "polyphony, n." OED Online. June 2013. Oxford University Press. Accessed August 16, 2013.

  2 "From the Translator: David Ball and Nicole Ball on Abdourahman A. Waberi's *Passage of Tears.*" http://wordswithoutborders.org/dispatches/article/from-the-translator-david-ball-and-nicole-ball-on-abdourahman-a.-waberis-pa. Accessed October 2, 2013.

  3 Of course, this notion of return is itself a myth, particularly in Condé's case. See Rosello (1995).

  4 "Pendant trois jours et trois nuits, le corps de Francis Sancher traîna sur le marbre froid des tables d'autopsie, jusqu'à ce qu'un médecin appelé de la Pointe en désespoir de cause fût formel. [...] Alors l'après-midi du quatrième jour, Francis Sancher revint chez lui..." (Condé, 1989a, 23–24). This recalls Chamoiseau's *Solibo magnifique* (1988), as the official police investigation of Solibo's death founders miserably, while popular understanding is rich in insights and interpretations.

  5 The novel presents the villagers' diverse attempts to understand Sancher's death, while never privileging any one version as authoritative. This structure recalls Umberto Eco's understanding of Baroque art (1989, 7): "it never allows for a privileged, definitive, frontal view; rather, it induces the spectator to shift his position continuously in order to see the work in constantly new aspects, as if it were in a state of perpetual transformation."

  6 With the notable exception of Suzanne Crosta, most critics have missed this dimension. Perret (1995, 663) attributes a theatrical quality to *Traversée de la mangrove*, and reads the novel as "an example of multiple voices, but in an alternating and recognizable fashion, like theatre." Fulton (2001, 307) highlights the place of oral storytelling in the text: "Story-telling itself thus becomes the link between characters; although their readings do not conjoin into a thematically or temporally consistent portrait of Francis Sancher, their entangled stories share his absence." Both critics thus attribute a vocal, theatrical quality to the novel, failing to pick up on the silent, interior status of the narratives. This point is critical to understanding what is so innovative about the narrative structure Condé puts into play. The narratives do not necessarily follow one another in succession, but could in fact unfold simultaneously within the minds of the characters. The

text thus does not merely unfold horizontally (in linear succession), but gains an important vertical and simultaneous dimension as well, by staging interior narratives that overlap with one another.

7   Francis Sancher is said to be from a slave-owning family of békés; according to one theory, his untimely death is the result of a curse on the family. Reputed to have treated their slaves with particular cruelty, all the male descendants in his genealogical line are doomed to die at the age of fifty, wherever they may find themselves at the time. Unlike many of his predecessors, Sancher comes back to Rivière au Sel to confront his destiny head on.

8   Celia Britton (1999, 19) offers an excellent account of Glissant's understanding of opacity.

9   Peterson (1993, 762–64) writes: "To my hearing, some of the finest and most refined applications of Bakhtinian analysis in the present day reconstruction of the African American literary legacy fall short, in their celebratory mood, of listening to the whole story." Peterson sees polyphony as a valuable alternative to both structuralism and deconstruction as it does not enclose meaning "within stable binary codes of opposed terms," nor make it subject to "an endless play of signifiers." He locates Bakhtin's key insight in the observation that "utterances come into the world [as] sites of social contestation."

10 OED Online. March 2014. Oxford University Press. Accessed April 14, 2014.

11 See, for instance, Jacques Coetzee (1998), Caryl Emerson (2002), and Stephen Benson (2003).

12 Condé, however, makes extremely productive use of the media in her fiction, exploiting its clichés and melodramatic character. This is partic- ularly the case in *Histoire de la femme cannibale* (2003) and *Célanire cou-coupé* (2000).

13 In her work on Condé, Sanders (2003, 151) argues that "polyphony can best be analyzed across long stretches of text and within the context of the novel as a whole." However, as this reading demonstrates, both approaches can be extremely useful to understanding Condé's poetics.

14 Kundera's later essays, *Testaments trahis* (1993) and *Le rideau* (2005), also play on these issues, although his most complete articulation of a theory of literary polyphony comes in *L'art du roman* (1986). The son of a musicologist, Kundera trained as a professional musician. He makes frequent reference to Bach, Beethoven, Janáček, and Messiaen.

15 See Lawrence Kramer (1995, 17–18) for a critique of the ideal wholeness that intellectuals ascribe to music. Kramer argues that form is associated with

unity and structure, "the idea that every note is necessary to the whole and no note is superfluous."

16 Note that in music, the term "polyphony" is used with similar flexibility: polyphony is often used as a general term for multivoicedness, whereas counterpoint implies more rigorous formal constraints.

17 Emerson (2002) argues that Kundera's "polyphony" is really a technique of variation.

18 As we saw in the Introduction, Assia Djebar prefers the term "*francographie*" over *francophonie*, as it places emphasis on writing rather than on voice.

19 Edward Cone refers to an identifiable composer's voice that comes across in music. As Stephen Connor (2001, 468–70) observes, Carolyn Abbate and Cone disagree over the status of the composer's voice in opera: Abbate subscribes to a Bakhtinian view of opera as structured by a multiplicity of voices, whereas Cone argues that all music can be thought of as "a form of purely symbolic utterance," linked to the implicit persona of the composer, and felt to convey a "sense of the composer's voice."

20 This is also the case with J. M. Coetzee, who similarly resists reductive, biographical readings of his work.

21 Condé describes how hearing local high school students dismiss her earlier novels as remote and uninteresting reinforced her conviction that writing must address the present (Broichhagen et al., 2006, 24). In both *La vie scélérate* and *Traversée de la mangrove*, Condé represents writers whom no one reads, confronting—and perhaps exorcising—this hazard of the profession with characteristic humor and irony.

22 "Néanmoins, la plante de cette médisance crût et fleurit dans le terreau du village et ne s'étiola que lorsque éclata la nouvelle de l'affaire avec Mira" ["Nonetheless, the plant of this rumor grew and blossomed in the rich soil of the village and only wilted when the news broke of the affair with Mira"] (Condé, 1989a, 36).

23 Personal communication with the author at Princeton University in the fall of 2003.

24 The relation Condé draws between writing and the act of crossing the mangrove recalls   Derrida's assertion (1976, 107–8) that "one should meditate upon all of the following together: writing as the possibility of the road and of difference, the history of writing and the history of the road, of the rupture, of the via rupta, of the path that is broken, beaten, *fracta*, of the space of reversibility and of repetition traced by the opening, the divergence from, and the violent spacing, of nature, of the natural, savage, salvage, forest."

25 Condé invited Chamoiseau to serve as the first public reader of her novel, and his response figured in the journal *Callaloo* in 1991.

26 "La pensée de la trace promet ainsi alliance, elle réfute possession, elle donne sur ces temps diffractés que les humanités d'aujourd'hui multiplient entre elles, par heurts et merveilles. Telle est l'errance violente du poème" (Glissant, 1996, 71). ["The notion of the trace thus promises alliance, refutes possession, opens onto these diffracted times that today's societies develop among themselves, through clashes and wonders. Such is the violent wandering of the poem."]

27 Condé asserts that *créolité* "effaces the history of slavery, of the plantation culture, and the economic foundations of the island. The term *créolité* makes the cultural laboratory more important than the memory of a sugar-based economy" (Apter, 2001, 94).

28 The novel ironically performs the commemoration that Loulou Lemeaulnes predicts: "Bientôt quelqu'un commencerait de broder une légende autour de Francis Sancher et ferait de lui un géant incompris" (Condé, 1989a, 124). ["Soon someone will start to embroider a legend around Francis Sancher and will make him into a misunderstood giant."]

29 Condé has expressed admiration for Chamoiseau's literary talent on numerous occasions, despite her irritation at the aggressive and prescriptive agenda he pursues in the *Eloge de la créolité*.

30 "Cyrille faisait ses pitreries ordinaires et les gens s'esclaffaient. Pourtant son cœur n'y était pas" (Condé, 1989a, 154). ["Cyrille clowned around as usual and people burst out laughing. But his heart wasn't in it."] "Qu'est-ce qui arrivait à leur conteur préféré de *déparler*?" (158) ["How come their favorite storyteller was talking nonsense?"]

31 In an interview with VèVè Clark in 1989, Condé discussed the dichotomy between written culture and lived experience. Interestingly, she flips the terms to evoke written experience and lived culture. "In other words, it is the writer who gave the people power, strength, unity, and faith. Césaire's was an intellectual attitude to culture that nobody believes in now—culture is a lived rather than a written experience in contemporary Guadeloupe" (Clark, 1989, 111).

32 Dash (1995, 43–45) cites Glissant's *Un champ des îles* to illustrate this point: "Durant que vous dormez dans cette plaine, le souvenir encourt les tournoiements de l'arbre, et plus haut son sang. Toute prose devient feuille et accumule dans l'obscur ses éblouies. Faites-le feuille de vos mains, faites-le prose de l'obscur, et l'éblouie de vos brisures."

33 As Smyth (2002, 18–19) points out, the mangrove is an important symbol for the founders of the *créolité* movement. In *Eloge de la créolité*, Bernabé, Chamoiseau, and Confiant proclaim: "Creoleness is our primitive soup

and our continuation, our primeval chaos and our mangrove swamp of virtualities."

34 This image alludes to Baudelaire's *Correspondances:* "La nature est un temple où de vivants piliers / Laissent parfois sortir de confuses paroles; / L'homme y passe à travers des forêts de symboles / Qui l'observent avec des regards familiers…" (Baudelaire, 1975, 11).

35 Morrison examines voicelessness in *La vie scélérate,* linking it to the trope of silence in contemporary writing by Caribbean women authors.

36 As Léocadie says, "Pour un peu je changerais de place et j'irais m'asseoir dans l'autre pièce ou sur la galerie où se tiennent ceux qui ne soucient pas de faire semblant, qui regardent la hauteur du rhum dans les bouteilles et vident leurs assiettes de soupe grasse en écoutant Cyrille crier ses 'yé krik' et ses 'yé krak'" (Condé, 1989a, 151).

37 My emphasis.

38 Condé comments in an interview, "In film, everything is communicated through visual means, through the acting […] I learned to externalize things" (Broichhagen et al., 2006, 10).

39 On these different narrative planes, see Genette (1972, 237). Genette opposes *diegesis,* the universe of the first narrative, to *metadiegesis,* the universe of the second degree of narration, a story within a story.

40 Joby and Xantippe are the two exceptions to this rule.

41 Leah Hewitt (1995, 641–51) suggests that Condé undoes this in her subsequent novel: "Unlike Condé's preceding novel, *Traversée de la mangrove, Les derniers rois mages* does not affirm female voices in any privileged way. It is as if *Les derniers rois mages* were meant to correct any (false) impression that Condé is a writer who promotes a feminist stance *over* and *against* men's concerns. Her rich dialectics of past and present, male and female, Antillean and American cultures, provide as many questions as answers."

Chapter 2: Edward Said and Assia Djebar: Counterpoint and the Practice of Comparative Literature

1 The occasion for Said's remarks was an interdisciplinary conference on Space, History, Identity at the American University of Beirut for which he was the keynote speaker. His presentation, "Unresolved Geographies, Embattled Landscapes," drew a standing-room-only crowd of more than one thousand Lebanese students.

2 At the time of the conference, Israel still occupied a "security zone" in South Lebanon. They withdrew from the zone in May 2000 in accordance with UN Security Council Resolution 425.

3 As I mention later in the chapter, many recent critical approaches suggest

a debt to Said and the model of counterpoint, including Kimberlé Crenshaw's intersectionality, Sarah Nuttall's notion of entanglement, Michael Rothberg's multidirectional memory, Mark Sanders' complicity, and Françoise Lionnet's and Shu-mei Shih's minor transnationalism.

4 Djebar's emphasis on relating architecture and music to the novel recalls Friedrich Schlegel's famous formulation in fragment no. 88 that the innermost form of the novel is mathematical, rhetorical, and musical (see Werner Wolf, 1999, 99).

5 For a different treatment of this subject, see particularly Mildred Mortimer (2005, 58–63). Mortimer offers a useful discussion of how Djebar extends Said's project to include women and non-canonical writers, although her definition of counterpoint as "reading back" and as the setting "of one narrative against the other" does not address the specifically musical foundations of counterpoint. It also misses the political aspirations of the term and the potential for reading more than two voices. Mai Al-Nakib's article on musical ekphrasis offers a compelling consideration of the relationship between music and literature in Djebar's work, as well as a broader overview of ekphrasis in general. In her discussion of counterpoint, Al-Nakib stresses the relation between voices, as well as the transformative potential of what she terms "paradoxical entanglements" (273). See also Moneera Al-Ghadeer (2008).

6 In his introduction to *Musical Elaborations*, Said (1991, xviii) writes: "Adorno is a creature of the Hegelian tradition, which presumes an inescapable historical teleology that incorporates everything in its relentless forward path. This I find unacceptable for all sorts of reasons. Rather than spelling them out here I shall briefly suggest an alternative based on a *geographical* or spatial idea that is truer to the diversity and spread of human activity."

7 These critics include Al-Nakib (2005), Jonathan Arac (1998), Stanthis Gourgouris (2004), Françoise Lionnet (2011), Mortimer (2005), May Telmissany and Stephanie Tara Schwartz (2010), and Alison Rice (2006).

8 John Docker (2007, 272–73) notes Said's "curious" disinterest in Bakhtin, and suggests that the fundamental difference between the two critics lies in Said's emphasis on the role of the individual in history, a position that clearly assigns to intellectuals the responsibility to act and intervene, whereas Bakhtin addresses literary and cultural forces at the impersonal level. Of course, Said's silence on Bakhtin's theory of novelistic polyphony could also be read as an instance of the anxiety of influence of the Russian precursor on the younger scholar. Said is interested in contested histories and geographies and how these play out in narratives; Bakhtin's interests lie in the novel.

9 According to *The Oxford English Dictionary*, the term "counterpoint" was

used in music as early as 1550, while the extra-musical usage of the term came later: in 1599, counterpoint was used to designate an antithesis, and in 1626, it was first used for a contrary point in an argument. On the relationship between music and rhetoric, see Patrick McCreless (2002).

10   While polyphony is universal, Bakhtin developed the notion of polyphony with Bach in mind.

11   Painter (2001, 222) discusses this in the German context as well, citing how German theorists in the early twentieth century attempted to deny the notion that the origins of Western polyphony might lie in the heterophony of folk and non-Western music by insisting that "counterpoint required planning and foresight, but 'heterophony' was improvised."

12   De Groot quotes an interview Said gave to Dutch television in 2000: "I think [Umm Kalthoum's music] is designed to send people, not exactly into a stupor, but it would induce a kind of melancholic haze, which people like. And I found it disturbing. Mentally it made you inactive... So I very early on rejected it and began to focus exclusively on Western music, for which I hungered more and more." Said (1991, 98) also discusses his early encounter with Umm Kalthoum in *Musical Elaborations*.

13   Anthropologist Paulla Ebron (2002, 39–40) critiques Said for avoiding "an analysis of the interactive relationship between Western art music and imperialism. The text on music offers only a little information on global interconnections... By ignoring the ways 'music' comes into being, socially and historically, Said eschews the question of how the West and its classical music are inscribed in global history. He fails to disrupt Western art music as a coherent, locally configured object." On the contrary, I would argue that Said's critical reflections on his own musical education and his exploration of the values associated with such forms as variation, counterpoint, and the sonata illustrate his attentiveness to these very issues.

14   The vertical point-against-point, note-against-note dimension of counterpoint is the one most readily used by critics currently working with the term. The horizontal development of simultaneous voices is less easy to transpose to the literary domain, but Kundera makes an attempt to do so in his discussion of Hermann Broch's *The Sleepwalkers* in *L'art du roman* (1986). Djebar's juxtaposition of multiple interlaced storylines (i.e., the simultaneously unfolding dramas of different characters) is one of the ways through which her text approximates the horizontal aspect of contrapuntal music.

15   On June 13, 2005, Djebar became the first North African woman writer to be elected to the prestigious Académie française, occupying the Chair of M. Georges Vedel. Only one other African writer had previously held

a chair in the Académie: Léopold Sédar Senghor of Senegal, who was appointed in 1983.

16 This was a recurring theme in interviews I conducted in Paris in October 2005, particularly with Sofiane Hadjadj, a founding editor of Éditions Barzakh.

17 Djebar (1994, 149) invests this traditional Berber writing with an irrepressible music and orality: "le sens même—et la musique, et l'oralité palpitante—de cet alphabet qui se ranime et réussit à ne pas être étouffée" ["the meaning itself—and the music and palpable orality—of this alphabet comes alive again and succeeds in not being stifled"].

18 *Quasi una fantasia* is also the title of a collection of essays by Adorno that discuss how Beethoven transcends the classical sonata form by incorporating contrapuntal material. Djebar may take her citation from Beethoven, or alternatively from Adorno.

19 At New York University in October 2004, Djebar and I discussed the links between democracy and polyphony. Djebar made these remarks several years before the popular uprisings that swept through Egypt and Tunisia in the spring of 2011; the Arab Spring clearly indicates the potential of the Internet as a venue for polyphonic exchange, and it now seems that the degree to which a society has access to Internet resources suggests its democratic potential.

20 In the French context, the power of film to transform the relations between different communities is particularly striking. Two recent works, Philippe Lioret's *Welcome* (2009) and Rachid Bouchareb's *Days of Glory* (2006), effectively changed public policy by fostering empathy for immigrants and veterans from the former colonies.

21 In *Nulle part dans la maison de mon père* (2007) as in her earlier novel *L'amour la fantasia* (1985), Djebar evokes her own near-suicide in front of an oncoming tram in Algiers. Following an argument with her lover, she ran off in the direction of the sea and was suddenly overcome by an irresistible urge to throw herself down on the tracks. It is unclear how we are to read Thelja's suicide: an act of despair; a momentary, self-destructive impulse like that which Djebar describes having experienced in her own life; a mystical desire for an irrecoverable wholeness; or perhaps the poetic fulfillment of her name, snow.

22 Djebar commented on the genesis of *Les nuits de Strasbourg* in a radio interview with Laure Adler on January 31, 2006, in which she explains she won a writer's fellowship from the city of Strasbourg and refers to the book as a *"pur roman de fiction"* ("a purely fictional novel"). Djebar wrote most of the novel itself in Louisiana.

23 The term "palimpsest" derives from the Greek and has come to connote

both erasure and retention. When scribes reused parchment, they would erase the original text and superimpose a new layer. Genette employs the term, notably in the essay "Proust Palimpseste" in *Figures I* (1966). Donadey (2001, 65–68) uses Genette in her insightful analysis of palimpsest in Djebar's fiction. The palimpsest is a key strategy in contrapuntal writing because of this simultaneous layering of different voices across disparate times and places. It allows the voices of the past to speak alongside contemporary voices.

24 Reda Bensmaïa (2003, 45) notes a similar chiasmic crossing of France and Algeria in Malek Allouache's film, *Salut Cousin*: "a becoming French of Algeria, or rather, a becoming Parisian of Algiers."

25 Barbé (2001, 134) provides an insightful discussion of the nomadic character of Strasbourg and characterizes the city as a "purely deterritorialized locus where only exile and wandering are possible."

26 Djebar (1999, 234). Taos Amrouche's *Jacinthe noire* (1947), one of the first francophone novels to be published by an Algerian author, also takes place entirely in France.

27 The French government gave 100,000 hectares of land to 8,000 incoming refugees from Alsace in 1871 (Bennoune, 2002, 53). Hugh Roberts also addresses this wave of immigration in his commentary to Gilo Pontecorvo's *Battle of Algiers* for Criterion Films.

28 Djebar's invention of an "Alsagérie" has drawn a great deal of critical attention. See particularly Rosello (2005), Rice (2003), and O'Riley (2002).

29 Algerian author Mohammed Dib also deploys sand and snow as interchangeable figures of emptiness and plenitude.

30 Fanon (1968, 22–24) famously argues, "Chaque voile rejeté découvre aux colonialistes [...] morceau par morceau la chair algérienne mise à nue [...] Chaque voile qui tombe exprime en négatif que l'Algérie commence à se renier et accepte le viol du colonisateur." ["Every rejected veil disclosed to the eyes of the colonialists [...] piece by piece, the flesh of Algeria laid bare. [...] Every veil that fell [...] was a negative expression of the fact that Algeria was beginning to deny herself and was accepting the rape of the colonizer."] Rita Faulkner (1996, 847–55) claims that Djebar rejects the theoretical constructs of patriarchal nationalist thinkers like Fanon.

31 "A voix nue" radio interviews, May 24–27, 1994. Rice (2006, 53–55) offers an insightful discussion of the improper name.

32 Interestingly, the significance of Assia as one who accompanies and consoles also accords well with the role that Antigone takes on with respect to her father, whom she accompanies into exile.

33 The phrase "toutes ces morts en marche" includes not only those who have not been properly buried, but also those who have died in exile, or whose

tombs have been uprooted and displaced as in the case of the Jewish graves
of Constantine.

34 Djebar trained as a historian at the Ecole normale supérieure, and was
an assistant in history at the University of Rabat, Morocco. From 1962 to
1965, she was the only Algerian woman to hold the post of professor of
history at the University of Algiers. In 1965, the government sponsored a
program of Arabicization, requiring professors to teach in Arabic. Djebar
left for France, and subsequently taught in the department of French at the
University of Algiers in 1975.

35 Carolyn Steedman (2007, 11) takes up Anderson's description of Michelet
as a young historian who went into the archive "in order to enact a
particular kind of national imagining": "the silence of the dead was no
obstacle to the exhumation of their deepest desires," and after Michelet,
"historians found themselves able to speak on behalf of the dead and to
interpret the words and acts that the dead themselves had not understood
in life." White (1973, 92) discusses Michelet's (1842) comment that the
dead require "an Oedipus who will solve for them their own riddle, which
made no sense to them, one who would explain to them the meaning of
their words, their actions which they did not understand."

36 I have in mind Judith Butler's probing work, *Antigone's Claim* (2000). See
also Catherine Holland (1998, 1108–32) for an analysis of Antigone's legacy
in feminist political theory.

37 See Donadey's discussion (2008, 65–88) of a similar relationship between
the French interrogation agent Costa and a captive Algerian woman
militant. The figure of Costa haunts Djebar's novels, particularly *L'amour,
la fantasia*.

38 Nicole Dombrowski Risser (2012, 70) documents this period in detail:
"Residents left without closing windows and shutters. Potted flowers stood
unattended on windowsills [...] Women even left their laundry drying on
the wash line. [...] The large plaza in the center of the city hall resembled
a giant Parisian flea market where furniture and household objects of
evacuated families sat like refugees themselves waiting for the next train
out of town."

39 Personal communication with the author at NYU in October 2004.

40 The Palestinian–Israeli conflict is an obvious instance of a historical context
fraught with violence and mistrust where performative encounters can be
extremely productive; several contemporary films, including Erez Tadmor
and Guy Nattiz's *Strangers* (2007), seek to open up new possibilities for
understanding by staging encounters between individuals from Israel and
Palestine in unanticipated settings, such as Berlin during the 2006 Football
World Cup finals.

41 As in Stéphane Mallarmé's "Salut," this oscillation demonstrates the productive ambiguity and simultaneity of which language is capable.

42 Derrida (2000, 5) also observes that the Foreigner "shakes up the threatening dogmatism of the paternal logos."

43 While Jane Hiddleston (2006, 154–55) sees Jean Anouihl's *Antigone* as the author's implicit intertextual reference, I contend that Djebar, on the contrary, makes every effort to call attention to multiple versions of Antigone. Djebar particularly favors the work of writers from outside metropolitan France.

44 After a century of silence, Djebar commemorates the victims of this episode: "Ces femmes, ces hommes, ces enfants pour lesquels les pleureuses n'ont pu officier (nulle face lacérée, nul hymne lancinant lentement dévidé), car les pleureuses se sont trouvées confondues dans le brasier... Une tribu entière!" ["Those women, men, and children for whom mourners were unable to officiate (no cut faces, no tormenting hymns slowly unfurled), since the mourners were among those in the flames... An entire tribe!"] (Djebar, 1985, 114).

45 Zimra (2004, 154). This admission is astonishing and cannot be taken at face value, considering that Djebar is exceptionally well read, has a pronounced interest in theory, and reflects at length on writing and voice throughout *Ces voix qui m'assiègent*. In this same text, Djebar (1999, 171) even quotes a lecture Derrida gave in Lisbon: "l'on n'invente que l'impossible."

46 The Civil War broke out shortly after the victory of the populist Islamist party (the FIS, or Islamic Salvation Front) in the first round of Algerian national elections in 1991. The FLN (National Liberation Front), which has dominated Algerian politics since independence, refused to relinquish power, declared a state of emergency, and canceled the second round of the elections, claiming that the platform of their rivals threatened democracy itself. Islamist militias and the national army then found themselves locked in a drawn-out struggle for power in which thousands of civilian non-combatants lost their lives.

47 This is a particularly powerful observation in the Algerian context, because proponents of French Algeria fought bitterly to keep the colony as they had sworn never to abandon the graves of their ancestors.

48 Many Algerians still lack information regarding the fate of loved ones who disappeared in the Civil War, but the government of President Abdelaziz Bouteflika passed amnesty legislation in 2006 that made it illegal for families even to pose the question. Women who previously had staged sit-ins to focus public attention on the disappeared, a strategy also deployed in Argentina's Plaza de Mayo, were forbidden by law to do so.

Critics accused the Algerian state of abdicating its responsibility to citizens and of closing down public debate.

49 October 17, 1961 is the subject of Michael Haneke's film *Caché* (2006), a psychological thriller which highlights how repressed memories of the massacres come back to haunt not only those responsible for the violence, but their children as well.

50 Cited in Dominic Thomas (2010, 198–99).

51 Calling itself a "theatre without walls," the Théâtre du Grabuge has made a practice of bringing theatre into unconventional public spaces. A recent production, for instance, situated the *Odyssey* in the Lyon TGV station, incorporating passers-by into the performance. *Le cri d'Antigone* was featured on the fringe at Avignon in 2009.

Chapter 3: Glenn Gould and the Birth of the Author: Variation and Performance in Nancy Huston's *Goldberg Variations*

1 *Les variations Goldberg* won the (appropriately named) Prix Contrepoint and was shortlisted for the Prix Femina. Huston's English translation of the novel appeared in 1996 as *The Goldberg Variations*, and earned the Governor General's Award for Translation.

2 Huston (2003, 65) recalls Barthes' insistence that "form and content [be] as inseparable as oil and vinegar in a good salad dressing."

3 In an insightful study, Ioanna Chatzidimitriou (2009, 24) describes the linguistic disruption at work within translingual narratives in terms that are particularly resonant for Huston's work: "the ever more silent, disappearing mother tongue and the deafening, overly self-reflexive presence of the foreign language."

4 Barthes lost his life in 1980 at the age of sixty-five due to injuries sustained in a road accident. According to Huston, his death coincided with her birth as a writer (Shread, 2009, 57).

5 Huston dedicates *Les variations Goldberg* to Barthes, "à celui qui est mort comme un enfant." ["To someone who died like a child."] In an autobiographical essay many years later, "The Mask and the Pen," Huston (2003, 65–66) recalls Barthes's inability to write fiction: "Barthes himself had fantasies of writing a novel but was brought up short by the first obstacle he encountered—namely, the difficulty of inventing proper names for his characters and then *believing* in them. [...] Like the proverbial centipede who can't figure out which leg to start with, Barthes was so paralyzed by his own need to understand how novels worked; therefore he had no choice but to renounce novel writing. [...] Not by chance did I make the leap at least in 1980—daring to embark upon fiction-writing at last, just a few months after the death of Roland Barthes." Ironically, Huston makes

Liliane a harpsichordist, notwithstanding the fact that Barthes openly proclaimed his distaste for the harpsichord in *Roland Barthes by Roland Barthes* (Noudelmann, 2012, 126). It was her instrument after all; she took up the harpsichord at the same time as she started learning French as a high school student in New Hampshire. In *Nord perdu*, Huston connects the piano to English and to the mother, and sees it as a vehicle for emotionalism, exaggerated dynamics, and manipulation; by contrast, she associates the harpsichord with neutrality, intellectualism, and the French language (Arroyas 2008, 93–105).

6 Huston was awarded the Governor General's Award for a French-language novel in 1993 for *Cantique des plaines*, although some argued that the novel should not qualify for the award since the author first published it in English as *Plainsong*, and later translated it herself into French. *Infrarouge/Infrared* (2010) won the less coveted *Literary Review*'s Bad Sex prize in 2012.

7 Huston is married to Franco-Bulgarian critic Tzvetan Todorov.

8 My aim here is to demonstrate how these aspects of Huston's work are inseparable.

9 See in particular Kaiama L. Glover (2010, 99–110). Huston has called herself a "faux bilingue" (a false bilingual) in *Nord perdu*. Reda Bensmaïa and Rey Chow (2005, 249–52) take Huston's comments on bilingualism as an "invitation to reflect on the connotations of bilingualism as a cultural condition."

10 Interestingly, Huston accords French this neutral quality in opposition to English, which she affiliates with the mother, emotion, and excess. If Assia Djebar similarly refers to French as a stepmother tongue, she does not accord it the same neutrality—French supplanted the Berber and colloquial Arabic spoken in her childhood home, even while it also gave her the freedom to express herself, access to higher education, and the ability to move about in society, unlike many other of her peers who remained cloistered at home.

11 Huston quotes Georges Sand in a collection of essays on contemporary literature, *Professeurs du désespoir* (2005): "L'homme est bon et mauvais. Mais il est quelque chose encore: la nuance, la nuance qui est pour moi le but de l'art." Huston, like Djebar, is interested in the nuances in human experience that connect people across national or historical divides. Among the questions her work explores are affiliation (how one inherits or elects an affiliation), the difference between genius and bricolage, and what writing or music can do in the face of violence and trauma.

12 Like many of her leading characters, Huston herself is an accomplished musician.

13 Huston recognizes the influence of Alain Robbe-Grillet and Sarraute on

her writing, and notes her special affinity for Marguerite Duras, Romain Gary, and Samuel Beckett.

14 Wolf considers music in *The Goldberg Variations* alongside film in David Lodge's *Changing Places* and painting in Thomas Hardy's *Under the Greenwood Tree*.

15 Thomas Forrest Kelly (2011, 2–4) corroborates this connection between the early music movement and social protests: "The protest movements of the 1960s and 1970s—civil rights, antiwar, and the like—produced what many called a 'counterculture' resisting all that was passed down as traditional and elitist. To the extent that early music was seen as traditional and participatory, it could be seen as part of a cultural trend toward music of the people, music without pretense, music that expresses a general union of popular and learned. It cannot be sheer coincidence that the [movement] arose at the same time as a number of other populist movements: the folk-music revival, for example, propelled by Pete Seeger, Alan Lomax, and others." Kelly speculates that early music performances appealed to audiences through their claim to offer spontaneous creativity in the moment; such performances drew on scholarship (not received ideas) and involved improvisation: "A substantial part of the activity of the modern early-music movement is an effort to evoke that excitement, the one-time, you-were-there effect of music being made *now*. [...] The impetus for its existence is grounded in the idea of spontaneity, of excitement, of recapturing experiences otherwise lost to us."

16 Theodore Ziolkowski (2010) considers four contemporary literary renditions of the Goldberg Variations, including Huston's, and speculates that the resurgence of interest in Bach's work comes from a postmodern nostalgia for order and a widespread fascination with Glenn Gould. The three other novels he examines are Thomas Bernhard's *Der Untergeher* [1983, *The Loser*], Richard Powers' *The Gold Bug Variations* (1991), and Gabriel Josipovici's *Goldberg: Variations* (2002). Unfortunately, his readings are primarily plot-based and he glosses over Huston's novel very quickly. In his view, "despite the virtuoso formal display and the shrewd insights into thirty different personalities, the work never succeeds in making clear any connection, other than the structural one, between Bach's Variations and the performance [it] depict[s]." It is a pity that Ziolkowski brings up Gould right at the very end of the essay, as it prevents him from developing what is otherwise an important insight.

17 While I do not wish to impose a psychological reading on Huston's work, it seems plausible that her fascination with Gould's sudden rejection of performance may stem from her own efforts to understand her mother's abrupt departure.

18 *Pérégrinations Goldberg* was released under the record label Naïve in 2000.

19 One character compares Liliane's halting way of speaking to the chords of Frescobaldi's music: "Elle pronounce plutôt une phrase, elle la laisse résonner comme l'accord de Frescobaldi, elle attend pour voir si l'arpège de quelqu'un d'autre ne viendra pas s'y intriguer, puis elle essaie une autre phrase" (Huston, 1981, 46). ["She pronounces a sentence, lets it resonate like a chord of Frescobaldi, waits to see if someone else's arpeggio will join in, then tries another sentence."]

20 *Pérégrinations Goldberg* consists of thirteen tracts. The first and last tracts feature Huston reading the first and last sections of the novel with the aria of the Goldberg Variations played on harpsichord in the background. The eleven intervening variations represent original compositions (with the exception of Frescobaldi's *Canzona Terza*) for harpsichord, percussion, serpent, and voice. They include: "Joual"; "L'Araignée" (Spider); "Mesure" (Measure); "Vert" (Green); "Figer" (Freeze); "Roche" (Rock); "L'Aile de la mort" (Death's Wing); "Tumeur" (Tumor); "Faux" (Out of Tune); and "Variation sur variation" (Variation on a Variation).

21 In Huston's recording, the counterpoint is primarily between the voice and the instrument, and between the text and the music; each variation unfolds in sequence, unlike Gould's vertical layering of voices. Gould's experiments in contrapuntal radio reflect his interest in Renaissance and Baroque composers whom he identified as "the first people who recognized that it was possible and feasible and realistic to expect the human mind and the human ear to be aware of many simultaneous relationships, to follow their diverse courses and to be involved in all of them" (Kostelanetz, 1988, 567).

22 The contrast between formal constraint and creative freedom figures at the very opening of the text in the two contradictory epigraphs: "Vous avez exactement quatre-vingt-seize minutes" ["You have exactly ninety-six minutes"] and "Vous avez tout votre temps" ["You have all your time"] (Huston, 1981: 10–11).

23 Mary Coldwell recalls that while the 1970s saw a prevalence of recordings labeled "authentic performance" on "original instruments," scholars in the 1980s (Taruskin, Dreyfus, and others) challenged the notion of "authenticity" on the grounds that it was "impossible to create a truly historically authentic Baroque performance 300 years after the fact, because among other things, contemporary audiences, venues, values, and contexts are so different. Also, in some cases the desire to create historically authentic replicas (a 20th-century 'modernist' idea) had led to rather boring, inexpressive performances—the opposite of 'authentic' performances in

the sense of performances that were truly imagined, created and owned by the performers." http://earlymusic.org/what-early-music.

24 In the sense that the concert brings together people Liliane loves or has loved, it recalls a scene from Proust's *Le Temps retrouvé*, in which many of the characters are reunited in the drawing room of the Princesse de Guermantes.

25 One of the speakers explicitly evokes Brecht in relation to the cinema, the theater, and music, to argue that desire and taste are not personal, but "fabriqués par l'appareil idéologique mis en place par le pouvoir" ["fabricated by the ideological apparatus established by power"] (Huston, 1981, 226).

26 Liliane reflects, "je ne dois penser qu'à mes doigts, et même à eux je ne dois pas vraiment penser. Sinon je sais qu'ils deviendront des bouts de chair, des boudins blancs, petits porcs frétillants, et je risquerai de m'interrompre horrifiée de les voir se rouler sur les morceaux d'ivoire" (Huston, 1982, 13). ["I should just think of my fingers, and still, I should not really think of them. If I do, I know they'll turn into bits of flesh, white sausages, wiggling little pigs, and I might interrupt myself, horrified at seeing them roll around on the ivory keys."] Gould made a similar observation in 1981: "Part of the secret in playing the piano is to separate yourself from the instrument in every possible way [...] I have to find a way of standing outside myself while at the same time being totally committed to what I'm doing" (Bazzana, 2004, 428).

27 A variant of this dream reappears in *Instruments of Darkness* where the writer Nadia has a nightmare that she is packing suitcases and playing the violin (her mother's instrument), but the notes disintegrate and fray, until only a single note remains. Nadia recalls that Schumann's madness at the end of his life consisted in hearing a single note in his head, a persistent, repeated "la" (A) that she interprets as a form of recovered innocence. Considering the wordplay Huston creates in *Les Variations Goldberg* between the note "mi" and me (the self), the "la" could well have something to do with the feminine and with questions of gender, signaling the way classical music has (until recently) marginalized women performers and composers. Liliane's inability to focus her thoughts on her performance recalls a passage in Barthes's autobiography, *Roland Barthes par Roland Barthes,* in which the author evokes his own struggle to keep his mind from wandering during a student performance of Aeschylus's *The Persians* at the Sorbonne. "I was fascinated by the temptation of thinking of something else; through the tiny holes of the mask, I could only see very high up and far way. As I delivered the dead king's speeches, my eyes came to rest on inert—free—objects and books, a window, a

cornice, a piece of the sky: they at least weren't afraid. I excoriated myself for getting caught in this uncomfortable trap—while my voice continued its smooth delivery, resisting the *expressions* I should have given it" (Barthes, 1977, 33). His voice continues to produce the text as required, while his thoughts are elsewhere, truant, detached. For Timothy Scheie, this scene reveals something essential about performance: a "reluctant subject constrained to 'be' in a particular way; a desiring body palpable beneath an ideological mask; language and voice severed from their expressive function; and finally, a utopian dream of liberation from this predicament forever deferred by the inability—or unwillingness—to remove the imposed mask of meaning and subjectivity." Scheie goes on to ask: "When is performance a liberating gesture and when is it a 'trap'?" (Scheie, 2006, 21–22).

28 An amateur pianist himself, Barthes extolled the virtues of amateur playing because its objective is pleasure rather than technical perfection (Noudelmann, 2012, 106–7).

29 The passage makes some very simplistic and problematic assumptions about translation; if Liliane had compared the translation of spoken-word poetry to music, form and timing would be absolutely critical, just as they are in rendering a piece of music. An interesting element of this comparison is that while both the performer and interpreter may be vehicles of another's meaning, the interpreter is effaced in the act, while the performer of a piece of music receives particular attention.

30 See Sisman's extensive discussion of the history and aesthetic problems of variation form in the *Grove Music Online*. She highlights a number of critical issues that come into play when analyzing any set of variations: What logic, if any, motivates the number and order of variations? How does the set of variations come to an end? Does the theme return, and if so, what kind of closure (artificial or revelatory) does this achieve? Elsewhere, Sisman observes that music critics tend to treat variations as "interpretations or criticisms of a theme," as Edward Cone does in writing on Schubert (Sisman, 1993, 36).

31 As is the case with much of Said's writing on music, critics have been quick to point out the flaws in his understanding of the Goldberg Variations: for instance, although she praises Said's efforts to consider music in relation to Vico's notion of history, Sisman (1993, 6) argues that one can hardly qualify the Goldberg Variations as "aberrant" as they adhere to a highly determined, mathematical logic.

32 Rosen's program notes to Jerome Robbins's 1971 version of the *Goldberg Variations* at the New York City Ballet.

33 In a sense, the novel—like other literary or artistic adaptations of musical

works—offers a highly creative response to Said and Daniel Baremboim's (2002, 156) question, "How does one give music a kind of resonance beyond itself? How does one give it a kind of extension?"

34 Even so, some musicologists contend that listeners experience the return of the aria in an entirely different way from the opening of the piece, because the listener's understanding of that aria has been expanded and transformed over the course of the variations.

35 Much as Barbara Johnson (1979) showed Baudelaire to do in his prose poems.

36 See John Caldwell's entry on "Invention" for *Grove Music Online*. Caldwell argues that the word invention has "affinities with 'ricercare', with its connotation of 'seeking out' or 'finding.'" He also notes that Bach used the word "invention" in the preface to the Clavier-Büchlein vor W. F. Bach (1720) to denote "original ideas."

37 These dimensions come together in the persona of Liliane, whose identity and self-expression as a woman is as much under critique as her musicianship. Liliane's controlled performance is explicitly contrasted to the highly sexualized, extroverted musical production of male performers who wield their instrument like a phallus that ejaculates on the public (Huston, 1981, 143–45). Feminine performance is at stake throughout the text, perhaps most remarkably in Variation XX: "Je plaque sur mon visage une expression quelconque en espérant que cet arrangement de ma physionomie correspondra à l'idée qu'ils se font d'une jeune fille 'animée' ou 'curieuse' ou 'intelligente'; j'essaie de me voir à travers leurs yeux. Mais ensuite, je m'affole à l'idée qu'ils vont réellement me juger là-dessus: toute cette comédie aboutira fatalement à un *avis* sur ma personne, alors qu'elle n'a rien à voir avec ce que je suis au fond" (162). ["I put any old expression on my face, hoping that this arrangement of my physiognomy will correspond to their idea of a 'vivacious,' 'curious,' or 'intelligent' young woman; I try to see myself through their eyes. But then, I panic that they will really judge me by it: this whole comedy will fatally lead to an assessment of me, even though it will have nothing to do with who I really am at heart."]

38 The Bibliothèque National de France in Paris houses one of the nineteen original manuscript copies of Bach's Goldberg Variations, including corrections and additions made by the composer.

39 Wolf (2002b, 21) calls attention to the "affinities between music, the 'song of the body', and a transgressive, anti-patriarchal écriture féminine, which disregards linear, rational discourse as described by Hélène Cixous with reference to musical terms." He argues that a "possible parallel in musicalized fiction between the feminine as the Other of the masculine

and music as literature's Other is indeed an intriguing perspective. It has not yet received its due attention, and I would at least like to point it out here as deserving further investigation although the majority of experiments with musicalization seems so far to have been written by men without consciously attempting an écriture féminine." Note that this movement from the masculine *roman* to the feminine *romance* is replicated in Variation XV; Bernald insists on contrasting music and meaning: he describes music as "roche" (a feminine term for rock that evokes a certain porosity) and meaning as "roc" (a masculine term that signifies hardness, solidity) (Huston, 1981, 127–28).

40   Biber's patron, the Archbishop Max Gandolf von Khuenberg, was a member of an Austrian society devoted to the veneration of Mary. The sonata uses *scordatura* in such a way that the strings of the violin cross; the high and low registers exchange their conventional positions. Arroyas (2008, 110–11) argues that Huston deliberately uses the sonata and its association with the Virgin Mary "to criticize and subvert Christian orthodoxy," "in opposition to the relegation of women to the role of procreation, [...] as paving a way for women to gain access to the spiritual and divine orders, to be creators and not only procreators."

41   "Le roman est d'une linéarité enrageante" (Huston, 1996b, 50–51). ["Novels are maddeningly linear!"]

42   According to Lévi-Strauss, musical performance holds the same social power as myth, since both music and myth are "instruments for the obliteration of time" (Dunsby, *Grove Music Online*).

43   Cameron Fae Bushnell (2009) offers an insightful analysis of tuning and difference in Vikram Seth's *An Unequal Music* and Daniel Mason's *The Piano Tuner* in "The Art of Tuning: A Politics of Exile."

44   Huston comments, "J'ai composé l'histoire alternée de deux femmes dans *Instruments des ténèbres*, en passant de l'anglais au français, chapitre après chapitre. Tous les jours, je me repassais d'une langue sur l'autre et y puisais un regain d'énergie" ["I wrote the alternating stories of two women in *Instruments of Darkness*, passing from English to French chapter after chapter. Every day, I'd switch from one language to the other, tapping into a new burst of energy"] (Gazier, Laval and Bouchez, 1997, 4). As critics have observed, even if the writer forced herself to respect the norms in each language, the French version contains anglicisms, like adjectives before the verb. It is impossible to label either version an original, due to the fact that Huston produced both texts simultaneously, side by side.

45   The narrative construction, focus on trauma, and historical concerns of the novel recall Nicole Krauss's fiction, particularly *Great House* (2011). In her insightful reading of *Fault Lines*, Katherine Kolb (2010) is particularly

attuned to the layers of meaning in Huston's title in both the French and English versions.

Chapter 4: Opera and the Limits of Representation in J. M. Coetzee's *Disgrace*

1   I come to this conclusion after having taught the novel several times to undergraduate and graduate students at the University of Massachusetts Amherst. Students invariably feel repulsed by Lurie's attitudes.

2   See Kerry Bystrom (2007) for a critique of the use of rape to imagine the genealogy of the new South Africa.

3   Lurie's effort to access other perspectives is seen in passages such as: "He can, if he concentrates, if he loses himself, be there, be the men, inhabit them, fill them with the ghost of himself. The question is, does he have it in him to be the woman?" (Coetzee, 1999, 160); and "Or do they think that, where rape is concerned, no man can be where the woman is?" Lucy repeatedly tells Lurie, "You weren't there. You don't know what happened" (140).

4   Condé's *Histoire de la femme cannibale* (2003) reworks several elements of Coetzee's novel, notably the academic setting, the disgraced professor, prostitution, and old age.

5   Byron's life and work inspired several nineteenth- and twentieth-century operas, including Giusseppe Verdi's *I Due Foscari* (1844) based on Byron's play, *The Two Foscari* (1821) (Johnson, 2005, 541), and Virgil Thomson's *Lord Byron* (1968), a three-act opera about Byron himself. The Ford Foundation at the Metropolitan Opera commissioned the opera, although the Met never produced it. It was finally premiered by the Julliard Opera (1972) with Gerhard Samuel as music director and Alvin Ailey as choreographer.

6   Note Coetzee's striking repetition of the word "passionate"; I come back to the question of passion later in my analysis of language and the lyrical.

7   Through this question of whether or not it would be appropriate to write an operatic role for the stray dog, Coetzee interrogates the boundaries of opera. Ironically, stray dogs have made an appearance in two recent operatic productions. First, in Russian composer Alexander Raskatov's *A Dog's Heart,* an operatic adaptation of Mikhail Bulgakov's satirical novel *Heart of a Dog* (1925) about a medical professor who implants a human pituitary gland into a stray dog, upon which the dog becomes human. Raskatov thus does exactly what Lurie contemplates: he writes the stray dog into opera, but the dog no longer remains a dog (although ultimately, a reverse operation returns him to his initial state at the end of the opera). The work premiered at the Netherlands Opera on June 7, 2010, and went on to La Scala and other venues. The second instance, *Laika, the Spacedog,* is a 2013 production of The English Touring Opera. A "science opera"

directed at young audiences, it recounts the story of Laika, the stray dog discovered in Gorky park in Moscow in 1957 who was sent into space as the first animal in orbit, becoming the most famous animal victim of the space race. Russell Hepplewhite composed the musical score to a libretto by Tim Yealland.

8   Lucy Valerie Graham (2003, 444) argues that the text omits the scene of violence against women: "Since the stories of Melanie and Lucy are elided in *Disgrace*, the responsibility for such an imagining is left with the reader. To consign rape to a space outside articulation may contribute to a wider phenomenon of silencing." Linda Seidel (2001, 22) reinforces this same point: "Someone else will have to write the stories of Lucy and Petrus and Pollox."

9   Steve Jacob's 2008 film adaptation of *Disgrace* does the novel a disservice in that it uses Graeme Koehne's arias, "Three Byron Poems," to give audial presence to Lurie's compositions. Aesthetically, this decision is very successful, as the music is haltingly beautiful and evocative; it does, however, compromise what I see as the ethical and performative function of the opera: to open up a space within the text that remains unreadable, opaque, and "other."

10 Ultimately, Parry (1996, 63) concurs that Coetzee's writing is nonetheless "ethically saturated" and a virtuoso "self-interrogation of narrative production and authority" and yet "diverts and disperses the engagement with political conditions it also inscribes."

11 Interestingly, when asked why he performed so badly at the university harassment hearing, Lurie claims it was for the principle of "[f]reedom of speech. Freedom to remain silent" (Coetzee, 1999, 188).

12 For an insightful discussion of non-verbal sounds in the novel, see also Michael Holland (2002).

13 Lucy's silence on the subject of the rape hauntingly recalls Wordsworth's Lucy: "And hers the silence and the calm / Of mute insensate things" ("The Education of Nature," 17–18).

14 Bystrom addresses these issues with respect to the TRC and land distribution.

15 In *Age of Iron*, Mrs Curren entrusts Mr. Vercueil to mail a long letter (a sort of posthumous confession) to her daughter in America after her death. This manuscript constitutes the novel we read. The end of the novel, however, tests the limits of narratability. Mrs Curren narrates her own death, describing the final embrace she receives from Verceuil, who serves as her Angel of Death. Her account of death—whiteness closing in all around her—makes an impossible claim on our credibility and exposes the hand of another author. One cannot write one's own death, so who completed her

narrative? The text thus comes to us necessarily tampered with, mediated, completed.

16 The name Vercueil further underscores the importance of music in the novel. Vercueil suggests a hybrid of Vinteuil, the piano teacher/composer in Proust's *A côté de chez Swann*, and Vercors, the pseudonym under which Jean Bruller published the resistance novel, *Le silence de la mer* (1942), alluding thus to two novels that engage extensively with music. Through the Vinteuil sonata, Proust explores the capacity of music to isolate and prolong an instant in time. In *Le silence de la mer*, the German officer stationed in a French home is an amateur composer who dreams of countering Bach's "musique inhumane" with his own "musique de l'homme."

17 The language in this passage recalls Rousseauist and Enlightenment theories on how music speaks. Sound penetrates the subject and acts directly on the emotions, on the heart. Note the almost parodic repetition of "heart."

18 This lecture, originally given in Graz, Austria in 1991 and then published in *Current Writing* in 1993, is the opening piece of the collection, *Stranger Shores* (2001). In *Age of Iron*, the music of Bach again epitomizes the classic. Many of these preoccupations return in *Diary of a Bad Year* (2008).

19 Coetzee is ambivalent in his attitude to criticism. While fiction allows a writer to stage his passions, "criticism is always either a betrayal (the usual case) or an overpowering (the rarer case) of its object" (Coetzee, 1992, 60).

20 See Eric Prieto (2002) for an excellent discussion of "Samuel Beckett, Music, and the Heart of Things" and also the long entry on music in *The Grove Companion to Samuel Beckett: A Reader's Guide to His Works, Life and Thought* (New York: Grove Press, 2004). Beckett's radio play, *Words and Music* (1961), explores the themes of love, aging, artistic creation, and the relation between music and language that also motivate *Disgrace*.

21 Another parallel between the two novels is a preoccupation with castration.

22 As the narrator of the novel is situated in Australia, it is unclear who precisely the "we" of this statement represents. Is it the West? The question is particularly nagging in that it opposes the vague, transnational "we, our people" whom the narrator holds responsible for Guantanamo, to a grounded, national subjectivity, the Finns.

23 Lurie is conscious of this, as he observes, "It is not the erotic that is calling to him after all, nor the elegiac, but the comic" (Coetzee, 1999, 184).

24 "The girl he has brought home is not just thirty years his junior: she is a student, his student, under his tutelage" (Coetzee, 1999, 12). Of course, Lurie is not just a middle-aged professor sleeping with a young

student, but a white man with a colored woman just years after the fall of the apartheid regime in South Africa. Incongruous couplings pervade Coetzee's fictions—Mrs Curren and Mr Verceuil in *Age of Iron*, Leda and the swan in *Elizabeth Costello*. Critics have read into these mismatched pairs Coetzee's desire to forge ties across radical differences, by locking two unlikely individuals into a reciprocal exchange. Attwell (1992, 7) calls our attention in particular to Coetzee's interest in reciprocity.

25 "There must be other, more productive ways of giving oneself to the world, or to the idea of the world. One could for instance work longer hours at the clinic. [...] Even sitting down more purposefully with the Byron libretto might, at a pinch, be construed as a service to mankind. But there are other people to do these things—the animal welfare thing, the social rehabilitation thing, even the Byron thing" (Coetzee, 1999, 146).

26 Lurie's dedication to ideas distances him from his daughter, as an early dispute between the two illustrates. Rooted to the present and the earth, Lucy asserts: "[The dogs] aren't going to lead me to a higher life, and the reason is, there is no higher life. This is the only life there is. Which we share with animals. [...] That's the example I try to follow. To share some of our human privilege with the beasts" (Coetzee, 1999, 74). Lurie, by contrast, aspires to transcendence, and pursues it through art. As several critics have noted, if he renounces this goal at the end of the novel, it is only because, as a result of Lucy's rape and subsequent conception, he is about to become a grandfather and will thus survive biologically through Lucy's progeny.

27 "A father had been watching beside his child's sick-bed for days and nights on end. After the child had died, he went into the next room to lie down, but left the door open so that he could see from his bedroom the room in which his child's body was laid out, with tall candles standing round it. An old man had been engaged to keep watch over it, and sat beside the body murmuring prayers. After a few hours' sleep, the father had a dream that *his child was standing beside his bed, caught him by the arm and whispered to him reproachfully: 'Father, don't you see I'm burning?'* He woke up, noticed a bright glare of light from the next room, hurried into it and found that the old watchman had dropped off to sleep and that the wrappings and one of the arms of his beloved child's dead body had been burned by a lighted candle that had fallen on them" (qtd in Caruth, 1996, 93).

28 "So faint, so faltering is the voice of Byron that Teresa has to sing his words back to him, helping him along breath by breath, drawing him back to life. That is how it must be from here on: Teresa giving voice to her lover, and he, the man in the ransacked house, giving voice to Teresa" (Coetzee, 1999, 183). The Orphic quality of this passage is unmistakable: "With the aid of

the banjo he begins to notate the music that Teresa, now mournful, now angry, will sing to her dead lover, and that pale-voiced Byron will sing back to her from the land of the shades" (186).

29 On this subject, see Abbate (1991), Smart (2000), and Clément (1988). Clément exposes opera's obsessive need to kill off the soprano heroine, in order to tame the ungovernable power of her voice.

30 My emphasis.

31 Need and passion overlap in this passage, subverting any clear-cut understanding of these two terms. The need to fill out the overlarge and rather empty human soul is like the need/desire that drives Lurie in his encounters with Melanie.

32 This portrayal of the degeneration of language recalls Wagner: "Science has laid bare to us the organism of language, but what she showed us was a dead organism, which only the poet's utmost can bring to life again, namely, by suturing the wounds with which the anatomist's scalpel has gashed the body of language and by breathing into it the breath that may animate it with living motion. This breath, however, is—music" (Lacoue-Labarthe, 1994, 119).

33 Zoë Wicomb (2002) argues that the English poets' vision of the landscape is an unnecessary filter, disrupting the spontaneous and immediate sensual relationship between people and their own country.

34 Graham Pechey (2002, 380) comments on this as well: "Words as song, he believes, are words in their ur-state, protected from all merely instrumentalizing uses."

35 Kofi Agawu (2001, 9) argues, "To the extent that speech rhythm and speech tone serve as defining characteristics of natural language, we might think of African languages as forms of music."

36 Rousseau gives a full account of his beginnings in music in the *Confessions*.

37 Abbate and Parker (2012, 7) address the issue of creative license, commenting on the current tendency to turn operatic performance into an activity "policed by a reverence for the work as a well nigh sacred object—a reverence in almost all cases not present at the time it was created."

38 Note the reference here to Broch's *Sleepwalkers* discussed in Chapter One.

39 My translation.

Conclusion

1 "When with a happy heart I hum a tune, it isn't always a Congolese rhumba. Am I a traitor? I express a substantial part of myself when I whistle a blues melody, a Jazz tune, a waltz, phrases from a Beethoven symphony, from a Verdi opera or the *Song of the Volga Boatmen*. Beyond the Congo, I feel African." My translation.

2 The contrapuntal approach developed here in relation to historical conflict in *Les Nuits de Strasbourg* provides a lens for considering many other contemporary novels that engage competing memories, including Amitav Ghosh's *In an Antique Land*, Alexander Hermon's *The Lazarus Project*, Nancy Huston's *Fault Lines*, or Boris Boubakar Diop's harrowing *Murambi or the Book of Bones*.

3 Carpentier (1988, 3). The score of Vivaldi's opera was long considered lost, but it was finally recovered in the Ukraine in 2002.

4 Carpentier develops these ideas more fully in his theoretical writing on "Barroquismo" where he argues that the "recurrent interaction (crossover) gives rise to continually new sources of identity as each expression becomes interwoven with others resulting in ever-shifing boundaries and borders" (Bromberg, 2008, 8).

Works Cited

Abani, Chris. 2004. *GraceLand*. New York: Farrar, Straus, and Giroux.

Abbate, Carolyn. 1991. *Unsung Voices: Opera and Musical Narrative in the Nineteenth Century*. Princeton: Princeton University Press.

—— and Roger Parker. 2012. *A History of Opera: The Last Four Hundred Years*. London, New York: Allen Lane (Penguin).

Adelson, Dorothy. 1942. "The Vinteuil Sonata." *Music and Letters*: 228–33.

Adichie, Chimamanda. 2003. *Purple Hibiscus*. Chapel Hill, NC: Algonquin Books.

Adler, Laure and Assia Djebar. 2006. "A voix nue." Five Interviews with Assia Djebar. *France Culture*, January 20–February 3.

Adorno, Theodor W. 1963, 1998. *Quasi una fantasia: Essays on Modern Music*. Trans. Rodney Livingstone. London: Verso.

——. 2002. *Essays on Music*. Selected and annotated by Richard Leppert. Trans. Susan Gillespie. Berkeley: University of California Press.

Agawu, Kofi. 1992. "Wrong Notes: Review of Edward Said's *Musical Elaborations*." *Transition* 55: 162–66.

——. 2001. "African Music as Text." *Research in African Literatures* 32.2: 8–16.

Al-Ghadeer, Moneera. 2008. "Conquest's Spectacle: Djebar's *L'amour, la fantasia* and Lacoue-Labarthe's *Musica ficta*." In "Anonymity" (special issue), *symplokē* 16.1/2: 241–71

Al-Nakib, Mai. 2005. "Assia Djebar's Musical Ekphrasis." *Comparative Literature Studies*, 42.4: 253–76.

Amrouche, Taos. 1947. *Jacinthe noire*. Paris: Charlot.

Anderson, Benedict. 1983. *Imagined Communities: Reflections on the Origin and Spread of Nationalism*. London: Verso.

Appiah, Kwame Anthony. 1991. "Is the Post in Postcolonial the Post in Postmodernism?" *Critical Inquiry* 17.2 (Winter): 336–57.

Apter, Emily. 2001. "Crossover Texts/Creole Tongues: A Conversation with Maryse Condé." *Public Culture* 13.1: 89–96.

Arac, Jonathan. 1998. "Criticism between Opposition and Counterpoint." In *"Edward W. Said"* (special issue), *boundary 2* 25.2 (Summer): 55–69.

Argand, Catherine. 2001. "Entretien: Nancy Huston." *L'Express*, March 1. http://www.lexpress.fr/culture/livre/nancy-huston_804287.html.   Accessed March 20, 2013.

Arroyas, Frédérique. 2007. *"Diabolus in musica*: La 'Sonate de la Résurrection' de Heinrich Biber, arme de détournement dans *Instruments des ténèbres* de Nancy Huston." *L'Esprit Créateur* 47.2: 88–100.

——. 2008. "Literary mediations of Baroque music: Biber, Bach, and Nancy Huston." In *Essays on Word/Music Adaptation and on Surveying the Field.* Ed. David Francis Urrows. Amsterdam: Rodopi: 93–105.

Ashcroft, Bill, Gareth Griffiths, and Helen Tiffin. 1989. *The Empire Writes Back: Theory and Practice in Post-Colonial Literatures*. London: Routledge.

Ashcroft, Bill. 2010. "Globalization, Transnation and Utopia." In *Locating Transnational Ideals*. Ed. Walter Goebel and Saskia Schabio. New York: Routledge.

Attridge, Derek. 1994. "Literary Form and the Demands of Politics: Otherness in Coetzee's Age of Iron." In Aesthetics and Ideology, ed. George Levine: 243–65. New Jersey: Rutgers University Press.

——. 1996. "Oppressive Silence: *Foe* and the Politics of Canonization." In *Critical Perspectives on J. M. Coetzee*, ed. Graham Huggan and Stephen Watson: 168–90. New York: St Martin's Press.

——. 2004. *J. M. Coetzee and the Ethics of Reading: Literature in the Event*. Chicago: University of Chicago Press.

—— and Rosemary Jolly, eds. 1998. *Writing South Africa: Literature, Apartheid, and Democracy, 1970–1995.* Cambridge and New York: Cambridge University Press, 1998.

Attwell, David. 1992. "Introduction." In *Doubling the Point: Essays and Interviews*, by J. M. Coetzee: 1–14. Cambridge: Harvard University Press.

——. 1993. *J. M. Coetzee: South Africa and the Politics of Writing*. Berkeley: University of California Press.

—— and Barbara Harlow, eds. 2001. *"South African Fiction after Apartheid"* (special issue), *Modern Fiction Studies* 46.1.

Aub-Buscher, Gertrude and Beverley Ormerod Noakes, eds. 2003. *The Francophone Caribbean Today*. Barbados: University of West Indies Press.

Bakhtin, Mikhail. 1973. *Problems of Dostoevsky's Poetics*. Trans. Caryl Emerson. Ann Arbor: Ardis.

——. 1981. *The Dialogic Imagination: Four Essays*. Trans. Gary Saul Morson and Caryl Emerson. Austin: University of Texas Press.

Banfield, Ann. 1991. "L'Ecriture et le Non-dit." *Diacritics* 21.4 (Winter): 20–31.

Barbé, Philippe. 2001. "Transnational and Translinguistic Relocation of the Subject in *Les Nuits de Strasbourg* by Assia Djebar." *L'Esprit créateur* 41.3 (Fall): 125–35.

Barca, Antonio Jiménez. 2009. "Entrevista con Nancy Huston: La inteligencia es catastrófica para la literatura." *El país*. (October 3). http://elpais.com/diario/2009/10/03/babelia/1254528747_850215.html Accessed March 26, 2014.

Barnard, Rita. 2003. "J. M. Coetzee's Disgrace and the South African Pastoral." *Contemporary Literature* 44.2 (Summer): 199–224.

Barthes, Roland. 1954. *Michelet par lui-même*, Paris: Editions du Seuil.

——. 1967. "The Death of the Author." Trans. Richard Howard. *Aspen* 5+6 (Fall/Winter).

——. 1977. *Roland Barthes by Roland Barthes*. Trans. Richard Howard. New York: Hill & Wang.

——. 1978. *Image Music Text*. Trans. Steven Heath. New York: Hill & Wang.

——. 1981. *Le grain de la voix: entretiens 1962–1980*. Paris: Editions du Seuil.

The Battle of Algiers. 1966. Gilo Pontecorvo. Criterion. DVD.

Bauchau, Henry. 1990. *Oedipus sur la route*. Arles: Actes Sud.

——. 1997. *Antigone*. Arles: Actes Sud.

——. 1999. *Journal d'Antigone 1989–1997*. Arles: Actes Sud.

Baudelaire, Charles. 1975. *Œuvres complètes*. Paris: Gallimard.

Bazzana, Kevin. 2010. *Wondrous Strange: The Life and Art of Glenn Gould*. Oxford and New York: Oxford University Press.

Becker, Florian, Paola S. Hernández, and Brenda Werth. 2013. *Imagining Human Rights in Twenty-First Century Theater: Global Perspectives*. Basingstoke, New York: Palgrave Macmillan.

Bédarida, Catherine. 1997. "John Coetzee dans son exil intérieur." *Le Monde*, October 10. http://www.lemonde.fr/cgi-bin/ACHATS/acheter.cgi?offre=ARCHIVES&type_item=ART_ARCH_30J&objet_id=287153. Accessed July 14, 2010.

Behdad, Ali and Dominic Thomas, eds. 2011. *A Companion to Comparative Literature*. Chichester: Wiley–Blackwell.

Benachour, Djamel. 2006. "Oran: Pièce théatrâle *Le cri d'Antigone: une tragédie ancestrale et actuelle.*" *El Watan*, April 13.

Benítez-Rojo, Antonio. 1992. *The Repeating Island: the Caribbean and the Post-modern Perspective*. Trans. James Maraniss. Durham: Duke University Press.

Bennoune, Mahfoud. 2002. *The Making of Contemporary Algeria*. Cambridge: Cambridge University Press.

Bensmaïa, Reda. 2003. *Experimental Nations*. Trans. Alyson Waters. Princeton: Princeton University Press.

—— and Rey Chow. 2005. "Editor's Introduction." In *"Between Languages"* (special issue), *Comparative Literature Studies* 42.4: 249–52.

Benson, Stephen. 2003. "For Want of a Better Term? Polyphony and the Value of Music in Bakhtin and Kundera." *Narrative* 11.3 (October): 292–311.

——. *Literary Music*. 2006. Aldershot: Ashgate.

Bernabé, Jean, Patrick Chamoiseau, and Raphaël Confiant. 1989. *Eloge de la créolité*. Paris: Gallimard, Presses universitaires créoles.

Bernhard, Thomas. 1983. *Der Untergeher*. Frankfurt am Main: Suhrkamp.

Bernstein, Michael. 1998. "Keeping the Conversation Going." *New Literary History* 29.4: 687–90.

Blanchot, Maurice. 1955. *L'espace littéraire*. Paris: Gallimard.

——. 2003 [1959]. *The Book to Come*. Trans. Charlotte Mandell. Stanford: Stanford University Press.

Bogue, Ronald. 1997. "Minor Writing and Minor Literature." *symploke* 5.1: 99–118.

Britton, Celia. 1999. *Edouard Glissant and Postcolonial Theory: Strategies of Language and Resistance*. Charlottesville: University of Virginia Press.

——. 2004. "Breaking the Rules: Irrelevance/Irreverence in Maryse Condé's *Traversée de la Mangrove*." *French Cultural Studies* 15: 35–47.

Broichhagen, Vera, Kathryn Lachman, and Nicole Simek. 2006. *Feasting on Words: Maryse Condé, Cannibalism, and the Caribbean Text*. Princeton: Program in Latin American Studies.

Bromberg, Shelley. "Which Way Did He Go? Identity, Culture, and Nation in Alejo Carpentier's *Concierto Barroco*." *Latin American Literary Review* 36.71 (January-June): 5–23.

Burke, Edmund. *A Philosophical Enquiry into the Origin of Our Ideas of the Sublime and the Beautiful*. Ed. J. T. Boulton. London: Routledge and New York: Columbia University Press.

Burton, Stacy. 2000. "Paradoxical Relations: Bakhtin and Modernism." *Modern Language Quarterly* 61.3: 519–43.

Bushnell, Cameron Fae. 2009. "The Art of Tuning: A Politics of Exile in Daniel Mason's *The Piano Tuner* and Vikram Seth's *An Equal Music*." *Contemporary Literature* 50. 2 (Summer): 332–62.

——. 2013. *Postcolonial Readings of Music in World Literature: Turning Empire on Its Ear*. New York: Routledge.

Butler, Judith. 2000. *Antigone's Claim*. New York: Columbia University Press.

Bystrom, Kerry. 2007. "Orphans and Origins: Family, Memory and Democracy in Argentina and South Africa." PhD Diss., Princeton University.

Caché. 2006. Michael Haneke. Sony Pictures. DVD.

Caldwell, John. "Invention." *Grove Music Online. Oxford Music Online*. Oxford University Press. http://www.oxfordmusiconline.com/subscriber/article/grove/music/13877. Accessed January 15, 2013.

Calle-Gruber, Mireille. 2001. *Assia Djebar, ou, la résistance de l'écriture: regards d'un écrivain d'Algérie*. Paris: Maisonneuve et Larose.

Carpentier, Alejo. 1974 [2011]. *Concierto barroco: novela*. Mexico: Siglo Veintiuno.

———. 1988. *Concierto Barroco*. Trans. Asa Zazt. Tulsa: Council Oak Books/ Hecate.

———. 1994. *Obras completas*. 17 vols. Ed. Felix Bacz-Jorge. Mexico: Siglo Veintiuno.

———. 1995 [1975] "The Baroque and the Marvelous Real." Trans. Tanya Huntington and Lois Parkinson Zamora. In *Magical Realism: Theory, History, Community,* ed. Lois Parkinson Zamora and Wendy Faris: 89–108. Durham: Duke University Press.

Caruth, Cathy. 1996. *The Unclaimed Experience: Trauma, Narrative and History*. Baltimore: Johns Hopkins University Press.

Cazenave, Odile and Patricia Célérier. 2011. *Contemporary Francophone African Writers and the Burden of Commitment*. Charlottesville: University of Virginia Press.

Césaire, Aimé. 1939. "Cahier d'un retour au pays natal." *Volontés* 20 (August 1939): 23–51.

———. 1972. *Discourse on Colonialism*. Trans. Joan Pinkham. New York: Monthly Review Press.

Chambers, Iain. 2001. *Culture After Humanism: History, Culture, Subjectivity*. London: Routledge.

Chamoiseau, Patrick. 1988. *Solibo magnifique*. Paris: Gallimard.

———. 1991. "Reflections on Maryse Condé's *Traversée de la mangrove*." Trans. Katherine Balutansky. *Callaloo* 14.2: 390.

Char, René. 1992. *Selected Poems by René Char*. Ed. Mary Ann Caws and Tina Jolas. New York: New Directions.

Chatzidimitriou, Ioanna. 2009. "Self-Translation as Minorization Process: Nancy Huston's *Limbes*/Limbo." *SubStance* 38.2(119): 22–42.

Clark, VèVè. 1989. "I Have Made Peace with My Island: An Interview with Maryse Condé." Trans. Cécile Daheny. *Callaloo* 12.1 (Winter): 87–133.

Clément, Catherine. 1988. *Opera and the Undoing of Women*. Minneapolis: University of Minnesota Press.

Clingman, Stephen. 2009. *The Grammar of Identity: Transnational Fiction and the Nature of the Boundary*. Oxford: Oxford University Press.

Coetzee, Jacques. 1998. "Unsettling the Score." In *Inter Action 6: Proceedings of the Fourth Postgraduate Conference,* ed. Hermann Wittenberg, Gabeba Baderoon, and Yolanda Steenkamp. Belleville: University of the Western Cape Press.

Coetzee, J. M. 1969. "The English Fiction of Samuel Beckett: An Essay in Stylistic Analysis." PhD diss., University of Texas at Austin.

———. 1980. *Waiting for the Barbarians*. London: Secker & Warburg.

——. 1983. *The Life and Times of Michael K.* New York: Viking Press.

——. 1987. *Foe.* New York: Viking.

——. 1990. *Age of Iron.* New York: Random House.

——. 1992. *Doubling the Point: Essays and Interviews.* Ed. David Attwell. Cambridge: Harvard University Press.

——. 1996. *Giving Offense: Essays on Censorship.* Chicago: University of Chicago Press.

——. 1999. *Disgrace.* London: Secker & Warburg.

——. 2001. *Stranger Shores: Literary Essays, 1986–1999.* New York: Viking.

——. 2003a. *Elizabeth Costello.* New York: Viking.

——. 2003b. "Fictional Beings." *Philosophy, Psychiatry, & Psychology* 10.2: 133–34.

——. 2005. *Slow Man.* New York: Viking Penguin.

——. 2008. *Diary of a Bad Year.* New York: Viking Penguin.

——. 2009. *Summertime: Scenes from Provincial Life.* London: Harvill Secker.

Cohen, Tom. 1996. "The Ideology of Dialogue: the Bakhtin/De Man (Dis) Connection." *Cultural Critique* 33 (Spring): 41–86.

Condé, Maryse. 1987. *La vie scélérate.* Paris: Editions Seghers.

——. 1988. *En attendant le bonheur (Heremakhonon).* Paris: Seghers. Reissue of *Heremakhonon* (Paris: Union générale d'éditions, 1976).

——. 1989a. *Traversée de la mangrove.* Paris: Mercure de France.

——. 1989b. "Habiter ce pays." *Chemins Critiques* 1.3 (December): 1–14.

——. 1993. "Order, Disorder, Freedom, and the West Indian Writer." *Yale French Studies* 83.2: 121–35.

——. 1995. *La migration des cœurs.* Paris: R. Laffont.

——. 1997. *Desirada.* Paris: Laffont.

——. 1999. *Le cœur à rire et à pleurer, contes vrais de mon enfance.* Paris: Laffont.

——. 2000. *Célanire cou-coupé: roman fantastique.* Paris: Laffont.

——. 2001. "La Francophonie dans tous ses Etats." Lecture given at the Graduate Center, CUNY, New York, March 9.

——. 2003. *Histoire de la femme cannibale.* Paris: Mercure de France.

——. 2006. *Victoire: les saveurs et les mots.* Paris: Mercure de France.

——. 2007. "Liaison dangereuse." In *Pour une littérature monde,* ed. Michel Le Bris and Jean Rouaud: 205–16. Paris: Gallimard.

——. 2010. *En attendant la montée des eaux.* Paris: Lattès.

——. 2012. *La vie sans fards.* Paris: Lattès.

Conley, Tom. 1993 [2006]. "Translator's Forward." *The Fold.* By Giles Deleuze. Trans. Tom Conley. Minneapolis: University of Minnesota Press.

Connor, Stephen. 2001. "The Decomposing Voice of Postmodern Music." *New Literary History* 32.3 (Spring): 467–83.

Cooper, Pamela. 2005. "Metamorphosis and Sexuality: Reading the Strange Passions of *Disgrace.*" *Research in African Literatures* 36.4: 22–39.

Cortázar, Julio. 1966. *Hopscotch*. New York: Pantheon Books.

——. 1980. *Queremos tanto a Glenda*. Mexico D. F.: Editorial Nueva Imagen.

——. 1983. *We Love Glenda So Much and Other Tales*. Trans. Gregory Rabassa. New York: Random House.

Crenshaw, Kimberlé. 1989. "Demarginalizing the Intersection of Race and Sex: A Black Feminist Critique of Antidiscrimination Doctrine, Feminist Theory and Antiracist Politics." *University of Chicago Legal Forum*: 139–67.

Crosta, Suzanne. 1992. "Narrative and Discursive Strategies in Maryse Condé's *Traversée de la mangrove*." *Callaloo* 15.1 (Winter): 147–55.

Dana, Catherine. 2004. "*Les enfants Antigone*." *French Forum* 29.1 (Winter): 113–25.

Dash, J. Michael. 1995. *Édouard Glissant* (Cambridge Studies in African and Caribbean Literature). Cambridge and New York: Cambridge University Press.

——. 1998. "The World and the Word: French Caribbean Writing in the 20th Century." *Callaloo* 34 (Winter): 112–30.

——. 2002. "The Madman at the Crossroads: Delirium and Dislocation in Caribbean Literature." *Profession* 2002: 37–43.

——. 2003. "Vital Signs in the Body Politic: Eroticism and Exile in Maryse Condé and Dany Laferrièrre." *Romantic Review* 94.3/4: 309–17.

Death for Five Voices: The Composer Carlo Gesualdo (1560–1613). 1995. Werner Herzog. Image Entertainment. DVD.

de Groot, Rokus. 2005. "Perspectives on Polyphony in Edward Said's Writings." *Alif* 25: 219–39.

Deleuze, Gilles. 1988. *Le pli: Leibniz et le baroque*. Paris: Editions de Minuit.

——. 1993. *Critique et clinique*. Paris: Editions de Minuit.

—— and Félix Guattari. 1975. *Kafka: pour une littérature mineure*. Paris: Editions de Minuit.

——. 1980. *Milles plateaux*. Paris: Editions de Minuit.

——. 1987. *A thousand plateaus: capitalism and schizophrenia*. Trans. Brian Massumi. Minneapolis: University of Minnesota Press.

Derrida, Jacques. 1967a. *L'écriture et la différence*. Paris: Éditions du Seuil.

——. 1967b. *De la grammatologie*. Paris: Minuit.

——. 1976. *Of Grammatology*. Trans. Gayatri Chakravorty Spivak. Baltimore: Johns Hopkins University Press.

——. 1985. *The Margins of Philosophy*. Trans. Alan Bass. Chicago: Chicago University Press.

——. 1996. *Le monolinguisme de l'autre, ou, La prothèse d'origine*. Paris: Galilée.

——. 1997. *De l'hospitalité*. Paris: Calmann-Lévy.

——. 2000. *Of Hospitality*. Trans. Rachel Bowlby. Stanford: Stanford University Press.

——. 2003. *Voyous: deux essais sur la raison*. Paris: Galilée.

Dib, Mohammed. 1994. *L'infante maure*. Paris: Albin Michel.

Diome, Fatou. 2003. *Le ventre de l'atlantique*. Paris: Anne Carrière.

Djebar, Assia. 1957. *La soif*. Paris: Julliard.

——. 1958. *Les impatients*. Paris: Julliard.

——. 1962. *Les enfants du nouveau monde*. Paris: Julliard.

——. 1967. *Les alouettes naïves*. Paris: Julliard.

——. c.1977 *La Nouba des femmes du Mont Chenoua*. Written and directed by Assia Djebar. NY: Women Make Movies.

——. 1980. *Femmes d'Alger dans leur appartement: nouvelles*. Paris: Des femmes.

——. 1985. *L'amour, la fantasia: roman*. Paris: J. C. Lattès.

——. 1987. *Ombre sultane*. Paris: J. C. Lattès.

——. 1991. *Loin de Médine*. Paris: Albin Michel.

——. 1995a. *Vaste est la prison*. Paris: Albin Michel.

——. 1995b. *Le blanc de l'Algérie*. Paris: Albin Michel.

——. 1997a. *Les nuits de Strasbourg*. Arles: Actes Sud.

——. 1997b. *Oran, langue morte*. Arles: Actes Sud.

——. 1997c. *L'écrivain francophone à la croisée des langues: entretiens*. Paris: Karthala.

——. 1999. *Ces voix qui m'assiègent: ...en marge de ma francophonie*. Paris: Albin Michel.

——. 2002. *La femme sans sépulture*. Paris: Albin Michel.

——. 2003. *La disparition de la langue française*. Paris: Albin Michel.

——. 2007. *Nulle part dans la maison de mon père*. Paris: Fayard.

Dobie, Madeleine. 2003. "Francophone Studies and the Linguistic Diversity of the Maghreb." *Comparative Studies of South Asia, Africa and the Middle East* 23.1/2: 32–40.

Docker, John. 2007. "The Question of Europe: Said and Derrida." In *Edward Said: The Legacy of a Public Intellectual*, ed. Ned Curthoys and Debjani Ganguly: 263–93. Melbourne: Melbourne University Press.

Donadey, Anne. 2001. *Recasting Post-colonialism: Women Writing Between Worlds*. Portsmouth, NH: Heinemann.

——. 2008. "African American and Francophone Postcolonial Memory: Octavia Butler's *Kindred* and Assia Djebar's *La femme sans sepulture*." *Research in African Literatures* 39.3 (Fall): 65–88.

d'Ors, Eugenio. 1935. *Du baroque*. Paris: Gallimard.

Dunsby, Jonathan. "Performance." *Grove Music Online. Oxford Music Online*. Oxford University Press. Accessed March 26, 2014.

Durrant, Sam. 2004. *Postcolonial Literature and the Work of Mourning: J. M. Coetzee, Wilson Harris, and Toni Morrison*. Albany: State University of New York Press.

Ebron, Paulla. 2002. *Performing Africa*. Princeton: Princeton University Press.

Eco, Umberto. 1989. *The Open Work*. Trans. Anna Cancogni. Cambridge, MA: Harvard University Press.

Emerson, Caryl. 1998. "Response to Thomas Pavel, 'Freedom, from Romance to the Novel: Three Anti-Utopian American Critics.'" *New Literary History* 29.4: 691–96.

———. 2002. "Milan Kundera on Not Liking Dostoevsky." Unpublished paper. American Association of Teachers of Slavic and East European Languages (AATSEEL) Annual Conference.

———. 2004. "On the Generation That Squandered Its Philosophers (Losev, Bakhtin, and Classical Thought as Equipment for Living)." *Studies in East European Thought* 56.2 (June): 95–117.

———. 2005. "In Search of the Dialogic Novel: *Anna Karenina* versus *The Brothers Karamazov*." Unpublished lecture given at the University of Pennsylvania conference, Dostoevsky Dismembered. April 15.

Erdinast-Vulcan, Daphna. 1997. "Borderlines and Contraband: Bakhtin and the Question of the Subject." *Poetics Today* 18.2 (Summer): 251–69.

Erlam, Rosemary. 1997. "Tentative de Communication dans *Traversée de la mangrove de Maryse Condé*." *New Zealand Journal of French Studies* 18.2: 29–38.

Ezra, Elizabeth and Terry Rowden, ed. 2006. *Transnational Cinema: the Film Reader*. London, New York: Routledge.

Fanon, Frantz. 1952. *Peau noire, masques blancs*. Paris: Éditions du Seuil.

———. 1959. "L'Algérie se dévoile." In *Sociologie d'une révolution: L'an V de la révolution algérienne*: 16–50. Paris: F. Maspero.

———. 1961. *Les damnés de la terre*. Paris: F. Maspero.

———. 1965. "Algeria Unveiled." In *A Dying Colonialism*: 35–63. Trans. Haakon Chevalier. New York: Grove Press.

Faulkner, Rita. 1996. "Assia Djebar, Frantz Fanon, Women, Veils, and Land." *World Literature Today* 70.4 (Autumn): 847–55.

Fish, Stanley. 2008. "Will the Humanities Save Us?" *New York Times*, January 6. http://opinionator.blogs.nytimes.com/2008/01/06/will-the-humanities-save-us/. Accessed July 14, 2010.

Foucault, Michel. 1977. *Language, Counter-Memory, Practice*. Trans. Donald F. Bouchard and Sherry Simon. Ithaca: Cornell University Press, 1977.

Fulton, Dawn. 2001. "Reading Death: Allegory in Maryse Condé's *Crossing the Mangrove*." *Callaloo* 24.1 (Winter): 301–9.

Gazier, Michèle, Martine Laval and Emmanuelle Bouchez. 1997. "Français dans le texte." *Télérama* (25 January). http://www.telerama.fr/livre/francais-dans-le-texte,69949.php. Accessed March 26, 2014.

Genette, Gérard. 1966. *Figures*. Paris: Editions du Seuil.

———. 1972. *Figures III*. Paris: Editions du Seuil.

Gikandi, Simon. 1992. *Writing in Limbo: Modernism and Caribbean Literature.* Ithaca: Cornell University Press.

——. 2001. "Globalization and the Claims of Postcoloniality." *The South Atlantic Quarterly* 100.3: 627–58.

Gilroy, Paul. 1993. *The Black Atlantic: Modernity and Double Consciousness.* Cambridge, MA: Harvard University Press.

Glenn Gould: the Goldberg Variations. 1981. Bruno Monsaigneon. Sony Classics. DVD.

Glissant, Edouard. 1969. *L'intention poétique.* Paris: Seuil.

——. 1981. *Le discours antillais.* Paris: Seuil.

——. 1987. *Mahagony.* Paris: Seuil.

——. 1990. *Poétique de la relation.* Paris: Gallimard.

——. 1996. *Introduction à une poétique du divers.* Paris: Gallimard.

Glover, Kaiama L. 2010. "The Ambivalent Transnationalism of a Literature-World— in French." *Small Axe* 14.3 (33, 2010): 99–110.

Goebel, Walter and Saskia Schabio, ed. 2010. *Locating Transnational Ideals.* New York: Routledge.

Goldmark, Daniel, Lawrence Kramer, and Richard Leppert, eds. 2007. *Beyond the Soundtrack: Representing Music in Cinema.* Berkeley: University of California Press.

Gould, Glenn. 1966. "The Prospects of Recording." *High Fidelity Magazine* 16.4 (April): 46–63.

Gourgouris, Stathis. 2004. "Transformation, not Transcendence." *boundary 2* 31.2: 55–79.

Gracyk, Theodore and Andrew Kania, ed. 2011. *The Routledge Companion to Philosophy and Music.* Abingdon, Oxon; New York: Routledge.

Graham, Lucy Valerie. 2003. "Reading the Unspeakable: Rape in J. M. Coetzee's *Disgrace.*" *Journal of South African Studies* 29.2 (June): 433–44.

Green, Mary Jean, Karen Gould, Micheline Rice-Maximin, Keith L. Walker, and Jack A. Yaeger, eds. 1996. *Postcolonial Subjects: Francophone Women Writers.* Minneapolis: University of Minnesota Press.

Guène, Faïza and Bernard Richard. 2002. *Mémoires du 17 octobre.* Les Engraineurs. Documentary film. 17 min.

Hardy, Thomas. 1873. *Under the Greenwood Tree.* New York: Henry Holt.

Hargreaves, Alec and Mark McKinney, eds. 1997. *Post-Colonial Cultures in France.* London and New York: Routledge.

Hartman, Geoffrey H. 1994. "Is an Aesthetic Ethos Possible? Night Thoughts after Auschwitz." *Cardozo Studies in Law and Literature* 6: 135–39.

Heidegger, Martin. 1959. *An Introduction to Metaphysics.* Trans. Ralph Manheim. New Haven: Yale University Press.

Hewitt, Leah. 1995. "Condé's Critical Seesaw." *Callaloo* 18.3: 641–51.

Hiddleston, Jane. 2006. *Assia Djebar: Out of Algeria*. Liverpool: Liverpool University Press.

Hirschkop, Ken. 1989. "Introduction: Bakhtin and Cultural Theory." In *Bakhtin and Cultural Theory*. Ed. Ken Hirschkop and David Shepherd. Manchester: Manchester University Press.

———. 2001. "Bakhtin in the Sober Light of Day: and Introduction to the Second Edition." In *Bakhtin and Cultural Theory*. Ed. Ken Hirschkop and David Shepherd. Manchester: Manchester University Press.

——— and David Shepherd. 1989. [2001]. *Bakhtin and Cultural Theory*. Manchester: Manchester University Press.

Hitchcock, Peter. 2010. *The Long Space: Transnationalism and Postcolonial Form*. Stanford: Stanford University Press.

Holland, Catherine. 1998. "After Antigone: Women, the Past and the Future of Feminist Political Thought." *American Journal of Political Science* 42.4: 1108–32.

Holland, Michael. 2002. "'Plink-plunk': Unforgetting the Present in Coetzee's *Disgrace*." *Interventions* 4.3: 395–404.

Huggan, Graham and Stephen Watson, ed. 1996. *Critical perspectives on J. M. Coetzee*. New York: St Martin's Press.

Huggan, Graham. 2008. *Interdisciplinary Measures: Literature and the Future of Postcolonial Studies*. Liverpool: Liverpool University Press.

Huntington, Julie. 2009. *Sounding Off: Rhythm, Music, and Identity in West African and Caribbean Francophone Novels*. Philiadelphia: Temple University Press.

Huston, Nancy. 1981. *Les variations Goldberg: Romance*. Paris: Seuil.

———. 1986. *Lettres parisiennes: autopsie de l'exil*. With Leila Sebbar. Paris: Barrault.

———. 1993. *Plainsong*. Toronto: Harper.

———. 1996a. *The Goldberg Variations*. Montreal: Nuage Editions.

———. 1996b. *Instruments des ténèbres*. Arles: Actes Sud.

———. 1997. *Instruments of Darkness*. Boston and Toronto: Little, Brown and Co.

———. 1999a. *Prodige: Polyphonie*. Arles: Actes Sud.

———. 1999b. *Nord perdu suivi de Douze France*. Arles: Actes Sud.

———. 2000. *L'empreinte de l'ange*. Paris: Babel.

———. 2001. *Dolce agonia*. Arles: Actes Sud. 2001.

———. 2002. *Losing North: Musings on Land, Tongue and Self*. Toronto: McArthur and Co.

———. 2003. "The Mask and the Pen." In *Lives in Translation: Bilingual Writers on Identity and Creativity*, ed. Isabelle de Courtivron: 55–68. New York: Palgrave MacMillan.

———. 2005. *Professeurs du désespoir*. Arles: Actes Sud.

———. 2006. *Lignes de faille*. Arles: Actes Sud.

———. 2010. *Infrarouge*. Arles: Actes Sud.

Indigènes/Days of Glory. 2006 [2007]. Rachid Bouchareb. Tessalit. DVD.

Irele, Abiola F. 2008. "Homage to Aimé Césaire." *Small Axe* 12.3: 124–27.

Jakobson, Roman. 1966. "Quest for the Essence of Language." *Diogènes* 51: 21–37.

James, David. 2011. "Testing Transnationalism." *Contemporary Literature* 52.1 (Spring): 190–209.

Johnson, Barbara. 1979. *Défigurations du langage poétique: la seconde révolution baudelairienne.* Paris: Flammarion.

Johnson, James. 2005. "The Myth of Venice in Nineteenth-Century Opera." *Journal of Interdisciplinary History* 36.3: 533–54.

Josipovici, Gabriel. 2002. *Goldberg: Variations.* Manchester: Carcanet.

Judkins, Jennifer. 2011. "Silence, Sound, Noise, and Music." In *The Routledge Companion to Philosophy and Music.* Ed. Theodore Gracyk and Andrew Kania. Abingdon, Oxon; New York: Routledge.

Kadir, Djelal, ed. 1996. *"Assia Djebar"* (special issue), *World Literature Today* 70.4 (Autumn)

Kassabian, Anahid. 2001. *Hearing Film: Tracking Identifications in Contemporary Hollywood Film Music.* New York: Routledge.

Kateb, Yacine. 1981 (1956). *Nedjma.* Paris: Editions du Seuil.

Kaup, Monika. 2005. "Becoming Baroque: Folding European Forms into the New World Baroque with Alejo Carpentier." *The New Centennial Review* 5.2: 107–49.

Kelly, Thomas Forrest. 2011. *Early Music: A Very Short Introduction.* Oxford: Oxford University Press.

Kemedjio, Cilas. 2013. "Maryse Condé and West Indian Complexity: The Writing of Monstrosity, Postcolonial Comparativism, and Cannibalistic Intertexualities." Trans. Ruthmarie H. Mitsch. *Research in African Literatures* 44.3: 176–89.

Kern, Anne-Brigitte. 1994. "A voix nue." Five Interviews with Assia Djebar. *France Culture,* May 23–7.

Kolb, Katherine. 2010. "Fractures and Recastings in Nancy Huston's *Lignes de faille.*" *Contemporary French and Francophone Studies* 14.5: 525–32.

Kostelanetz, Richard. 1988. "Glenn Gould as a Radio Composer." *The Massachusetts Review* 29.3 (Fall): 557–70.

Kramer, Lawrence. 1989. "Dangerous Liaisons: The Literary Text in Musical Criticism." *19th-Century Music* 13.2 (Autumn): 159–67.

——. 1995. *Classical Music and Postmodern Knowledge.* Berkeley: University of California Press.

Krauss, Nicole. 2005. *The History of Love.* New York: Norton.

——. 2010. *Great House.* New York: Norton.

Kristeva, Julia. 1970. "Une poétique ruinée." Introduction to *La Poétique de*

Dostoièvski, by Mikhail Bakhtin, trans. Isabelle Kolitcheff: 5–27. Paris: Seuil.

———. 1973. "The Ruin of a Poetics." In *Russian Formalism*. Ed. Stephen Bann and John E. Bowlt. Edinburgh: Scottish Academic Press.

Kritzman, Lawrence, ed. 2006. *The Columbia History of Twentieth-Century French Thought*. New York: Columbia University Press.

Kundera, Milan. 1986. *L'art du roman*. Paris: Gallimard.

———. 1988. *The Art of the Novel*. Tr. Linda Asher. New York: Harper & Row.

———. 1993. *Testaments trahis: essai*. Paris: Gallimard.

———. 2005. *Le rideau: essai en sept parties*. Paris: Gallimard.

Lachman, Kathryn. 2010. "The Allure of Counterpoint: History and Reconciliation in Edward Said and Assia Djebar." *Research in African Literatures* 41.4 (Winter): 162–86.

Lacoue-Labarthe, Philippe. 1994. *Musica ficta*. Trans. Felicia McCarren. Stanford: Stanford University Press.

Lambert, Gregg. 2004. *The Return of the Baroque in Modern Culture*. London and New York: Continuum Press.

Lamming, George. 1960. *The Pleasures of Exile*. London: Joseph.

Le Bris, Michel and Jean Rouaud, eds. 2007. *Pour une littérature-monde*. Paris: Gallimard.

Leppert, Richard. 2007. "Opera, Aesthetic Violence, and the Imposition of Modernity: *Fitzcarraldo*." In *Beyond the Soundtrack: Representing Music in Cinema*, ed. Daniel Goldmark, Lawrence Kramer, and Richard Leppert: 99–119. Berkeley: University of California Press.

Lindley, Mark. 2012. "Temperaments." *Grove Music Online. Oxford Music Online*. http://www.oxfordmusiconline.com/subscriber/article/grove/music/27643. Accessed June 5, 2012.

Lionnet, Francoise. 2011. "Counterpoint and Double Critique in Edward Said and Abdelkebir Khatibi: A Transcolonial Comparison." In *A Companion to Comparative Literature*, ed. Ali Behdad and Dominic Thomas: 387–407. Oxford: Blackwell.

—— and Ronnie Scharfman, eds. 1993. *"Post/Colonial Conditions"* (special issue), *Yale French Studies* 82.

—— and Shu-mei Shih, eds. 2005. *Minor Transnationalism*. Durham: Duke University Press.

Lodge, David. 1975. *Changing Places: A Tale of Two Campuses*. London: Secker and Warburg.

Lopes, Henri. 2003. *Ma grand-mère bantoue et mes ancêtres les Gaulois*. Paris: Gallimard.

Mallarmé, Stéphane. 1998. *Œuvres complètes*. Paris: Gallimard.

Mann, Thomas. 1997. *Doctor Faustus*. Trans. John E. Woods. New York: Knopf.

Mansell, Darrel. 1985. "Glenn Gould: The Idea of South by North." *The Iowa Review* 15.3 (Fall): 58–65.

Marais, Mike. 2006. "J. M. Coetzee's *Disgrace* and the Task of the Imagination." *Journal of Modern Literature* 29.2: 75–93.

Marranca, Bonnie and Edward Said. 1991. "Criticism, Culture, and Performance: An Interview with Edward Said." *Performing Arts Journal*: 21–42.

McCreless, Patrick. 2002. "Music and Rhetoric." In *The Cambridge History of Western Music Theory*, ed. Thomas Christensen: 847–79. Cambridge: Cambridge University Press.

Meschonnic, Henri. 1982. *Critique du rythme*. Lagrasse: Verdier.

Meudal, Gérard. 2000. "Maryse Condé, l'inconvenante." *Le Monde,* November 11.

Miller, Christopher. 1996. "After Negation: Africa in Two Novels by Maryse Condé." In *Postcolonial Subjects: Francophone Women Writers*. Ed. Mary Jean Green et al. Minneapolis: University of Minnesota Press: 173–85.

———. 2006. "Francophonie." In *The Columbia History of Twentieth-Century French Thought*, ed. Lawrence D. Kritzman: 235–38. New York: Columbia University Press.

—— and Farid Laroussi, eds. 2003. *"French and Francophone: The Challenge of Expanding Horizons" (special issue), Yale French Studies* 103.

Morrison, Anthea. 1995. "Emanicipating the Voice: Maryse Condé's La vie scélérate." *Callaloo* 18.3: 616–25.

Morrison, Toni. 1992. *Jazz: A Novel*. New York: Knopf.

Morson, Gary Saul and Caryl Emerson, eds. 1989. *Rethinking Bakhtin: Extensions and Challenges*. Evanston: Northwestern University Press.

———. 1990. *Mikhail Bakhtin: Creation of a Prosaics*. Stanford: Stanford University Press.

Mortimer, Mildred. 2005. "Edward Said and Assia Djebar: A Contrapuntal Reading." *Research in African Literatures* 36.3 (Fall): 53–67.

Moudileno, Lydie. 1995. "Portrait of the Artist as Dreamer: Maryse Condé's *Traversée de la Mangrove* and *Les Derniers Rois Mages*." Trans. Francis Higginson. *Callaloo* 18.3 (Summer): 626–40.

———. 2006. "Positioning the 'French' 'Caribbean' 'Woman' Writer." In *Feasting on Words*, ed. Vera Broichhagen, Kathryn Lachman, and Nicole Simek: 123–46. Princeton: *PLAS*.

Murdoch, H. Adlai. 2001. *Creole Identity in the French Caribbean Novel*. Gainesville: University of Florida Press.

—— and Anne Donadey, eds. 2005. *Postcolonial Theory and Francophone Literary Studies*. Gainesville: University of Florida Press.

Nesbitt, Nick. 2003. *Voicing Memory: History and Subjectivity in French Caribbean Literature*. Charlottesville and London: University of Virginia Press.

Noudelmann, François. 2012. *The Philosopher's Touch*. New York: Columbia University Press.

Nuttall, Sarah. 2009. *Entanglement: Literary and Cultural Reflections on Post-Apartheid*. Johannesburg: Wits University Press.

O'Riley, Michael. 2002. "Translation and Imperialism in Assia Djebar's *Les Nuits de Strasbourg*." In "The Seventy-Fifth Anniversary Issue," *The French Review* 75.6 (May): 1235–49.

Ors, Eugenio d'. 1935. *Du baroque*. Trans. Agathe Rouart-Valéry. Paris: Gallimard.

Painter, Karen. 2001. "Contested Counterpoint: 'Jewish' Appropriation and Polyphonic Liberation." *Archiv für Musikwissenschaft* 58.3: 201–30.

Pamuk, Orhan. 2006. "Freedom to Write." Trans. Maureen Freely. *New York Review of Books* 53.9 (May 25).

Parry, Benita. 1998. "Speech and Silence in the Fictions of J. M. Coetzee." In *Writing South Africa: Literature, Apartheid, and Democracy, 1970–1995*. Ed. Derek Attridge and Rosemary Jolly. Cambridge: Cambridge University Press: 149–65.

Pavel, Thomas. 1998. "Freedom, from Romance to the Novel: Three Anti- Utopian American Critics." *New Literary History* 29.4: 579–98.

Pechey, Graham. 2002. "Coetzee's Purgatorial Africa: The Case of *Disgrace*." *Interventions* 4.3: 374–83.

Perret, Delphine. 1995. "Dialogue with the Ancestors." *Callaloo* 18.3 (Summer): 652–67.

—— and Mary-Denise Shelton, eds. 1995. "*Maryse Condé*" (special issue), *Callaloo* 18.3 (Summer).

Peterson, Dale. 1993. "The African American Dialogue with Bakhtin." *American Literature* 65.4 (December): 761–75.

Pfaff, Françoise. 1996. *Conversations with Maryse Condé*. Lincoln: University of Nebraska Press.

Philcox, Richard. 2001. "Translating Maryse Condé: A Personal Itinerary." *Sites* 5.2: 277–82.

Powers, Richard. 1991. *The Gold Bug Variations*. New York: W. Morrow.

Prieto, Eric. 2002. *Listening In: Music, Mind, and the Modernist Narrative*. Lincoln, NE: University of Nebraska Press.

Proulx, Patrice J. 2000. "Writing Home: Explorations of Exile and Cultural Hybridity in the Correspondence of Nancy Huston and Leïla Sebbar." *L'Esprit Créateur* 40.4 (Winter): 80–88.

Proust, Marcel. 1987–89. *À la recherche du temps perdu*. Ed. Jacques Tadié. Bibliothèque de la Pléiade. Paris: Gallimard.

Ramsay, Raylene. 2000. "The Nature of Hybridity in Maryse Condé's *Traversée de la mangrove*." *Nottingham French Studies* 39.2 (Autumn): 213–335.

Randal, Don Michael, ed. 1986. *New Harvard Dictionary of Music*. Cambridge: Belknap Press of Harvard University Press.

Rejouis, Rose-Myriam. 1999. "A Reader in the Room: Rose Myriam Rejouis Meets Patrick Chamoiseau." *Callaloo* 22.2: 346–50.

Rice, Alison. 2003. "Alsagérie: croisements de langues et d'histoires de l'Algérie à Strasbourg dans *Les nuits de Strasbourg* d'Assia Djebar." *Paroles déplacées* 2 (September): 55–68.

———. 2006. *Time Signatures: Contextualizing Contemporary Francophone Autobiographical Writing from the Maghreb*. Lanham, MD: Lexington Books.

Risser, Nicole Dombrowski. 2012. *France under Fire: German Invasion, Civilian Flight and Family Survival during World War II*. Cambridge, UK: Cambridge University Press.

Robbins, Jill. 1991. "Visage, Figure: Reading Levinas' *Totality and Infinity*." *Yale French Studies* 79 ("Literature and the Ethical Subject"): 135–49.

Rosello, Mireille. 1995. "Caribbean Insularization of Identities in Maryse Condé's Work: From *En attendant le bonheur* to *Les derniers rois mages*." *Calalloo* 18.3: 565–78.

———. 2005. *France and the Maghreb: Performative Encounters*. Gainesville: University of Florida Press.

Rothberg, Michael. 2009. *Multidirectional Memory: Remembering the Holocaust in the Age of Decolonization*. Stanford: Stanford University Press.

Rousseau, Jean-Jacques. 1959–. *Œuvres complètes*. Ed. Bernard Gagnebin and Marcel Raymond. 5 vols. Paris: Gallimard.

———. 1990. *Essai sur l'origine des langues où il est parlé de la mélodie et de l'imitation musicale*. Ed. J. Starobinski. Paris: Gallimard.

———. 1992. *Discours sur l'origine et les fondements de l'inégalit; Discours sur les arts et les sciences*. Paris: Garnier-Flammarion.

Said, Edward. 1978. *Orientalism*. New York: Random House.

———. 1991. *Musical Elaborations*. New York: Columbia University Press.

———. 1993. *Culture and Imperialism*. New York: Vintage Books.

———. 1999. *Out of Place: A Memoir*. New York: Knopf.

———. 2000. *Reflections on Exile and Other Essays*. Cambridge, MA: Harvard University Press.

———. 2002. *Parallels and Paradoxes: Explorations in Music and Society*. With Daniel Barenboim. New York: Pantheon Books.

———. 2006. *On Late Style: Music and Literature against the Grain*. Introduction by Michael Wood. New York: Pantheon Books.

———. 2012. "The Public Role of Writers and Intellectuals." In *The Public Intellectual*, ed. Helen Small: 19–39. Oxford: Blackwell Publishing.

Salibi, Kamal. 1988. *A House of Many Mansions: The History of Lebanon Reconsidered*. Berkeley: University of California Press.

Sanders, Carol. 2003. "'Une si belle enfant ne pouvait pas être maudite': Polyphony in Maryse Condé's Novel *Les Migrations du cœur*." In *The Francophone Caribbean Today: Literature, Language, Culture*, edited by Gertrud Aub-Buscher and Beverley Ormerod Noakes: 151–68. Barbados: University of the West Indies Press.

Sanders, Mark. 2002a. *Complicities: The Intellectual and Apartheid*. Durham: Duke University Press.

———. 2002b. "Disgrace." *Interventions* 4.3: 363–73.

———. 2002c. "Ethics and Interdisciplinarity in Philosophy and Literary Theory." *Diacritics* 32.3/4: 3–16.

Sarraute, Nathalie. 1963. *Les Fruits d'or*. Paris: Gallimard.

Scheie, Timothy. 2006. *Performance Degree Zero: Roland Barthes and Theater*. Toronto: University of Toronto Press.

Scher, Steven Paul, ed. 1992. *Music and Text: Critical Inquiries*. Cambridge: Cambridge University Press.

Sebbar, Leila. 1999. *La Seine était rouge*. Paris: Thierry Magnier.

Seidel, Linda. 2001. "Death and Transformation in J. M. Coetzee's Disgrace." *Journal of Colonialism and Colonial History* 2.3 (2001): 22 paragraphs.

Sereda, Stefan. 2008. "Riffing on Resistance: Music in Chris Abani's *Graceland*." *ARIEL: A Review of International English Literature* 39.4 (November): 31–47.

Shread, Carolyn. 2009. "Redefining Translation through Self-Translation: The Case of Nancy Huston." In *Translation in French and Francophone Literature and Film*, ed. James T. Day: 51–66. Amsterdam and New York: Rodopi.

Silverstein, Paul. 2004. *Algeria in France: Transpolitics, Race, and Nation*. Bloomington: University of Indiana Press.

Simon, Julia. 2011. "Rousseau." In *The Routledge Companion to Philosophy and Music*, ed. Theodore Gracyk and Andrew Kania: 317–27. London and New York: Routledge.

Sisman, Elaine. 1993. *Haydn and the Classical Variation*. Cambridge, MA: Harvard University Press.

———. "Variations." *Grove Music Online. Oxford Music Online*. Oxford University Press. http://www.oxfordmusiconline.com/subscriber/article/grove/music/29050. Accessed February 19, 2013.

Smart, Mary Ann, ed. 2000. *Siren Songs: Representations of Gender and Sexuality in Opera*. Princeton: Princeton University Press.

Smyth, Gerry. 2008. *Music in Contemporary British Fiction: Listening to the Novel.* Basingstoke: Palgrave Macmillan.

Smyth, Heather. 2002. "Roots beyond Roots: Heteroglossia and Feminist Creolization in *Myal* and *Crossing the Mangrove*." *Small Axe* 12 (September): 1–24.

Sophocles. 2001. *Antigone.* Trans. Paul Woodruff. Indianapolis and Cambridge, MA: Hackett.

——. 2005. *Oedipus at Colonus.* Trans. Eamon Grennan and Rachel Kitzinger. Oxford: Oxford University Press.

Spivak, Gayatri Chakravorty. 1988. "Can the Subaltern Speak?" In *Marxism and the Interpretation of Culture,* ed. Cary Nelson and Lawrence Grossberg: 271–316. Urbana: University of Illinois Press, 1988.

——. 2002. "Ethics and Politics in Tagore, Coetzee, and Certain Scenes of Teaching." *Diacritics* 32.3/4: 17–31.

Starobinski, Jean. 1971. *Jean-Jacques Rousseau: la transparence et l'obstacle.* Paris: Gallimard.

Steedman, Carolyn. 2007. "Something Called a Fever: Michelet, Derrida, Dust (Or, in the Archives with Michelet and Derrida)." In *Archives, Documentation, and Institutions of Social Memory: Essays from the Sawyer Seminar,* ed. Francis X. Blouin and William G. Rosenberg: 4–19. Ann Arbor: University of Michigan Press.

Stora, Benjamin. 1991. *La gangrène et l'oubli: la mémoire de la guerre d'Algérie.* Paris: La Découverte.

——. 2005. *Le livre, mémoire de l'histoire: réflexions sur le livre et la guerre d'Algérie.* Paris: Préau des collines.

—— and Mohammed Harbi, eds. 2005. *La guerre d'Algérie: 1954—2004, la fin de l'amnésie.* Paris: Laffont.

Strangers. 2007. Erez Tadmor and Guy Nattiz. 2007. United Channel Movies. DVD.

Telmissany, May and Stephanie Tara Schwartz, eds. 2010. *Counterpoints: Edward Said's Legacy.* Cambridge: Cambridge Scholars Publishing.

Thomas, Dominic. 2010. "Documenting the Periphery: The Short Films of Faïza Guène." *French Forum* 35.2/3 (Spring–Fall): 191–208.

Thomas, Downing A. 1995. *Music and the Origins of Language: Theories from the French Enlightenment.* Cambridge and New York: Cambridge University Press.

Tolbert, Elizabeth. 2001. "The Enigma of Music, the Voice of Reason: 'Music,' 'Language,' and Becoming Human." *New Literary History* 32.3 (Spring): 451–65.

Tomlinson, Gary. 1999. *Metaphysical Song: An Essay on Opera.* Princeton: Princeton University Press.

Urrows, David Francis, ed. 2008. *Essays on Word/Music Adaptation and on Surveying the Field*. Amsterdam and New York: Rodopi.

Valéry, Paul. 1957–60. *Œuvres*. Paris: Gallimard.

Vallaeys, Béatrice and Nathalie Levisalles, eds. "Francophonie: ma langue vivante." Supplément à *Libération* No. 7730, March 16, 2006.

Vargas Llosa, Mario. 2011. *Making Waves: Essays*. New York: Farrar, Strauss, Giroux.

Vertovec, Stephen and Robin Cohen, ed. 1999. *Migrations, Diasporas, and Transnationalism*. Cheltenham, UK, Northampton, MA: Edward Elgar.

Waberi, Abdourahman. 2003. *Transit: roman*. Paris: Gallimard.

——. 2012. *Passage of Tears*. Trans. David and Nicole Ball. Kolkata and London: Seagull Books.

Walker, Paul. "Fugue." *Grove Music Online*. *Oxford Music Online*. Oxford University Press. http://www.oxfordmusiconline.com/subscriber/article/grove/music/51678. Accessed February 16, 2013.

Welcome. 2009 [2010]. Philippe Lioret. Film Movement. DVD.

White, Hayden. 1973. *Metahistory: The Historical Imagination in Nineteenth-Century Europe*. Baltimore: Johns Hopkins University Press.

——. 1992. "Commentary." In *Music and Text*, ed. Steven Paul Scher: 288–319. Cambridge: Cambridge University Press.

Wicomb, Zoë. 2002. "Translations in the Yard of Africa." *Journal of Literary Studies* 18.3/4: 209–25.

Williams, Peter. 2001. *Bach: The Goldberg Variations*. Cambridge: Cambridge University Press.

Wolf, Werner. 1999. *The Musicalization of Fiction: A Study in the Theory and History of Intermediality*. Amsterdam and Atlanta: Rodopi.

——. 2002a. "Intermedial Iconicity in Fiction: Tema con variazioni." *From Sign to Signing: Iconicity in Language and Literature* 3: 339–60.

——. 2002b. "Toward a Functional Analysis of Intermediality: The Case of Twentieth-Century Musicalized Fiction." In *Cultural Functions of Intermedial Exploration*, ed. Erik Hedling and Ulla Britta Lagerroth: 15–34. Amsterdam and New York: Rodopi.

Yaeger, Patricia. 2007. "Editor's Column." *PMLA* 122.3 (May): 633–51.

Young, Robert. 1995. *Colonial Desire: Hybridity in Theory, Culture, and Race*. London, New York: Routledge.

Zambrano, Maria. 1989. *La tumba de Antigone*. Madrid: Mondadori.

Zamora, Lois Parkinson and Monika Kaup, ed. 2010. *Baroque New Worlds: Representation, Transculturation, Counterconquest*. Durham: Duke University Press.

Zimra, Clarisse. 2004. "Hearing Voices, or, Who You Calling Postcolonial? The Evolution of Djebar's Poetics." *Research in African Literatures* 35.4 (Winter): 149–59.

Ziolkowski, Theodore. 2010. "Literary Variations on Bach's Goldberg." *Modern Language Review* 105.3 (July): 625–40.

Žižek, Slavoj. 2002. *Welcome to the Desert of the Real: Five Essays on September 11 and Related Dates*. London, New York: Verso.

Index